BLOODLINES

BLOODLINES

A JOURNEY INTO EASTERN EUROPE

MYRNA KOSTASH

DOUGLAS & McINTYRE
Vancouver/Toronto

Douglas & McIntyre
1615 Venables Street
Vancouver, British Columbia
V5L 2H1

Canadian Cataloguing in Publication Data

Kostash, Myrna.
  Bloodlines : a journey into Eastern Europe

ISBN 1-55054-110-2

  1. Kostash, Myrna – Journeys – Europe, Eastern.
2. Europe, Eastern – Description and travel – 1981-
I. Title.
DJK19.K68 1993   914.704'854   C93-091520-8

Editing by Barbara Pulling and Charis Wahl
Cover design by Tania Craan
Cover collage by Barbara Klunder
Map by Fiona MacGregor
Design and typesetting by George Vaitkunas
Printed and bound in Canada by D. W. Friesen & Sons Ltd.
Printed on acid-free paper ∞

This book is for my hromada in Edmonton,
with whom the journey began,
and for David Albahari, Tomaz Mastnak,
Sonja Liht and Milan Nikolic,
born Yugoslavs, with whose brave imagination
the nation will begin again

CONTENTS

ACKNOWLEDGEMENTS

Written with the assistance of the Alberta Foundation for the Literary Arts and the Multiculturalism Program, federal Department of Multiculturalism and Citizenship.

Portions of this book have appeared in earlier versions in *Capilano Review, Prairie Fire* and *This Country, Canada.*

Over the course of thinking about, planning and writing this book, I benefited from the resources and expertise of many people to whom I owe thanks:

For their critical reading of parts of the manuscript in various draft stages: Brian Fawcett, John-Paul Himka, Olenka Melnyk, Frank Sysyn and Lyle Weis;

For hospitality and unflagging conversation about Eastern Europe: Miki Andrejevic and Nena Andrejevic-Jocic, Marko Bojcun, Peter Gowan, John Hannigan, Mrs. Daria Hornjatkevyc, Halya Kowalska, Roman Onufrijchuk, Andrew Pakula, Igor and Lena Pomerantsev, Ann Snitow, Paul Wilson and Halena Wilson;

For translation of bedevilling Slavic vocabulary, Andrij Hornjatkevyc; for laser printing beyond the call of duty, Ray Wintonyk; for contacts in East/Central Europe: Jars Balan, Chrystia Chomiak, Bohdan and Halya Klid, Bohdan Krawchenko, Branka Magas, Sofija Skoric and Zdena Tomin;

For their writer's encouragement: Patrick Friesen, Mary Ann Hushlak, Julie Landsman, Erna Paris and Merrily Weisbord;

For their friendship: Duane Burton, Lida Somchynsky and Cori Stent;

For their ingenious editorial interventions: George Melnyk, Charis Wahl and the impeccable Barbara Pulling;

For their willingness to talk with me, for their courage and civic virtue, all those with whom I spoke in Poland, Czechoslovakia, Yugoslavia and Ukraine.

"I can do you blood and love without the rhetoric,
and I can do you blood and rhetoric without the love,
and I can do you all three concurrent or consecutive,
but I can't do you love and rhetoric without the blood.
Blood is compulsory – they're all blood, you see."

Tom Stoppard
Rosencrantz and Guildenstern Are Dead

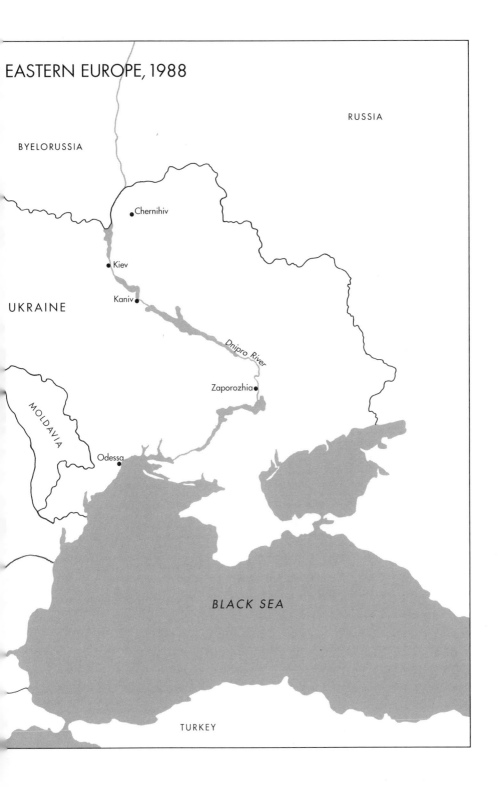

EASTERN EUROPE, 1988

RUSSIA

BYELORUSSIA

•Chernihiv

•Kiev

UKRAINE

Kaniv•

Dnipro River

MOLDAVIA

Zaporozhia•

Odessa•

BLACK SEA

TURKEY

INTRODUCTION

In the spring of 1982, I began the first of the travels into Central and Eastern Europe that gave rise to this book. I travelled to Bucharest (once, and never again) and to Budapest and Belgrade. In 1984, I visited Ukraine, Poland and Czechoslovakia, all for the first time, and revisited Yugoslavia (Croatia and Bosnia as well as Serbia). 1986: Yugoslavia once again. 1987: Poland, Czechoslovakia and again Yugoslavia (Slovenia and Serbia). 1988: Ukraine, Poland, Czechoslovakia and Yugoslavia (including Kosovo and Macedonia). All told, these trips added up to some ten months of travel.

I did not know in 1988 that everything was about to change – visits to Serbia and Ukraine at the end of 1991 were a kind of coda to my journeys – and so this is not a book about the revolution. This is a book about memory. About the territories that exist in the imagination of a Canadian writer, in that of her interlocutors, and in the space between them.

I did not travel haphazardly. I had a plan. Initially, my idea was to interview writers of my generation, bred by the events of the 1960s, who were writing from within the opposition in their respective societies. I was most interested in how they coped, as creative people, with the *political* demands of their situation. In 1980 my book about Canadian politics and culture in the sixties had been published, and I was feeling keenly the split in my own country between the creative intelligentsia and the "men" of action. Provided with contacts by friends and friends of friends, I set off, sometimes with a companion but usually alone. Occasionally I had an invitation – from the Writers' Union of Ukraine or the journal *Literatura na swiecie* in Warsaw or the PEN Centre in Slovenia – but I was just as happy to make my way as an independent traveller.

I limited myself to Slavic Central and Eastern Europe (excluding, therefore, Rumania, Hungary and Bulgaria) as I felt, in some still unformulated way, that my project was also "about" ethnicity.

My third traveller's hat was that of the New Left socialist: the anguish I had been feeling in coming to terms with the nature of the Soviet Union had been provoked mainly by books and casual encounters with dissident exiles. I wanted to see for myself how "actually existing socialism" looked and wondered how this might affect my own political beliefs.

This all sounds neat and tidy. The *experience* of these travels, however, was turbulent and very upsetting. I lost control of my plan as I met more and more people who took me further and further afield in my inquiries and as I realized that much of the solidarity I felt with them – political, generational and ethnic – was illusory, or at least ambiguous. Between trips, I did a prodigious amount of reading (see the notes at the back of the book for a partial listing of my sources) and sat in on several university courses, and this too widened the scope of my curiosity. My travels and my reading threw into question all the assumptions I had leaned on, on the basis of my limited awareness in Canada, to interpret events in Eastern and Central Europe. I learned to speak Ukrainian. I went to movies, I subscribed to underground publications, I corresponded with friends in Belgrade and Warsaw and Odessa (I sent postcards to Prague but knew I would never get anything back) and with relatives in western Ukraine. Each time I travelled I was turned inside out again in what was proving to be the most difficult work of my life as a writer.

Take a second-generation Ukrainian Canadian, a feminist, a writer, an alumna of the 1960s, and put her on a train in Belgrade heading north. What exactly is her business?

How does the "old country" live on in the citizen of the new? How may I understand these people and their extraordinary history – my blood relations, as it were, from whom I was separated by the accident of being born into the new family line in Canada? How do they imagine the place I come from? Can I trust what I see of theirs? What is the source of my feelings – feelings I didn't even know I had – about their history, their landscape, their languages, their sites of collective memory? What is their claim on me? Mine on them? In other words, what has this part of the world got to do with me?

This book is by way of an answer.

A few notes about my methods: I interviewed without a tape recorder for obvious reasons. My interviews in Czechoslovakia and Poland were done almost exclusively in English. I also conducted interviews two or three times in French and, on my second trip to Ukraine, frequently in Ukrainian. I never spoke Russian (although it was sometimes assumed I was speaking Russian when I was speaking Ukrainian). As for getting along in the shops and cafés, on the buses, at the cinema and so on, I made use of a "generic Slav" speech, a little bit of everything – Serbo-Croat, Slovene, Slovak, Polish and Ukrainian. It worked rather well. Reading the various languages – posters, newspaper headlines, slogans, advertisements and the like – was much less of a problem. There is enough mutual intelligibility among the Slavic languages that, if you know one or two of them, you can read your way through the rest.

I have not always used an interviewee's real name in the book, and few of the conversations are reported verbatim, as I always took notes after the interview. For transliteration from the Serbian, I have followed popular press style in using the Croatian orthographical equivalent; from the Ukrainian, I have followed the eminently readable system employed in Dr. Orest Subtelny's history of Ukraine. Where a place name is sufficiently familiar in its English-language usage, I have chosen that spelling rather than the local one: Odessa for Odesa, Warsaw for Warszawa, Belgrade for Beograd, and so on. I have kept the names of countries as they were known when I visited: Czechoslovakia, Poland, Yugoslavia and Soviet Ukraine.

To give readers a historical context for each country's situation since the 1940s, I have included a summary of key historical events at the beginning of each chapter.

CZECHOSLOVAKIA

1946: *Communists win 38 per cent of popular vote in free elections* **1948**: *taking advantage of trade union support during political crisis, Communists seize power* **1949-52**: *show trials of Communist "renegades," socialization of economy and Stalinization of cultural policy* **1960s**: *economists debate reforms, writers debate Marxist humanism, New Wave cinema an international success* **1967**: *reform Communist Alexander Dubcek to power* **1967-68**: *"Prague Spring" experiments with socialist pluralism* **1968**: *Warsaw Pact armies invade and occupy Czechoslovakia* **1969-70**: *"normalization" process purges reformers* **1977**: *opposition group, Charter 77, organizes* **1989**: *Velvet Revolution – street demonstrations, general strike, collapse of Communist power* **1990-92**: *presidency of Vaclav Havel, former political prisoner* **1993**: *separation of Czechoslovakia into the Czech Republic and Slovakia*

LIVING IN THE TRUTH

I meet Zdena in her subsidized flat somewhere beyond Islington High Street, several bus stops off the wretched Northern Line of London's underground. She is round-bodied, rather elegant and only three years out of Prague. She speaks an English that sounds la-di-da to me, only occasionally slipping into middle-European vowels. She is trying to make a living as an English writer, having paid her dues with numerous Czech-in-exile stories in worthy British and diaspora publications.

These are her instructions: on my way to Prague, I am to telephone her from the continent. I am to ask her how the weather is. If she tells me it is cold and wet, I am not to go to Prague or to attempt any contacts there. If she tells me the weather is fine, I may proceed. Her friends will be waiting for me. "You need only one name and one address. Marketa. 7 Jecna. Give her my love."

I telephone London from a provincial post office in Slovakia. Zdena is in Wales, says her son, and will be gone for two weeks. I ask him what the weather is like. Not bad, he answers, but it's rainy in Wales. I decide I will go to Prague.

PRAGUE, 1984: Prague is the Paris of the East – so said travel guides and travellers before me. Compared to the unlovely Stalinist renovations of Kiev and Warsaw and ramshackle Belgrade, Prague is a feast at first sight. A splendid skyline of Gothic and Baroque towers, domes and steeples, statuary on the bridges over the Moldau and pretty cobblestoned mediaeval alleyways – all washed in shades of ochre, pink and verdigris – have enchanted visitors for centuries. I am delighted.

Only a hundred metres from my hotel in Wenceslas Square there are butcher shops with racks of fresh meat, music stores displaying rock 'n' roll records, a bookshop selling a translation of Joseph Heller's newest novel, and pleasant wine bars and cafés packed with the youth of Prague. Just off the square, in the restaurant of the Alcron Hotel, waiters in black tie deliver hors d'oeuvres and little glasses of chilled, amber-coloured plum brandy to guests seated under chandeliers. The dance band, silhouetted against the potted plants in the French windows, plays "Cheek to Cheek" for the courtly fathers waltzing with their daughters. In the theatres, *Love's Labour's Lost* and *Our Town*.

The Czechs, I have been told, have a droll sense of humour. I hear a joke. Question: Why do Prague police travel in threes? Answer: One can read, one can write, and the third one is there to keep an eye on the two intellectuals.

I allow myself the brief respite of thinking this city is kind to strangers. Later, I will come to terms with other observations: the savage obscenities of the man who bumps into my suitcase in the alleyway, the sullen indifference of the hotel staff, the waiter barking at me because it is the end of his shift and I have not finished my lunch.

Wedged between the joie de vivre of the Mediterranean Slavs (so goes one theory) and the melancholia of the northerners, the Czechs have settled temperamentally into the bourgeois stolidness of *Mitteleuropa*. There are harsher judgements of their character: stricken by self-doubt and hesitation, Czechs have a "distaste" for revolution and disorder and have condemned themselves to mere survival, as though the very pettiness of this ideal matched their geopolitical inferiority complex. Have they no memory, I wonder, of what they had brought into being in the spring of 1967, the summer of 1968 – the most radical and comprehensive program of change yet attempted in Eastern Europe. Alas, this is to be a sore spot. For the memory of the one – the glorious audacity of their vision of "socialism with a human face" – is collapsed into the memory of what immediately followed in August 1968 – the invasion of the country by armies of the Warsaw Pact, the brutal ending of the cheerful political experiment and the beginning of twenty years of occupation and government by quislings.

There is no general disgrace in military defeat. Yet Czech exiles excoriated their erstwhile national army with charges they had become "weak-kneed" in their settlement with the occupiers and quislings. "Remember," they reminded the rest of us, "while Czech army officers were crying, their rifles dangling at their sides – they had not fired a single shot – citizens stood up uselessly with bare hands against the tanks. Now there are

Czechs learning that submission without a fight does not pay."

"People have never had it so good," I will write later in my notebook. "Bad cars and plain food and bad television, but it *is* meat and cars and TV." Czechs themselves will speak to me of that "mess of potage" – the meat in the butcher shops, soft-core porn on Sunday television and indolent afternoons in the taverns – for which they have traded their self-respect and now can't look each other in the eye. "The fact that it is difficult to obtain a particular consumer item is not enough to move people to decisive political action," exiled Chartist Jaroslav Suk observed in an article published in Sweden that I read before arriving. Some even accuse certain Czechs of collaboration. But who of them is *not* a collaborator when to acquire parts for their car engines, a place in the music school, an imported antibiotic, they must consort with thieves and cheats? They have kids, debts, an application in for a passport, a half-built cottage waiting on baksheesh in the brickyard. Ask them who they think they are and more than half will say "democrats."

Prague is a "Potemkin village," Frantisek will tell me. "Look: cosmetic renovations of the façades of buildings, of what *tourists* can see from the street. Inside it's still dank and mouldy and falling apart. Charm for you; ruin for us." He means moral as well as architectural spaces. The every-day bribes people pay just to get a tooth filled or a fan belt replaced, and the envy of other people's wealth (I remember a crowd of boys and men staring morosely at a Mercedes-Benz outside my hotel). The contempt for their own, less favoured countrymen: in tourist season, I learn, Czechs are not welcome in certain bars and restaurants around the charming squares of the Old Town. Theatres full of Shakespeare? Villagers are brought in by the busload; the women go to the show, the men to the pubs. Depressed by their own indecisiveness – careerism in a despised Party? danger and poverty in the underground? isolation in private life and the dream of owning a VCR? – people evade self-examination by an extraordinary investment of energy in endless, finicky renovations to their humble summer cottages, to housekeeping, to mushroom picking and cultivating roses. It is a phenomenon.

I look out my hotel window onto Wenceslas Square, which is thick with the walking wounded of 1984 and the ghosts of the screaming students and human socialists of 1967. I think of the bare-handed resistance of '68 and of that same hot summer in the West, where the riot of police against antiwar protestors in a park in Chicago had been our moral correlative, we felt, to the students facing down the tanks of Russian impe-rialists. *Welcome to Czechago.* Out there are those Czechs who remember.

I descend to the underground, ride in one direction for a few stops, cleverly reverse my journey and emerge at the corner of Jecna and Karlovo Namesti. I stand for a few minutes to make sure there are no suspicious characters in my wake. To be doubly sure, I sit on a park bench. No one follows suit. The coast clear, I make my way along the dusky street to number 7.

The entry to the courtyard stands next to a filthy shop displaying Party literature. The shop shows no sign of life; could its basement har-bour a listening post of the secret police? I dart through the entry, knocking against garbage cans on my way to the elevator cage, where I discern the figure of a middle-aged man waiting in the gloom. He smiles wanly at me and takes no further interest. We ride together to the fourth floor where he turns left and I, right. I knock decisively. The door swings open and a young, fair-haired man with his mouth full of food invites me to step inside, not even bothering to hear out my little speech of introduction, "... from Zdena in London." I am swept into the kitchen and seated in the company of Marketa and several other women who, laughing and swigging beer, are baking for that weekend's wedding of the son and daughter of two dissident families.

The cheerful people of the Prague underground do not skulk around. I have my first lesson in living human.

I visit Marketa at work. She waits table and washes dishes at the coffee bar at Charles University. This menial job gives her lots of time to sit and chat with interesting customers, some of whom have come expressly to see her. In fact, this little coffee bar is a bit of a drop-in cen-tre for the disgruntled and disaffected who have not yet made the plunge to the underground.

Just that morning Marketa had been summoned to an interrogation with the security police. This happens every month. They always ask, "Who have you been seeing? What do you talk about?" She always answers, "It is not a crime to meet my friends and to talk about what-ever we want." Then, in a little ritualized dialogue, they offer her emi-gration. She refuses.

She is twenty-three years old, fair of face and sturdy, the daughter of a philosopher exiled to Vienna and an activist mother sentenced to five years' surveillance and three years' conditional discharge under supervision. All her brothers and sisters and their spouses are blacklisted oppositionists. Could she study art history, work for the Ministry of Museums and National Monuments, save for a television set and a Skoda? Even if she could, she would not want to.

In a group photograph taken in 1979 outside the Prague municipal court, Marketa stands in the back row, long bangs hanging over her glasses. She is eighteen years old but looks about fifteen. The group – a couple of grown-ups, several teen-agers, a toddler and a dog – waits in solidarity with their parents and friends on trial inside. They are in the resistance.

Yet Marketa, swabbing down the counters, is not a "dissident." She bristles at the word used by sympathizing westerners who conflate all anti-Soviet resistance. Nor will she name her commitment "political," another word that westerners employ, imagining they are flattering their Czech interlocutor. Marketa says she is simply a citizen trying to live like a human being in a garbage dump. As soon as she could, she signed the illegal document, Charter 77, and joined that tender swarm of oppositionists moving en masse from clandestine press conferences to illegal rock concerts to political trials to weddings and funerals.

Charter 77 is not an organization; it has no statutes, no permanent bodies or formally organized membership. Anyone who agrees with its ideas, takes part in its work and supports it belongs to it.

Chartists do not harangue. They are reasonable. Starting tomorrow, they point out, you too can begin to speak the truth. Workers can claim their constitutional right to elect their union representative. Students can exchange views. Believers can go to church. Artists can show their work to their friends. Nobody is asking you to be a hero.

The tumult of revolution is not necessary. Be modest, be patient. Conserve your energy. Be kind and courteous to each other, do not shove each other around in the queues or scowl across the meat counter or cheat one another. Do not be guilty of self-abuse: of apathy, resignation and moral nihilism. Is it not true that, if we grasp these few existing possibilities of civil and civic behaviour, we can begin to reinvent the world?

It seemed to me at the time that they could have gone on forever as they were, fulfilling personal commitments to civic virtue, submitting rhythmically to the song and dance with the authorities, serene in the knowledge of their unbetrayed consciences.

Is a signature an act? Is being nice?

They lived in the truth and did not seek to overthrow anything. They had, it seemed to me, worked out a modus vivendi with the system. As long as they could ignore the unmarked police cars parked in the streets, they could go on like this, hand to mouth, embracing on the dance floor of their private apartments to the rhythms of a blacklisted band.

The water is turning to wine and the cigarette smoke hangs like a blue canopy over the heads of the revelers at the wedding party, their voices an oratorio of gossip and argument. Marketa rushes about, flapping a copy of a press release from a defence committee for the "unjustly prosecuted." A young man in Moravia has been arrested for having collected signatures on a petition pressing for the withdrawal of Soviet missiles from Czechoslovakia. Vicissitudes in the provinces! A projector is being dragged out of a closet. People take paintings off the wall to clear a space for the home movie of the gang's big party last fall. The same faces, sticking out their tongues at the camera, and the same congestion, smiles and seductions at the kitchen sink, earnest heart to hearts by the coat rack. Camaraderie in the deep freeze.

A morose, thirtyish engineer contemplates the profundities of his beer glass while unburdening himself of his grievances towards his parents. His mother, who had wept copiously in 1968 at the sight of the tanks outside the windows, has become an activist in the Czech-Soviet Friendship Society; his father, a computer technician in the Ministry of Communications, professes to admire the Russian people, frequents international conferences, putters around his dacha and breeds bloodhounds. The son refuses to join the Party. He doesn't like the people. People like his mom and dad. He has committed himself to "passive resistance." He never votes and never goes to the May Day parade. His voice is so flat I cannot tell if he is proud of this or merely lackadaisical.

I am introduced to Frantisek who, two and a half weeks ago, got out of prison. He'd been put away for two years for "hooliganism," code for editing an illegal publication. He was the editor of *Vokno*, meaning "window." *Vokno*'s logo was a rectangle divided into six "panes" by cell bars. He is philosophical. "They can close down a paper here today, and tomorrow a new one will appear over there." He intends to get back to the business of hooliganism as soon as he can, but for the next three years, he must report to his neighbourhood police supervisor at ten o'clock every night, submit to house searches and be prepared to show the police monthly confirmation of his earnings.

He had been held in a medium-security prison, which was fine by him. Hardened prisoners don't collaborate, inform or brownnose. It's the first-timers in a minimum-security institution, still wet behind the ears and in shock, who are keen to be "co-operative."

At midnight they roll back the carpets and put on dancing music: the Beatles.

BIBLIOMANIA

PRAGUE, 1984: In Nikolaj's recurring nightmare, he is stumbling about in great darkness wearing only his pyjamas.

In 1971 he was seized from his house at three in the morning, driven out of the city and abandoned on a country road wearing his pyjamas and one shoe. In 1977 he became one of "them" – the signatories of the Charter. He has never practised his profession, librarianship, but has worked for years as the night shift operator in an apartment building. Bulky, rather frayed about the edges, he shuffles around the Old Town with a shopping bag. In it may be empty beer bottles, manuscript pages, radishes, old paperbacks. He frequents second-hand bookshops where friends are employed. Sometimes consignments of books include prohibited titles. The bookshop employees are supposed to destroy these, making note of who brought the consignment in. Instead, they hide them under the counter for Nikolaj. The book closest to his heart is Orwell's *Down and Out in Paris and London*. He's never been to Paris or London.

We are riding the tram. Nikolaj pulls out a magazine from his shopping bag. It looks old but it may just be the worse for wear. He opens it to an article over which I make out his by-line. His real name. This librarian/translator/film critic has found the one place where he may appear in print: a mycological journal. Nikolaj has discovered a mushroom.

FESTIVAL OF TOILERS

SLOVAKIA, 1984: Tomorrow is the Ukrainian festival of song and dance at Svidnik, close to the border with Soviet Ukraine. Tonight in Presov my companion and I visit friends of friends, the disaffected

Ukrainian intelligentsia of this university town. It takes three of us half an hour to drink two litres of white wine in the pub on the ground floor of Roman's apartment building. We are there to drink, not to talk. The plainclothesmen are everywhere. Up in his apartment, it takes four hours to drink a bottle of gin. We talk.

I stick my tongue in the gin. Roman drinks it in gulps. He is becoming wild. He pulls at his hair, leaving exasperated shocks of it sticking straight up. He has a degree in Ukrainian literature but hasn't published a word in thirteen years. Out there are Doctors of Literature not even *born* in his heyday who are rubbing up against ideas he hasn't a goddamned clue about, doesn't even have the goddamned *vocabulary* to discuss.

He's a dispatcher for a trucking company. In 1968, he was a bloody naïf in the provinces, cheering on the heroes of the Prague Spring. The Soviets would not invade – after all, the Spring was about a better socialism, right? Maybe the people of Prague were a little giddy from living close to the borders with western Europe, but what was *his* excuse, shoved up close to the u.s.s.r., the border laid straight across the Carpathian Ukrainian people?

By the early 1970s, he was smarter. He joined an unofficial circle of nationally conscious Ukrainians in Presov. This is how he met Mykola, the ethnographer. The circle had made contact with dissidents in Ukraine and were smuggling samizdat across the border. In 1972, during a customs check at the Soviet-Czech border station at Chop, Mykola was discovered to be carrying nineteen illegal documents, including a typescript of the notorious book by the Soviet Ukrainian journalist Ivan Dziuba, *Internationalism or Russification?* In Ukraine, Dziuba was sentenced to five years' imprisonment and five years' internal exile. The circle in Presov was rounded up and Roman lost his teaching job.

After a brief imprisonment, Mykola was assigned, as punishment, to the job of shepherd on the collective farm in his father's village. Stretched out on the slope of the pasture lands, released from conversation, he had all the time in the world to contemplate the vanity of the short term.

We are Mykola's house guests, and we learn more about him. His peasant father was a sincere Communist. Before Communism, one third of his harvest, good, bad or indifferent, was taken in tax; when he couldn't pay the taxes, they threw his kids out of school. After Communism, the landlord was gone, the kids stayed in school and wore shoes. He inherited seven hectares divided into seventy-seven parcels, so irrational an apportioning that he even supported collectivization: handed over his property, signed up with the state farm and earned two and a half times the salary of a professor.

His son, Mykola, became a professor. Now ex-professor, Mykola may not be mentioned in any Ukrainian-language publication, although he may be cited in Slovak-language texts. He's the director of an amateur folk dance group that, although it has performed on state television and at the Svidnik festival, may not publicly acknowledge him as director. Now, in 1984, he is a monitor in a water heating plant in Presov. He has half his library there, a writing desk, a tea kettle.

He is still an ethnographer. "Look," he says. He shows us suitcases of research notes; transcriptions of interviews and statistical tables meticulous in longhand; dozens of file folders holding bibliographies, commentaries on and exegeses of the work of suppressed Ukrainian sociologists; a huge cardboard box that contains his unpublished articles and the four thousand typewritten pages of his unpublished books.

Vodka and appetizers, vodka, beer, fried cabbage, meat sauce and knoedel.

I follow Mykola up the creaky staircase to the attic, bumping my head on the pictures hanging on the walls of the stairwell. The work of Oleksa Novakivsky, for example, an important Ukrainian expressionist landscape painter from Cracow who died in 1935, twenty years before the Soviets were willing to talk about his work. The National Gallery in Kiev has fifteen of his pictures; Mykola has fifty-two. A wild goose chase around Czechoslovakia led him to a house in Prague where the keeper of Novakivsky's pictures, the daughter of his patron and biographer, had committed suicide one week earlier. Mykola got the pictures, having convinced the authorities they were of no value.

Oils of the Moravian landscape, the work of an artist in Prague who, as proprietor of her own art academy, was declared a bourgeois class element in 1949 and chased out of home and academy. She was reduced to begging in the streets, went mad and died. A portrait of the publisher of an uncensored edition of the work of Ukrainian poet Taras Shevchenko. The publisher leaped to his death the day the Red Army arrived in Prague in 1945. A portrait of a composer celebrated in Prague in the 1920s and 1930s, unheard of since. A still life – the artist died at hard labour in the forests of Siberia. A street scene – the artist died of tuberculosis in Cracow. Charcoal sketches of the Adriatic coast – the artist now designs chocolate boxes in New York.

Mykola has books. Editions from the 1840s and 1880s, published in St. Petersburg, about the history of Ukraine by Ukrainian scholars – all in Russian because, until 1905, the Ukrainian language was forbidden in print. Thin, crackling collections of poems rescued from the mildew of an old woman's basement. Ukrainian literary criticism pulled from a bonfire lit to clear up the garbage, the junk, the detritus of generations whose scholarship, hard won, lasted no longer than the luck of their youth.

SVIDNIK: A large audience, in a very good mood, is seated in front of a large stage on a beautiful summer's day. The performances are exceedingly colourful and executed in a smart and vigorous manner – a wedding dance, a ritual game, a soldiers' dance, dances of field work, of housework, of courtship and leave-taking – as though the festival were a convention of ethnographers and not a reunion of the Ukrainian minority in Slovakia, quaffing beer and chomping on sausages, the grease running down their chins.

From the festival brochure: "The Svidnik Festival has become a mighty manifestation of the unity of peoples and nationalities, and of our inseparable brotherhood with the Soviet Union, our liberator."

Group after group of village dancers from the western slopes of the Carpathians weave and hop across the stage doing dances I have never seen before. They stamp their heels and slap their knees and do a lot of mincing little jumps in circles in the manner of the Hungarians, under whose unsympathizing influence both they and the Slovaks lived for a century. It is also, let it be said, the way mountain people dance.

The Hungarians belong to their past. This is a Soviet festival, and so we have the Soviet consul from Bratislava, who makes a diplomatic speech about peace in Slovak, Russian and Ukrainian, the Byelorussian dance troupe on its way to performances in Prague, and the chorus and band of the Red Army unit stationed in the area since 1968, who take up a full hour of the program.

The Red Army boys are singing "Katyusha," which always brings the house down, from Novosibirsk to Vancouver. The roly-poly woman sitting in front of me, her jelly-arms jiggling in rhythm to her smacking hands, is singing along with an enthusiasm I find beyond the call of duty. But I have got it wrong. These are songs of an army of liberation, the Red Army that burst out of the Carpathians, scourged the local fascists and drove out the Nazis. That other Red Army, which rolled in under cover of night in August 1968, is not mentioned. I refuse to clap. I refuse to be charmed. I will not tap my foot. I glare at the stage, even at the boys who may be from the Carpathians just on the other side of the mountains, in Uzhhorod, in Ukraine.

Beyond the concert stage are scores of little booths, all selling identical species of sausages and vodka, a few selling trinkets and books and records of folk music, none of them of Ukrainian provenance. Everyone standing around here is drunk – drunk gypsies, drunk workmen, drunk dancers in costume.

The sun is going down behind the gentle foothills in a spectacular flourish of crimson red, and the boys from Svidnik pass around the bottle, the sausage and the massive loaf of rye bread while the musicians tune up their accordion, their fiddle and their little marching drum. The light is draining away. The music bursts out in a clattering, screeching roundeley of hillbilly rapture and the boys whirl each other around, tossing each other back and forth inside their stomping circle. It does not look very Ukrainian to me. It's dark. Somebody passes me the bottle. I take it.

USE YOUR IMAGINATION

PRAGUE, 1984: I stand in the small street across from the synagogue, not sure whether to admire its dark, mediaeval brick steadfastness or to feel sorry about this temple that has lost most of its congregation, this crenellated roof line that echoes under heaven the skyline of the vanished ghetto. Jiri has asked me to wait for him here, and then we'll have lunch. Jiri has become a Jew, I'm told. Whether he was born one is unclear, but his seraphic face and moist, tender eyes inhibit me from asking.

The men file out from services. Jiri signals me over and I join him in the line shuffling into the communal hall next door. The congregation, this Saturday, has many Americans in it.

The relatives. We all have relatives, don't we? The ones who got away, Jiri, and saved the bloodlines – people in America who remember their grandmothers' maiden names, who were paying attention in their cribs when the names of the grandfathers' villages were shouted out from the letters that arrived between the wars. Thank God for that, Jiri, and do not resent our luck.

The women are in the hall. They have cooked the lunch and set the tables and arranged for the bottles of cold beer (redeemed with tickets sold at the door) while the men were praying. Like the regiment of women in my childhood (my mother brisk, thin, in a homemade apron) who conveyed platters of ham and bowls of perogies slathered with sour cream from the ovens and cauldrons in the church kitchen to the men and children posted in long rows, as though to sit and eat, just sit and eat, were *our* labour.

In the Jewish hall in Prague, I am seated behind a bowl of chicken noodle soup. Am I meant to eat it? Shouldn't there be a prayer, a grace? Shouldn't we all sit down together, instead of this milling about, the Americans and their relatives holding beer bottles and speaking each other's language brokenly, while my soup cools and Jiri sits forehead to forehead with a rabbi and intones prayers from a small, crackly prayer book, oblivious to my bewilderment? I ache with the familiarity of this soup, ladled out into a flat-bottomed basin, the pattern of the china washed by the clear, yellowish, fatty broth, thin egg noodles afloat like a water plant. It is my baba's chicken soup. I sat in her kitchen, under the slanted roof, and slurped the greasy broth from a large, silver-plated soup spoon too big to put entire in my mouth. This *was* the taste of chicken noodle soup: chicken fat, salt and a pinch of silver plate.

It's all right, isn't it, Jiri? I can sit here while you pray for me too. I can relax in this hubbub and these odours that remind me of where I come from, where I started out from, and not mind overly much that I am afraid to say so here. I am a Ukrainian Canadian surrounded by Jews; if I were to shout out that I felt at home, would I be asked to leave? Would I be seen as a kind of uncleanliness in this hall of the justified, bearing in my psyche of the seventh generation the memoranda of the pogrom?

Because it is the Sabbath, we walk back to Jiri's flat, a rather long walk over the bridge and up a long hill, and when we arrive at his apartment, his Gentile wife opens and closes the doors, turns on the lights, fetches the dictionaries. We sit in buttery sunshine at either end of a long oak table, one of several pieces of furniture he has acquired from departing friends going into exile, and try to understand each other.

"There was a time," I begin, "when I considered myself to be a citizen of Prague, in the spring of 1968."

"It was an illusion," says Jiri.

"No, it was an act of imagination."

"You can imagine whatever you like," he says, "but the soul of a system can never change. The goal of a system is precisely *not* to change."

"If I believed that," I say, "I wouldn't be able to make any sense of what I've seen: Polish Solidarity, Ukrainian poets surviving the gulag and writing more poems – "

"Excuse me, but didn't Budapest, 1956, tell you all you needed to know?"

Look at this photograph, Jiri. We are in the grade six class in Delton School in Edmonton. Our names are Filipchuk, "Stinko" Stako, Helbriecht, Algajer, Takas, Beeler, "Chop Suey" Cherwaty, Wakeruk, "Kotex" Kostash. Our fathers wear coveralls and our mothers run up and down the back alleys in aprons, calling us to supper. Look at how we're dressed: rubber boots, boys' hand-me-down jeans on girls, head scarves over our limp hair, second-hand coats too short in the sleeve, white socks in a heap at our skinny ankles. But clean, very clean.

One morning, Miss Clarke introduces us to a new classmate. She has him by the arm, as though to hold him up. His hair is black and flat upon his round skull; his skin is dusky. I think he's a gypsy, gypsies being the darkest people I know of, although I've never seen one. Indians are dark too, but I've seen Indians; he doesn't look like an Indian. He's a Hungarian. His name is Gabor and he stands in front of us in a sweater probably unpacked from a box sent to the refugee camp in Austria; same for the pants and shoes. He wears these garments like a small dog who's been forced into baby clothes by silly girls playing house. He seems to be living in the centre of some private mortification behind large, dark, unfocussed eyes.

I think I understand that. But his misery mingles in my little heart with the thrill of looking upon a refugee – *a tatterdemalion blown in from that cold and dark and evil zone where the Russians live. It is very far away and surrounded by high, blank walls. It is very hard to get out but Gabor has got out. Little Gabor comes as an ambassador of Freedom Fighters on the hills of Buda. He stands before us in an aureole of anti-Communist glory. Even children have stood their ground in the streets of Budapest, throwing stones at the Russians. Later, when I repudiated that cosmology, I threw off Gabor, too.*

"They were magnificent," says Jiri.

"Because they took up arms? Because they aren't like Czechs?"

"The Czech opposition could be rounded up and liquidated in an hour."

When Jiri had had the chance to study, in 1967, he worked in a factory. When all hell was breaking loose in August 1968, when his friends were making decisions that would change their lives forever, he was bumming around France and Italy. He returned, found work in a film studio and drank away the 1970s. When his friends in the pubs, elated by the beer, confessed to some hope that things would change "soon," he said that hope was just another doctrine. It was all an illusion, he said. His generation had hit the streets for a few weeks of adolescent political ardour, were repelled and fell away.

"We thought *you* were magnificent," I say. "You took on Stalinism, we took on Yankee terror."

"Oh, yes. Our newspapers were full of the war in Vietnam and the student protests. Only 10 per cent of it was believable, of course. I mean, about the war. As for the protests, if you'll pardon me, what exactly did you have to protest about?"

He does not wish to offend, merely to understand. There is much to wonder about. We in the West had said we wanted to be "in solidarity" with the Czech students of the spring of 1968, the summer of 1968, and one understood that, yes, hippies singing Beatles' songs together on Charles Bridge was a fine thing, even a necessary thing (but not the *cause* of the invasion, as a wistful reporter from the hippie Los Angeles press believed). But what then was this "solidarity" with the Communists of Vietnam, these socialist hordes in black pyjamas slithering through the jungles to deal a mortal blow to the one force on earth that could roll back the Russian Empire from central Europe, the American army? In 1968, the students of Prague were absorbed by a carnival of the deadly serious – beer bottles in hand, firecrackers sizzling at the monuments, a banner reading, "The only good Communist is a dead Communist!" Just who was it we in the West were friends of?

We were the *New* Left, I rejoin, reconstituting society around notions of radical democracy. We were hostile to Marxism-Leninism: we didn't support *that* kind of socialism. "We got a lot of our ideas from you, about socialism with a human face."

"You want socialism? Look around."

"No," I reply. "Not *that* kind of socialism."

"We call this the real one."

There is no way around this. The language we deployed, about a future that would be socialist, was already polluted by its own history in Czechoslovakia.

But looking back to 1968 I do not see the ghosts of the victims of power but those of our own youth. Like the Rumanian writer Petru

Popescu, who wrote elegiacally in 1976 of the loss of Prague, under guns and tanks, to his generation, we had thought Prague was a real place (the "heavy, peaceful heart of Europe") when in fact, in dreams of freedom and music, what we spent there were "our unlived lives." After 1968, the people of Prague had somehow to live on without freedom and music. And we without our adolescence.

Later, I will imagine a line of black, bobbing ciphers on the western horizon. I squint. They are doing a little dance and seem to be waving their arms in my direction. Later I will be told that this was the revolution in my country.

STILL LIFE WITH SIGNATURE

PRAGUE, 1987: I track Nikolaj and his wife, Olga, down to their new flat. They have been moved here by the municipal authorities, their former flat having been declared unfit for habitation. This was a stroke of luck: hoping to move, they had had their names on an accommodation list for seven years. The "new" flat is located in a two-hundred-year-old building that was a tavern and brothel in the fifties. Nikolaj takes me down the outside steps into the courtyard and through a heavy wooden door that grates horribly on its hinges. I can see for myself the row of wretched toilets, smell the old odours of sewage and malt. The pub had been called *Peklo*, which means Hell.

They live in two rooms. There is a shower stall in the kitchen; their lavatory is outside with the others. What had choked up the space in their former, four-room flat is now stuffed like sausage meat into the casing of these seven walls: papers stacked to the ceiling, books two and three rows thick upon the open shelves. Paintings are hung on wires in front of the books, so that to get at a dictionary one has to lift up a small, dark still life of flowers in a brass vase. They have only a coal-burning stove. All winter long a fine layer of dust sieves down upon their heads.

For five years it had been their modest pleasure to go to the country for the summer, staying as lodgers in the house where Olga's family had vacationed for fifty years. But neighbours, perhaps envious of the landlord's ability to enrich himself in this way, tipped off the local police that he had been renting to dissidents. The landlord cancelled their reservation. It would cost them seven months' wages to take a holiday to the Bulgarian coast. It is as though they have been condemned to perpetual confinement here, under the coal dust and dismal oil paintings, with geraniums dying on the window ledge and the miasma of ancient sewers seeping through the walls. They console each other with a bit of mordant make-believe.

"I'm not going to Paris this year. How about you?"

"Well, I'm definitely not going to Stockholm, and I've heard that Lena isn't going to Los Angeles."

But tomorrow a friend is going to be released from prison, and two months ago they had a smuggled copy of Josef Skvorecky's *Pribeh inzenyra lidskych dusi* (*The Engineer of Human Souls*), which they took turns reading. They would sleep, then read some more, until they had to pass on that "encyclopedia of fate," as Nikolaj calls it, clutching each other under the blankets and sobbing at the death of Nadia, "whom the gods love."

On the way to the local alehouse to fill up the beer jug, Nikolaj runs into a neighbour, a middle-aged man in the blue smock of a worker. He sways drunkenly, grinning at us with spittle in the corners of his mouth. He used to be a screenwriter and playwright. At nineteen, he had his first play produced at the National Theatre. He was the talk of the town, the darling of the film and theatre set as they careered brilliantly towards their best moment. A year after the Prague Spring of 1968, at thirty, he had lost everything, including his own future. Now he works as a night cleaner. Nikolaj says he is mad.

"Only once, during a late-night police raid on our flat in Prague in the early spring of 1980, was my typewriter in real danger. One of the Leather Jackets (a particularly nasty breed of secret policeman) was approaching it with greed and menace in his eyes.... I was almost blind with fury and frustration.... I sprang between the Leather Jacket and my typewriter just in time. No, you won't take it, I said, and he said he'd kick me, and I replied go right ahead – and then there was a whistle and he had to leave. The raid was over. I sat down, cooled my forehead on the smooth blackness of my typewriter, and cried." – Zdena Tomin, "The Typewriters Hold the Fort"

They aren't all mad. Possessed, perhaps, but not mad. Nikolaj takes me to meet Jan, indefatigable underground literary editor. His last name, nicely, means "shovel."

We meet Jan in the leafy courtyard of a restaurant not far from the American embassy. He has issued a collection of critical essays in a samizdat edition of thirty copies and believes it has had four or five hundred readers. He wants me to know these are quality readers! Some young writers have published *only* in samizdat – the clandestine distribution of onion-skin typesheets *is* publishing – they are magnificent!

There's a strong breeze and it flaps around all of Jan's manuscript pages. He is working on an anthology of Czech poetry that will eventually make a samizdat book in Polish translation for the Polish underground. He slaps plates and cutlery in exasperation onto the flimsy sheets and glares at me from behind his round spectacles: it's all my fault, dragging him out to this disorder. But coming here was Nikolaj's idea, an insistence, perhaps, on the normality of writers working at café tables.

Jan speaks a tormented English. I have no German or Czech, he no French or Ukrainian. We're stuck with his torment. He insists I hear him out, even as he tears at his moustache while he ransacks his brain for a word he once knew. I am in an agony of empathy. Nikolaj, hoping to be helpful, withdraws a number of dictionaries from his shopping bag and strews them among the bread basket and beer mugs, offering up several possibilities for each of Jan's vanished English words. (Nikolaj will do this for me again and again: a tankard of pilsner, a friend possessed of a story I must hear, his own cloudless smile closing the gaps in our faltering speech.)

Once while working several weeks as a dishwasher, Jan tells us, he read forty books by official writers, none of whom had published before 1970. He has survived to tell the tale; will they? By day they write garbage – sentimental stories about animals, say – and by night they read samizdat. Perhaps by now they are schizophrenic.

"What about the next generation?" I ask.

"Waiting for the climate to change so they may enter the literary profession through the front door. Or frittering away their energy in small and inconsequential contributions to fly-by-night alternative publications. Waiting."

You could grow old, waiting.

—

PRAGUE, 1988: I sit with Olga and Nikolaj under the chestnut tree in their back yard, in the deep, soft night and breathless air of August, a quarter moon moving out from behind the towers of a Gothic church to lay its shimmering track down upon the Moldau at our feet. We snack by candlelight on ham, peppers, tomatoes and bread and pass the bottle of schnapps. It's a green humpy bottle of Stara Myslivecka, the Old Huntsman. There he is on the label, a red-cheeked, pipe-smoking mountain man, smiling cheerfully at us and holding up a bottle of ... Stara Myslivecka. This drink, says Nikolaj, is known as "alcohol with a human face."

The branch of the Moldau called Devil's Creek dribbles along the embankment at the base of Nikolaj and Olga's apartment building. Next year the city will begin a lengthy renovation of the creek bed below their window and they will have to live without running water, with the roar of the compressors and the stench of the canalization.

The creek, like all Bohemian streams and rivers, is the home of a *vodnik* or water spirit. The vodnik drags unwary swimmers to their deaths and captures their souls in glass jars. With the draining and renovation of Devil's Creek, he will be driven from his lair. Where then is he to make his residence, he and his collection of glass jars? Nikolaj says he will be welcome to use their toilet tank.

Months later, in Canada, I come across a book published in the United States by Charter 77's foundation in Sweden. It's a picture album of the everyday life of the opposition: dissidents going to trials and funerals, performing *Macbeth* in the living room, jogging with the dog and consoling their children.

There is a set of photos from a Christmas party. In a large dining room balloons are hanging in bunches from the ceiling and candles flicker on the table. "St. Nicholas Day presents for the children of Charter signatories jailed in political trials," reads the caption. No one is identified, but I am sure I recognize Nikolaj as St. Nick. The figure is slimmer, the beard darker and thicker, but it's the same nose, long and straight, and the same full lower lip. He looks quite splendid in his homemade mitre and pastoral tunic, surrounded by little girls crowned with paper stars and a little black devil with horns.

Nikolaj, patron saint of the orphans of the signature.

THE POETS AND THE COMMISSARS

PRAGUE, 1987: On a breezy, balmy Sunday, I am walking along Stresovicka Street on my way to see Zdenek. There is no one about. I slow my pace from the long, purposeful stride I habitually assume when I want to signal that I am not an idler, not a snoop. I pause to admire the gardens of high summer – the roses in aromatic profusion, the succulent, heavy pears – and the clean, fresh paint of the garden gates. I have time to notice that several metres ahead of me on the asphalt sidewalk someone has written something in chalk. Large white letters come into view, a single word, and then I am on top of it. DUBCEK. I stop, my toes on the B. I look around to see if anyone has joined me in the street and then immediately feel sheepish.

But I want to remember this. I want to remember the sensation of seeing DUBCEK, in bold, unscuffed letters – am I the first to pass this morning or have we all walked around the inscription to leave it legible for the next passerby? – on a sidewalk in a city in a time where I thought it had been erased. I had not expected that, eighteen years after his banishment into obscurity, there would be any magic left to evoke in the name. I had not expected that out there in the bustle of the city was a graffiti artist held in the same nostalgic moment as I. I imagine a teenage boy in T-shirt and sneakers (perhaps even watching me from behind a chintz curtain) scrawling in the middle of the night the one word that pulls together the separated strands of my memory and his learning: the camaraderie of the westerner who can know nothing of what happened after Dubcek in 1969 and the Czechoslovakian kid who knows nothing else.

Dubcek wore a tight blue suit with a white handkerchief folded in squares in his breast pocket. The lapels were narrow, the tie was narrow. He looked as if he would burst through his shirt. He was a Slovak, not a Czech, and his cheekbones squeezed his eye sockets, so that when he smiled he looked half Mongol. He held his clenched fists up to shoulder height and smiled triumphantly – toothy, spontaneous, radiant – as if to say, "Aw, shucks." He was the General Secretary of the Communist Party of Czechoslovakia, and when first the students of Prague and then westerners talked of "socialism with a human face," we had his slightly goofy face in mind.

It is delicious to sit in Zdenek's roomy study, the window pushed open to let in the sounds of his garden and the Sabbath drone of an occasional automobile and the dilatory exchanges of neighbours. He offers me tea – I have a choice from among a rank of Twinings tins, gifts of visitors who have preceded me – while elsewhere in the house his daughter, son-in-law and two grandchildren quietly mind their own business.

It is the study of a gentleman and a scholar, a translator of Shakespeare and Joyce, a man with the souvenirs of his previous life to remind him he is a cosmopolitan: the yellowing Penguin paperbacks, a poster from the Metropolitan Museum of Art, snapshots of friends in Paris, hardcover editions of American, English, French and German novels and, in a neat pile, months-old copies of the *New York Review of Books*, the *New Statesman* and *Newsweek* that he must pass on in a few days to their next reader. He will not tell me how he got them.

I sit in an armchair; he sits across from me on a divan under two paintings. In one, a solitary figure is standing on a vast stretch of pavement. The outline of the fence and watchtower of what we decode to be a concentration camp lies across the horizon. At its base, the word ALCYON has been imprinted in the pavement like the last word from a lost tribe before their vanishing. When Zdenek admired his friend's work, his friend told him he could have it if he first wrote a short story based on what he saw. Zdenek wrote a story about the last human being alive after the atomic Armageddon.

I have come to Zdenek to talk about the fifties. I excavate the lives of my generation and hit rock, sparks flying, at the layer of their parents' lives. Zdenek could be our grandfather.

"If," Zdenek begins, "we think of the fifties as an era of devastation, then they began in 1938 when the Germans closed our universities." Many writers made the decision at that time to give no comfort to the enemy – not to publish as long as Czechoslovakia was under occupation. Month by month, the abstaining literati felt their readers slip away, the possibility of civilizing intercourse blocked by the writers' speechlessness. As the fascist state oozed into every available civic cranny, the public was condemned to cynicism or wishful thinking. Finally, two of Zdenek's professors approached him with the proposition that, as silence bred despair and not resistance and as the only weapon to hand was the "spiritual," it was time to start writing again. The universities were shut down but the university library remained open. Zdenek went every day to research his new project: the life of Cervantes.

In 1987, Zdenek is forbidden to use the university library.

"The total surveillance of the entire population has been spread more gently over everyone and everything, it is devoid of the former spasms of hate. Is this better or worse? It is an attack on the very concept of normal life. I

consider it more dangerous than in the fifties, yet we find it easier to live with." – Ludvik Vaculik, *A Cup of Coffee with My Interrogator*

Zdenek is refilling the teapot when the telephone rings. I assume it's tapped, but he seems to be speaking completely openly to Jan, the blacklisted editor, about Charter 77's arrangements for the funeral of Vaclav Cerny, eminent critic, blacklisted teacher and one of the Charter's first signatories. As we take up our conversation again, Ludvik Vaculik arrives, bristly and vivacious. He is one of the sixties' enfants terribles, author of a speech to the Writers' Union that led to his expulsion from the Party and now the writer of funny and bitter feuilletons about everyday life in the "alternative city" of the underground. He gives me a ferocious look, not at all happy, I guess, to run into a foreigner at Zdenek's today. He has come to take delivery of an underground edition of the short stories of an ex-teacher who had once vowed never to write again. Bundles in his arms, Vaculik leaves us, but not ten minutes later the poet Pavel is at the door, a newspaper rolled under his arm. Zdenek inserts an envelope into the paper. The conversation turns on the publication of some of Pavel's poems in an émigré journal in Munich. I assume the envelope contains his royalty earnings in hard currency.

Pavel stays for tea. The doorbell rings again. Two window cleaners, in the vicinity on a job, drop by to say hello: blue coveralls, a mop, a bucket, rags folded over their arms like a wine steward's white towel. One is a historian, the other a critic of French literature. They too stay for tea. The critic tells us a little joke.

"I was on a cleaning job right in the city centre and overheard a French couple not two metres away from me who had obviously got lost and were trying to find their bearings on a map. I put down my mop, walked over to them and gave them directions, in French. They were very grateful and, as they strolled away, I heard the woman say to her husband, 'Such cultivated workers they have here in Czechoslovakia!' And now they're probably back in France, telling their friends about the astonishing progress of the Czech working class under socialism."

—

"We sometimes argue whether things are worse now than in the fifties or if they are better. We can find sufficient evidence for both contentions." – Ludvik Vaculik, *A Cup of Coffee with My Interrogator*

PRAGUE, 1988: Zdenek talks about the liberation in 1945, the Communist "coup" in 1948: days of mass demonstrations by Communist supporters until the ailing President, disarmed by a mass resignation of non-Communist ministers, invited the General Secretary of the Communist Party to form a government. In 1948, the newspaper where Zdenek was employed was shut down and it became impossible for him to earn his living in publishing. "Some of us realized," he says, "that because there is a close connection between what one writes and the state of one's soul, it would be worse than pointless to write under Party approval." Others had no choice: Catholic authors, the democratic camp, even the pro-Communist avant-garde were all proscribed. Desert time.

People collapsed. They made "confessions." These became a literary genre of their own, edited and polished and rehearsed. Like so: "I have committed grave crimes against the people's democratic order, against the Communist Party and against the Czechoslovak people. I was a treacherous enemy within the Party. Even after my arrest I denied my guilt and it was long before I decided to admit the full depth of my crimes. I am justly an object of contempt and deserve the maximum and the hardest punishment." Who was going to argue? Confessions came from the same people who, a few months earlier, had been complaining of "insufficient Bolshevik vigilance" in the matter of unmasking the agents of imperialism – often, old friends.

Important members of the university faculties suddenly joined the Party's front organizations, made denunciations and sent in anonymous notes to the Party press revealing that X was the son of a "millionaire" or Y was "too friendly" to American literature. The worst period was 1950–53. Zdenek had the feeling that at any moment the secret police would enter his house, take him away and hang him. Some of his friends broke down, writing doggerel and glib texts of celebratory socialist realism. Others retreated into private life, into close friendships if they were lucky, or simply into glum and sullen domesticity, cutting off contact with other families who might – who knows? – betray them. And, anyway, there was no longer anything to say.

"If a writer remains silent," said the poet Jaroslav Seifert in a famous speech to the Writers' Congress of 1956, "he's lying." It would be another ten years before the poets would finally gag on the silence. In that lead-up to the Spring, it was hard to know how best to survive. It seemed inflexibility might save you: to defend yourself against the incessant lying in the press and official literature, you simply stopped reading. You never turned on the radio. At television news time, you went out for a walk in the streets where, to avoid the exhortation and the language of rapture (translated from Russian) on the posters, you walked with your eyes on your shoes.

Zdenek can look up now; in 1988 he can buy the *Financial Times* and he is no longer being followed. On the other hand, his translation of *Long Day's Journey into Night*, which he is revising, will have to be published under a colleague's name. He tells me that months ago, his friend, the writer Ivan Klima, submitted a novel to an official publisher. There's been no reply. This is a good sign. A silent publisher is one who isn't vilifying you.

Zdenek tells me that Bohumil Hrabal has been invited to (re)join the Writers' Union. Does the collaborationist literary establishment sniff the wind and open its doors to the blacklisted writers one at a time? No, rather one old man is terrified of dying in obscurity.

Hrabal had been a law student when the Nazis closed down the universities. Until 1963, he wrote for the desk drawer; one story, *mirabile dictu*, appeared in a short-lived literary journal, but any novels that got as far as the typescript stage were ordered destroyed. Then, in the exhilarating season of the sixties, publishers competed for Hrabal's manuscripts; his books were displayed in the shops and reviewed in the newspapers. Readers wanted to shake his hand. And then the catastrophe. Expulsion from the Writers' Union in 1969, the banning of all his books and his distraught and despondent exile in the blacklist again. Long years of anonymity, growing old among oblivious generations.

In 1975, Hrabal made a deal: for an indirect "self-criticism" (he had been wrong, he wrote, to have called the invasion of his homeland a "national tragedy"), his heavily censored books would be published. He now writes two versions. The first he works on in close consultation with the official censor. The second is the unexpurgated edition, which he submits for publication to the underground.

And which one of us has not done the same, reserving for ourselves in the private keep of our imagination the book we could have written?

To his friends, Hrabal pointed out that it was precisely the current cohort of underground writers who had pushed him into literary life after the war. What was he supposed to do now, damn it – just walk away from the displays in bookstore windows and the chats on television and the pay cheques for a job well done? He was a Czech writer. He wanted to be published in Czechoslovakia and be read by Czechs. Let overheated undergraduates burn his books in the garbage cans in the parks, but let them answer this: what is the duty of the writer, to die or to write?

Some writers joined the Party very sincerely. They believed in the promise of radical reorganization of society and they believed in their role as spokespersons for this transformation: "deepening the consequences of the postwar liberation," they called it. There is the case of the provincial bard who, before his arrival in Prague, the Spring, the occupation, the escape west, the international reputation, wrote of the Great Helmsman: "When Stalin lights his pipe in the morning, the whole world is illuminated." Do we wish now that he actually believed it or that he didn't? Which is unforgivable – naiveté or perjury?

Zdenek says that during the confrontations in the 1960s between the members of the Writers' Union and the Ministry of Culture and the hot discussions about "freedom of creativity" and censorship and bureaucracy and "Party lines," the postwar Communist writers' ambition to "speak for" the submerged consciousness of the nation suddenly fused with their conscience. "At the Writers' Congress in 1967, I entered the hall just as Ivan Klima was comparing censorship by the Party to the worst of the Austro-Hungarian Empire. I couldn't believe my ears. Why had it taken him twenty years to see it?"

Zdenek recalls another scene, this one from the late seventies. He was uneasy about having these two men together in his sitting room: the Communist (freshly ex-) and the former political prisoner who had been sentenced in the 1950s to eight years' hard labour in the uranium mines. The one was as ruddy and plump as the other was tallow-faced and sunken in the chest. But the meeting did not seem to bother them. As Zdenek fussed over the canapés, they poured out his vodka in cupfuls.

"To your health!"

"To yours!"

The ex-Communist penitents who became signatories of Charter 77 lost all formal status and privilege; some went to prison. They were interrogated and humiliated by former comrades. Having let go of the youthful and ardent selves who had believed in Communism and been rewarded with power, they had then to construct middle-aged selves who had zeal and purpose in an illegal organization. Zdenek still hides their books, couriers their royalties and pours them tea. "But there is a danger," he says, in thinking about it now, "in forgiving them too quickly."

WHERE IS UZHHOROD?

PRAGUE, 1987: As a little boy, Zdenek tells me, he was taken to the hills of Uzhhorod for his summer holidays. He thinks of Uzhhorod and gives a little sigh. Why does he sigh? Because Uzhhorod used to be in Czechoslovakia but now lies in Ukraine, and so is "lost." Czechs and Slovaks were never more than a minority there, and now those people they called "Rusyns" call themselves Ukrainians, but still he is regretful. He loved his Uzhhorod.

Cool and bucolic on the western slopes of the Carpathians, a refuge from the dusty, cloying summer heat of Prague, a flight from bourgeois pastimes into rustic entertainments among the Rusyns. (I imagine these Rusyns in sheepskin vests, red stockings, funny hats.) The little boy, Zdenek, is holding fast to his mama's gloved hand, agog at these hillbillies driving their bleating, piss-stained flocks up into the hills from the hardened dirt alleyways of Uzhhorod, yelling and cursing in their odd, sibilant Rusyn tongue: Zdenek's lost Carpathian trolls.

In Slovakia during the war, the Nazis recruited local Ukrainians into a special brigade formed for the purpose of assaulting the local Slovak villages. This is what I've written on a torn piece of paper, loose among my notebooks. I don't know who told me this or even if it's true. But it has the ring of truth: you can be persuaded to assault your neighbours if they are revealed to be strangers after all.

Vaclek, whom I will meet in Belgrade, graduated from Prague film school in the late 1950s. One of his first professional assignments was to shoot an athletic event held at the Slovak/Ukrainian border: Czechoslovak athletes bearing a torch on a relay race across the border into the u.s.s.r. – Uzhhorod. The image that endures for him is that of hundreds of Soviet Ukrainians pressed in a heap against the wire fences at the border, staring in an agony of longing, trying to see relatives last seen before the war, before the border went in, before Uzhhorod slipped away.

I once thought of visiting Uzhhorod, on a trip to Ukraine. "How may I get to Uzhhorod?" I asked the travel agent in Edmonton. I had in mind a trip into the mountains of western Ukraine or, rather, a trip *through* the mountains, for Uzhhorod lies in a terrain known as Beyond the Carpathians. *Away* from Galicia where my relatives live, on the other side of the mountains, westward.

"You don't want to go there," he said. "It takes a very long time from Chernivtsi on a very bad train."

And so I have never been to Uzhhorod.

I sit in the hand-me-down desk in the church basement on Saturday mornings, staring at the map hanging on the wall. I see a large land mass, rather shapeless, billowing in all directions from the Black Sea. It has a lot of cities: Donetsk in the east, Kiev in the middle, Lviv in the west, Odessa in the south and Uzhhorod in the southwest. This is the Ukrainian Soviet Socialist Republic, known to us as "Ukraine." This is "where we come from," "ours." This is perfectly normal. Ukraine is the billowing country of the Ukrainians.

Ah, but what did I know? All these years later, I try to reimpose that map on the geography of my conversations. Its borders bleed away into the lost territories of Central European childhoods: Chernivtsi, lost by the Rumanians. Lviv, lost by the Poles. Uzhhorod, lost by the Czechs and the Slovaks. And suddenly the Ukraine I thought I "came from" has slipped into the dream time of its neighbours, and I cannot get to Uzhhorod by Ukrainian train.

ON THE TRAIL OF THE MASTER

PRAGUE, 1987: He seems a gentleman of the old school, educated in interwar Bohemia – our guide, leaning against the hood of the mini-van and smoking a cigarette in an ebony cigarette holder. As we slide crablike into our seats, he greets us with pleasantries in French, German and English. Of these languages, he speaks English the best and, despite the fact there is only one anglophone in the group, conducts the excursion almost exclusively in that language, except for the odd turn of phrase from the others. "This *je ne sais quoi*," he says, with a flick of his cigarette holder, now empty; or, "*Bitte schön!*" as he pretends to kiss the fingertips of the ladies descending from the van.

He is a retired something-or-other who offers his services to the state tourism agency as chauffeur and guide. He implies that retirement did not suit him.

We will be two hours on the road to Tabor. We will have lunch, then set off for a second stop at a Bohemian castle, Hluboka, before turning back to Prague. I don't know what Hluboka is famous for; my reason for joining the tour is to see Tabor, which had been the seat of the great fifteenth-century peasants' rebellion called the Hussite.

On July 6, 1415, in the southern German city of Constance [Konstanz], Jan Hus, Rector Magnificus of the University of Prague and preacher at Prague's Bethlehem Chapel, was burned at the stake as a heretic, having suffered arrest, imprisonment and torture at the hands of the bishops of the Roman church. The invitation to a church council and the safe conduct offered by King Sigismund of Hungary had been a trap. The bishops' peasants had already gathered and tied the faggots for Hus's pyre. His death would inspire a movement among whole communities of Czechs and lead to wars that recast the fate of the Czech lands in the heart of Europe.

Spread out around us are the broad grain and corn fields of the collectivized farms of Bohemia; they remind me unexpectedly of home and the ambitious plantings of the farmers near Two Hills, Alberta, crops rolling to the horizon, broken only by windrows and wood lots and the occasional sheds and barns of a collective dairy or poultry farm. A phalanx of combines moves in stately formation under a sky as high and wide and blue as Alberta's.

These are the lands of Bohemia's great uproar and agony on the cusp of the modern age, a story that rears up from the rubble of five centuries to claim me: injustice committed upon the weak, radical ideas of resistance, the assault on the gates of the rich, the untimely death of Jan Hus, master, hero, martyr. And so I wait for our guide/chauffeur to name the names, point out the places – the village squares, the rivers and their bridges, the valleys and the crossroads – where it all happened. To evoke the ghosts of the defiant followers of Hus who took this route, withdrawing to Bohemian Tabor from Germanized, Catholic Prague. For surely he is a Czech patriot, this raconteur at the wheel?

But he only moves his right arm in slow arcs to point out to us, every twenty kilometres or so, the birthplace of some Party notable or the headquarters of a textile mill or the outbuildings of a chemical plant. The languor never leaves him.

Hus's words: "Seek out truth, listen to the truth, know the truth, love truth, hold on to truth, defend truth, even unto death." He preached rapturously for the poverty and humility of the Church and against celibacy and monasticism, the blasphemous veneration of saints and relics, and recruiting bishops and cardinals and popes from the corrupted ranks of the wealthiest families. He preached in Czech. To Czech-speaking peasants, to artisans and labourers and, over at the university, to beggared students, he was the parish priest. Against him stood the Germans, and their Czech minions, and a Church that owned 51 per cent of the land. In 1410, when the archbishop of Prague excommunicated Hus and put the whole city under interdict, three students marched in protest. They were arrested by Church authorities and executed. The Master, as Hus is known in the legends, called them martyrs.

The Pope also excommunicated Hus, and the Master fled Prague for the countryside, where he continued his preaching among the peasants and villagers until summoned to Constance, and the torture rack, and the pyre.

Jan Hus's ashes were scattered on the Rhine, probably by his persecutors. His mourners took what was left.

Five hundred and fifty-eight years later, on May 3, 1968, thousands of students, protesting the overweening power of the Communist Party and of its appendages at the university, would stream in through the twisting cobble-stoned streets of the old city of Prague and, in an exhilarated mass, converge in the square at the base of the statue of Hus.

Tabor is much renovated, at least those parts of it facing the central square. Once more our chauffeur leans comfortably against the hood of the van and screws a cigarette into his little black holder. He will wait for us here, in this parking lot. At one o'clock we should regroup and drive away for lunch. I hesitate, hopeful of a bit of history. In the little street directly opposite the museum, he says, there is a very good ice-cream shop. Then he looks meaningfully at his watch. We have forty-five minutes.

I dash into the museum. A dozen rooms confront me, chock-full of Hussiana – maps, documents, portraits, battle plans, miniature reconstructions of the fifteenth-century town – and panels of barely intelligible text. Where is that damned guide now that he could be useful? I imagine him strolling languidly around the square, licking an ice cream. I concentrate ferociously on one or two texts and explanatory markers, deciphering what I can of the Czech. I have come to the heart of the Hussite idea and can only stumble through it like a child playing blindman's bluff.

With the country at the point of civil war twenty years after Hus's execution, the Hussites dug in at Tabor. Using guerrilla tactics and mobile field fortifications, they were able three times to throw off the forces of the enemy. But in 1434 they were finally defeated, not by papal or imperial armies but by a breakaway Hussite faction known as the Utraquists. These were the "moderates" who would eventually reconcile themselves with Rome and elevate their own man to the Bohemian throne. (But who now remembers the Utraquists?)

Inspired by Hus's radical theology and the necessary democracy of a field camp, the Hussites in Tabor had waged a war of liberation not only from the German aristocracy and the papacy but also from certain ideas: that any person should be placed higher than other citizens or that there was a separate morality for priests or separate privileges for landlords. Landlords, said the Hussites, were "social idlers" living off the fruits of others' toil. In their own communities the Hussites organized a communism of goods and abolished feudal obligation among the peasants. Girls were educated alongside boys, women preached and fought in the army. In Hussite lands, the priesthood was abolished and confession was prohibited.

This glorious experiment would invigorate reformers and radicals for centuries. Surely, I think, as we speed towards lunch, it would be claimed by even a twentieth-century Czech? Had not the modern Father of the Nation, Tomas Masaryk, himself described the inheritance of the Hussites as clarity, reasonableness, morality, fraternity? Had not Huss's countrymen, even in dispersal, kept the faith? But I have not counted, in my zeal of solidarity with the elegant polyglot chauffeur dipping his fork into the luncheon casserole, on a rejection *on principle* of ideas or historical characters associated with the Communist Party of Czechoslovakia. As I sip the pilsner and listen to the chitchat about hotel rooms in Prague, I realize that, because the state held Hus and his ideas up for admiration, Czech citizens are bound to find them humbug. I can understand, but I do not approve, and my biliousness does not subside all the way to the castle.

The mini-van swings into a vast parking lot full of tour buses. The chauffeur's excitement is palpable. With beatific expansiveness and a sweep of his arm, he announces the splendour we are about to visit: an exact replica of Windsor Castle, the latest version of a thirteen-century castle of venerable lineage: the house of Schwarzenberg.

Aroused at last, our guide is perfervid in his admiration of this august branch of the German aristocracy that had been so gracious as to set up house in humble Bohemia. For three hours he narrates tirelessly all the achievements of the remarkable Schwarzenbergs and their complex and fascinating genealogy. He points out for our delectation room after room of paintings, carpets, silverware, crystal, furniture, weaponry. He does not say how Germans came to be lords and masters in the Czech lands.

The anti-papist Czech nobility confronted Ferdinand of Habsburg and the Holy Roman Empire on November 8, 1620, at the Battle of White Mountain. They lost.

On June 21, 1621, three nobles, seven knights and seventeen burghers were publicly executed in Prague, their properties redistributed among foreigners and their followers given the choice of conversion or emigration. The Church recovered its land and its serfs. The Jesuits, given absolute authority over education, emptied the libraries and burned Hussite books. One Jesuit boasted that he had personally put 60,000 volumes to the torch.

From the surrounding Protestant countries, old and new books were smuggled into Czech lands and copied in a miniature hand, varnished to look like small blocks of wood and inserted into the beams of rooms or barns to conceal and protect them. These were the first Czech samizdat.

Fifty years after the Battle of White Mountain, most of the noble families returned to their estates, much chastened. They reembraced the Church of Rome, learned to speak and write German, and resumed their pleasant way of life in the bucolic Bohemian countryside, admiring their vineyards; the peasants resumed their indentured labour in the fields.

Then too began the era of the great building of Prague – the Prague of the opening night of Mozart's *Don Giovanni*, of the splendid creamy façades of villas and theatres so much admired by today's tourists. The baroque, one writer has observed, is the style of the Czech national disaster.

Still smarting from the forty-five frustrating minutes in the museum of Tabor, and because I know it will annoy him, I insist on asking our guide about the peasants who worked the Schwarzenberg fields. Were they enserfed? Did they have an education? Were the women literate? He frowns at me, then waves his hand airily, as though to dispel my mood of earnestness. He is our host and does not wish to fatigue his guests with the uncouth past.

The Party would have him revile the Schwarzenbergs. But if he, the suave gentleman-citizen of a weak country, must have a master, he will take the glittery courtier from Vienna and repudiate the peasants' hero, the parish priest with manure on his boots.

FILLING IN THE BLANKS

PRAGUE, 1987: It is drizzling a bleak, cold rain and we have all come inside the National Museum to seek shelter, hundreds of us in a long, enervated queue waiting to give up our sodden umbrellas and rancid coats to the cheerless custodian of the cloakroom. In a shoal of tow-headed schoolchildren, I drift into the rooms of the exhibit called "Czechoslovakia in the Twentieth Century."

In the first room, we gape at photographs of Emperor Franz Josef taken during Bohemia's heyday just before the Great War, at some fancy women's dresses hung on mannequins, at crystal ware, tea caddies, shop signs, stained-glass art-nouveau window panels. It is like being at a garage sale of the Empire; these are the leftovers after the best items have been carried off by a better clientele.

The second room: A few dull photographs of glum and frowning crowds massed together to greet the bloodless arrival of the Nazis, a girl's black jacket hung to display the yellow star sewn on its sleeve, another group of photographs of the band of partisans who shot Acting Protector Reinhard Heydrich and then were martyred in the basement of the Orthodox Church of Saints Cyril and Methodius in Prague. The drama is veiled and muted: if this was a time of protracted agony and resistance, the curator is not telling us.

But the books I have read fill me in. I know that on the morning of May 27, 1942, Herr Stellvertretende Reichsprotektor, Obergruppenführer der SS und General der Polizei Reinhard Heydrich was shot by two Czech resistance workers, Jozef Gabcik and Jan Kubis, as he was driving into Prague from his country home. He died in great agony and was buried in solemn, Fascist pomp in Berlin. To avenge his death, the entire village of Lidice was destroyed by order of the Chief of Security Police in Prague: 173 men shot on the spot, 198 women shipped to Ravensbruck, 81 children gassed in Chelmno and 17, of more Aryan features, adopted into German families.

Gabcik and Kubis, who had been dropped into the country by British aircraft, took refuge in the basement of the church of Saints Cyril and Methodius with five other parachutists. On June 18, the church was surrounded by SS troops and police who exchanged fire with the Czechs until, exasperated by the inconclusive battle, the SS cut a hole in the church wall, introduced a hose and pumped water into the basement to flush the fighters out. It is said that the Czechs used the last seven bullets on themselves.

Vecna Pamet. Eternal be their memory.

The third room: History skips to a version of 1948. Of the journey between liberation in 1945 and the socialist republic of 1948, nothing. Of the arrests, tortures, confessions, trials and hangings until 1952, nothing. Exhortation has taken the place of narration. *Proletari vsech zemi spojte se! Za sozialismus a mir!* Proletarians of the world, unite! For socialism and peace! It wasn't until 1968, during the Prague Spring, that the story was finally publicized of how the police chauffeur in charge of the ashes of the dead – the ones who'd been hanged in 1952 and sent to the crematorium – boasted that he had driven around all over north Bohemia scattering the ashes here and there. There was another version of this tale: that he had simply put the ashes in a potato sack, slung it into the back of his car and made for the suburbs of Prague. On hitting an icy patch in the road, he thoughtfully scattered the ashes on the ice and then turned around and drove back. In both versions, the punch line is the same: it was the first time, the chauffeur quipped, that he'd been able to fit eleven passengers into the back seat of his car.

I have also heard stories from friends: "My father was a businessman. In 1951, he was arrested. Whole trades were arrested: furriers, jewellers, realtors. They sentenced him to three years for the crime of 'self-enrichment.' They even interrogated my mother, charged her with having 'co-operated' with the enemy, who was her husband. It was the first day of school. The police arrived at 4:00 A.M. so I missed the whole first day. On the second day, the policeman took me to school, which marked me for a long time. My father was an enemy of the people. But I knew something was wrong with this. I knew it."

The fourth room: Pinned to a black felt board at the back of a small glass cabinet are four documents – typed notices – pertaining to the events of 1968. "Because of capitalist-imperialist collaboration with certain reactionary elements in Czechoslovakia, the armies of the fraternal socialist nations were forced to come to the assistance of the imperilled homeland." Sovietized banalities. The language is perfectly intelligible.

That is 1967–68 in its entirety. No photographs, no newspapers, no leaflets or pamphlets, no dishonoured insignia or scorched and shredded proclamations ripped off telephone posts. No banners, no poems, no girls in miniskirts jiving on film sets, no hippies on Charles Bridge playing guitars and singing, "We all live in a yellow submarine." No soldier from Tadzhikistan peering down from his turret and weeping in front of the students who jeer at him and tell him to go back home. He would if he could, but he is going to stay where he is for the next two decades.

"After the tanks had come, my father wanted the whole family to get out of the country," another friend has told me. "Before the war, he had been an organizer for the Social Democrats. After the Communist coup in '48, he was sentenced to hard labour in the uranium mines. There were 20,000 prisoners in one of those mines alone – Jachymov. Cursed be its name! He was finally released in 1960. Not even the death of Stalin in 1953 had sprung him. When the tanks came, he wasn't going to hang around for more."

The rest of the exhibit: Life for the next twenty-one years is, as they say, normal. We drift off to the rooms dedicated to paleontology.

LIVING HUMAN

PRAGUE, 1988: Marketa has married a furnace stoker who works in a maternity hospital. He has got her the job in the basement, monitoring the heating plant. Three times a day she flits about among the pipes, ducts and furnaces, checking dials and gauges and thermometers. Between inspections, she reads. Chartists do not have career paths.

Marketa is no longer summoned to interrogation. Upon marriage, she ceased to be of much interest to the police; now her husband, gentle and sweet-faced Premek, endures the ritual. "Who does your wife meet with? What do they talk about?"

When I visited her in 1987, she was alone in the basement. Now, a year later, Marketa's unemployable brother, David, has begun to alternate shifts with her. They have a little room with a cot, a cassette player, a shower stall and a small fridge, and it is here that they receive visitors. I come bearing the expected provisions – coffee, Marlboros, chocolate – feeling like a GI in Yokohama. We munch and chat.

Marketa wants the life of a Christian mother: to have several children and to stay at home with them until they go to school, rearing them in an atmosphere of domestic affection. This is an end in itself, she says, and a far more humane occupation than her job at the hospital. Perhaps the uterine compulsions pulsate down through the maternity wards above, I think. Outside the building, gripping drooping bouquets of flowers, the new papas of Prague stare up at the windows for a glimpse of their phantom wives and babies.

I mention the women's movement in the West, its ideas concerning the patriarchal family and the struggle of women for equality in the workplace. But I have misjudged this young woman of the Prague resistance, too glibly assumed her agreement. Normally she's as cool as a cucumber, but now she flares up. "I've never understood women in the West, why you would choose a dull and stuffy office job doing stupid work all day when you could be at home with your children!" She casts her eyes around the little basement room beside the furnaces to make her point. "You would choose *this*?"

Don't I understand that the rearing of children is humanizing, that even housework can be a labour of love? she asks. She acknowledges that "generally" Czech men don't lift a finger around the house, but says even this is changing in the underground, where blacklisted men, out of work or working the menial night shift, take up the slack of childcare and housework for their wives busy at better-paying jobs.

Marketa is prepared to sacrifice her family's standard of living to stay at home with her children. This is, in fact, a point of principle, a strike for pietistic, Christian values and a blow against the inhuman mobilization of women's labour by the Communists. By refusing to provide mothers with what they need – cheap and healthy food, decent living space, affordable appliances – the state has forced women into the work force, covering up this compulsion with resounding slogans and a flower from the boss for every female employee on International Women's Day.

Marketa is not fooled. She has not been in the streets agitating for her rights. She hasn't had to: her "rights" are delivered by the Party. And how, she asks rhetorically, is she supposed to put her faith in such an emancipation when this is the same Party that has delivered a constitution it perverts and a dictatorship of the proletariat composed of anxious and exhausted women trapped in clangorous factories, bus queues and the crowds of May Day, each waving a red flag?

Marketa and Premek take me to Strelecky Island under First of May Bridge to catch the last performance at a theatre festival. Although legal, the festival is unofficial. At the gate we are greeted by a lopsided, hand-painted sign informing us without explanation that all remaining performances have been cancelled. We wander among the closed-up tents, the vacant stages, silenced puppet theatres and comatose marionettes. Perhaps the performances have been too popular.

A group of loitering actors who have come upon a bottle of wine behind the counter of a food kiosk invite us to drink. When the wine runs out, we make our way back across the river in search of other entertainment, but it is Monday and the jazz clubs are all closed. The beer cellars have stopped serving food, so we wander next to Wenceslas Square and join a long line of tourists queuing for grilled sausages and chunks of rye bread. It is nine o'clock in downtown Prague.

"Behold," says Premek, "a capital city of socialism!"

He gesticulates towards the badly lit, emptying spaces of the square, conjuring up for me the day in 1969 when he had travelled with pride and apprehension from his factory in northern Bohemia to a protest rally here, right where we stand now in the gloom. He had hoisted a placard in the name of his buddies back home: "This Factory Is Not in Agreement with the Occupation!" He had felt the mission to be a signal honour and remembers being amazed at the nonchalance of the people of Prague going about their daily business, passing through ranks of tanks to the grocery store.

We decide on the open air taverna of Slovansky Island, but the beer runs out just as we arrive. It is a beautiful night, gentle and warm under the linden trees, and we do not want to go home, to disappear into the dark on a clattering tram. Marketa, who has many friends, suddenly spots a table full of young musicians who hail us over: eight people and a bottle of wine. One of the young men dashes around the corner and is back again with another bottle; he uncorks it and pours it out in an exuberant round of salutations and toasts. He is the lead singer in an unofficial rock group called Joseph's Gypsy Orchestra. He passes around his Walkman so we can all have a listen.

Marketa slips a videocassette into my purse and asks me to get it out to Toronto, to friends, which I do, knees knocking at Customs and Passport Control at the Prague airport. In Toronto it will sit gathering dust. It cannot be played on a North American VCR. Never mind, in another year and a half, it will be November 1989, and Marketa will go to meet her friends in broad daylight in Wenceslas Square to plan Day Two of the revolution.

STATIONS OF THE UNDERGROUND

PRAGUE, 1988: World premiere of *Video Journal Number Four.* The images are foggy and they wobble, as though the hand that held the camera were trembling. I wonder if, deprived of this room, these people I am with, I would recognize the event. After all, the milling crowd, the anguished expressions of civilians, the studied nonchalance of the soldiers huddling together as if in self-defence, even the grey grittiness of the setting (a European city, at night) is almost archetypal: war, in our time.

"We don't know who still can hear us in Czechoslovakia," a weary and disconsolate narrator announces in voice-over. "Please, everyone, distribute the news everywhere. Our borders have been crossed. We can no longer defend our republic. It is useless to fight." And then there was nothing: a camera run out of film, a microphone clicked off, just the oceanic sounds of the atmosphere at midnight, the radio waves already on their journey through the cosmos while the ant-people below shook their tiny fists at the tanks and then went, weeping, home to bed.

It is almost the twentieth anniversary of these events, of the Soviet invasion of 1968.

Our host, Sasha, is a wizard of technology, his apartment a warehouse for the media productions of the underground. I note a JVC stereo, a Sony colour television, a VCR, a film projector and an IBM clone computer. Video cameras and spare parts must be smuggled into Czechoslovakia; film stock too must be smuggled in or purloined from workplaces. When all the cassettes are used up, the originals have to be erased and reused. Copies are made after hours in film labs where the underground has sympathizers: it takes two full days and nights to make fifty. Sasha is very nervous about the VCR: he has "borrowed" it from a friend's workplace for the weekend and is desperately anxious about damaging it.

More jittery camera work. Alexander Dubcek, the woebegone Slovak, General Secretary of the Communist Party in the unexpected role of darling of the masses. A May Day parade. *The* May Day parade, May 1968. A forest of flags and banners and placards. "Of our own free will, for the first time!" Veterans of the International Brigades who went to Spain, former political prisoners, hippies. "Love not war!" "Long live the U.S.S.R. – but at its own expense!" The beaming Dubcek upon the reviewing stand, waving. King of the May.

"That was the first time I saw Communists smiling," says Marketa, from the back of the little room. She was twelve in 1968.

I can barely understand the language of the narration and I recognize only here and there a politician's face. The street corners, the living rooms, the clubs so familiar to my companions are only street corners and rooms and clubs to me. I was twenty-three when I first saw these images. The Communist hero with the loopy grin, the crowds with human faces, the students singing Beatles songs and the tanks at rest under flickering street lamps.

Now, in 1988, *Video Journal*'s own roving reporter accosts men and women in the streets of Prague. "What," she asks, "does 1968 mean to you?" They shuffle, scrape their feet, puff on cigarettes; they look over their shoulders, drop their voices, bite their lips. "We don't want to discuss it" or "Everyone says we are not to discuss it but, since we have no information, there's nothing not to discuss." Or, from a sunbathing schoolgirl: "It was an explosion of antisocialist elements." Or: "I'm not interested in politics." Or: "It's a personal question which I have no wish to discuss with you in public." Finally, an old woman from the countryside, stout and bent, her head in a white kerchief, clasps her hands over her heart. "Many, many things happened in 1968. I haven't been able to breathe for the twenty years since." She sighs deeply, as though the breath were being pressed out of her.

Next the interviewer talks to Marta Kubisova. After the occupation, Kubisova, "the queen of song," became even more famous for her protest songs – and for the kiss she planted on Dubcek in public when even his associates had stopped greeting him. Now she is a member of Charter 77 and has not sung publicly for eighteen years. Her records were withdrawn from shops and jukeboxes and the master tapes erased. Her image was excised from old television programs. Kubisova's erstwhile singing partners, the Golden Kids, who did not kiss Dubcek, kept on singing, toured the entire Soviet bloc and became rich. The interviewer asks her what she has lost. "Not much," she replies.

Video Journal Number Four concludes. A theatrical performance at a youth club, a parody of Raymond Chandler on the hundredth anniversary of his birth: drunks in a bar, an American bar, sloppily demanding whiskey, listing leftwards off the bar stool; babes jumping around in a swell version of the Charleston, hoods in spats with hats smashed down over their brows. What a mishmash.

The photography assistant lets us in the back door off the alley and we join a crowd packed around a film projector in the middle of a small, hot, smoky room. It is Sunday evening. Because she sometimes works late, the assistant has a key to the lab, a bit of official privilege that unlocks the door to this illegal screening.

The images flit over a bare white stone wall; underneath the poly-chromatic pictures of a Slovak village lies the textured shadow of coarse, flaking stone, the bedrock of these flickering, light- and airborne images snatched from Carpathian Rumania. A village on the mountain slope, in the rain, its roadways turned into sucking bogs of mud, ancient wooden dwellings tottering in the mist, leathery faces and thick, knobby hands around the table, around the blackened pot of soup. An old man: "I've lived under the Austrians, now I live under the Rumanians. It's all the same to me who's boss." Stout and furrowed women sing as they pluck skinny chickens. Two horses, a woman and a wooden harrow labour on the hillside. A child reads ponderously from a schoolbook: "I am a citizen of the Rumanian Socialist Republic and I live in a beautiful, rich land."

There is a grumble of indignation around the projector.

The film is the work of a graduating student of a film school. Submitted to the faculty to satisfy the requirements of the degree, it was disqualified on the grounds it gave offence to a fraternal socialist repub-lic. This screening, then, is her defence.

In the back rooms of a television studio, a friendly engineer makes the eleventh-generation copy of a videocassette of *The Deerhunter*, which, in its unsubtitled version, is widely believed to be an anti-Communist work.

Marketa takes me to an unofficial rock concert. It is hours by slow tram and bus, and then another half hour on foot, to get to the dacha owned by the parents of the boy who's arranged the show. (Where are the par-ents? Do they know what's going on?)

We are not invited into the dacha. We spread ourselves out on the broad grassy slope of the yard, fanning out from a makeshift stage, speakers and a sound board. There are about seventy-five of us: babies and dogs, skinny men with ponytails and women in bare feet, peasant skirts, headbands and beads passing a wine bottle from hand to hand. They look like hippies who haven't quite got it right: there's no dope and there's no dancing. The music is discordant, raw, aggressive (is tuning up a Bolshevik conspiracy?), no longer recognizably rock but a percussive subtext to the gesticulations of the berserk: both form and content, it is explained to me, are the "concrete expression" of rock artists' acute frustration in the face of artistic repression.

The lyrics are passed around with the wine bottle, sheets of samizdat dribbled with Bohemian plonk. Three groups perform – Asphalt, Frou Frou and Dogs of War. It's the last of these that the fuss is all about. They were once professional rock musicians, lost their status in the post-1968 "normalization" and are performing now for the first time in three years. They have subscribed to the tenet of the underground that "it is better not to play at all than to play what the establishment demands."

Such festivals are rare, for good reason. Unofficial musicians have been raided in rehearsal and their unlicenced equipment confiscated. Those who have made their property available for rehearsals or performances have lost their houses to sudden municipal improvements such as rights-of-way or bus turnabouts or to zealous application of the local bylaws. A dacha in the countryside was confiscated on the grounds its garden was attracting wild pigs – or could, or would, or might.

Nikolaj invites me to a vernissage. The show features the work of artists prohibited from exhibiting for the last fifteen years. Its organizers have been granted permission to place small notices in the newspapers and to hang a festive banner over the entrance with big red letters announcing VYSTAVKA (Exhibition). But official tolerance is grudging: the venue is a *Kulturni Dum* (cultural centre) located in an industrial neighbourhood far from the gilded false fronts of central Prague. We get there by clattering streetcar along avenues of drab and decomposing flats and factories.

Nevertheless, *le tout* Prague of a certain milieu is in attendance, streaming in under a big red star hoisted onto the roof. Just inside the doors, at the beer and wine concession, the mob is intense, seeking drink and refuge from the din inside the hall, where a punk band called All the Beautiful Machines is playing with a fervour to summon up the dead. I stand in front of a painting in the company of a social worker who assists former prisoners to find jobs and places to live. "Including political prisoners?" I ask. "Oh, yes, but not Havel," she replies. "Havel's rich." I hadn't asked.

The paintings depress me. They are the work of the painters of my generation, who erupted from their studios in 1967 and 1968 only to be hurled back into isolation, painting private pictures of the absurd. Bad technique, weak drawing, bad design, ugly colours: fifteen years of painting incommunicado, refusing all discourse with socialist realism and denied contact with Munich, Paris, Los Angeles. And yet, perhaps the medium – violent, unattractive, aggressive, energetic – is the message? That, and the virtual absence of the human figure.

Premysl invites me to visit his studio. He lost his chance to attend art school when his father, a human rights lawyer, was dismissed during the normalization and went to the countryside to seek the honest work of a farm labourer. Premysl instructed himself from books and posters and the banned canvases of art school graduates. He has set himself up in a private studio at the top of Neruda Street to which he invites stray foreigners to view his work.

He describes his style as "hyperrealistic" with "fantastic overtones." Such critics as he's had take a different view: they have attacked his work as "imperialistic," meaning "aping western values." But as Egon Bondy, the celebrated underground critic, points out in an essay printed in samizdat – Premysl passes it over to me so that I may verify this – there are no references in Premysl's work that are specifically western, unless a toothbrush is western, a bathing suit, a motorcycle, a mirror, an elevator. He has no collectors in his homeland, but two of his canvases hang in the home of a dentist in Los Angeles.

He's been invited to send some paintings to an exhibition in Copenhagen. He's already packed them up but offers to show me photographs instead. I take my place at a paint-splotched table with three young Italians; Premysl met these kids in the street and has given them shelter in his studio. Nobody says a word. I wait for the Italian girl to pass me a snapshot. She has no arms; she passes it between her teeth. It's a painting of a fat blonde woman in aviator goggles sitting in a swimming pool.

THE JAN PALACH SCRAPBOOK

PRAGUE, 1988: Sometime in January 1969, on the steps of the National Museum, he doused himself with gasoline and set himself on fire. In his agony he ran berserk down into the square that lies in the heart of the city, and he died at the base of the statue of good king Wenceslas. So I had been told. So I remembered: a black-and-white photograph in a Toronto newspaper, some details of gruesome suffering, a dead student, bitter, charred, martyred, one of us.

I want to be photographed at this monument, just outside the heavy chain loop encircling it. During the first days of the occupation, an eleven-year-old boy, standing on the statue's pediment, had tried to push a Czech flag down the nose of a Soviet tank and was shot dead. The spot instantly became a shrine – candles, flowers, pictures of ousted leaders Dubcek, Svoboda and Smrkovsky. Because I think that my motive must be obvious to everyone, including plainclothes policemen, I look furtive and impatient, as though I am just passing by on my way to the museum.

The record shop just one street over from Wenceslas Square has out-door speakers. I stand in front of the shop and listen to the yelping voice of Bob Dylan. The young people inside were probably not even born at the time of the death of Jan Palach, student. It feels oppressively odd to be a foreigner here and the only one remembering.

In 929, Saint Wenceslas, the Christianizer, the Premyslovic prince of Bohemia, was murdered by his brother, Boleslav, the pagan, at the door of a church.

Jan Palach was a twenty-two-year-old student at the Philosophy Faculty at Charles University. The day after his death, thousands of his fellow students demonstrated in Red Army Square in front of the Philosophy Faculty building. They tore down the street signs and, under the dark and ponderous portico, set up a big placard that read, "Jan Palach Square."

Palach came from the village of Vsetaty, and because his grave in Prague became a point of pilgrimage and demonstrations for his mourners, the authorities activated an obscure regulation that required bodies to be buried at the birthplace of the deceased. Version one: Palach's mother came to Olsany cemetery and took his coffin home. Version two: One night a group of secret policemen crept into Olsany cemetery, dug up his coffin and delivered it to a crematorium. In the village of Vsetaty, his mother received the urn of ashes and reburied her son.

Ordeal by fire: once, and then again.

I had imagined Jan Palach as thin and blond and agitated. Eventually, I come across a high-schoolish picture of him – a sweet-faced youth with a mild smile on a wide, flattened upper lip, one eyebrow higher and thicker than the other, very short, dark hair. He has no character yet, no agitation.

"The Ten Commandments: 1. I don't know. 2. Don't care. 3. Don't tell. 4. Don't have. 5. Don't know how to. 6. Don't give. 7. Don't go. 8. Don't sell. 9. Don't show. 10. Do nothing." *Vecerni Praha* (*Evening Prague*), August 26, 1968

Students rose up in 1848 throughout the Austro-Hungarian empire. In Cracow in March, in Prague in June, in Lemberg (a.k.a. Lwow, Lviv) in November. In the Whitsunday Uprising in Prague, students and workers erected barricades in the narrow streets of the old quarters and held them for five days against the Austro-Hungarian army. They were finally crushed by the bombardment of the guns of General Windischgratz.

They were buried in Emaus cemetery, now destroyed. Czech patriots duly made the pilgrimage to lay heaps of flowers at the graves until – so the writer Jiri Grusa tells us in his feuilleton "A Bride for Sale"– Austrian Minister of the Interior Alexander Bach, tiring of the ceremony, had the remains dug up in 1851 and transferred under cover of night to an unknown place.

On January 19, 1988, at three in the afternoon, three Charter 77 spokespersons laid a wreath at the statue of Wenceslas in Wenceslas Square and flowers at the Philosophy Faculty building. Police removed the wreath after twenty minutes and the flowers within two hours.

(A year later, on January 15, in spite of an official prohibition, some four thousand people would show up in Wenceslas Square to mark the twentieth anniversary of the immolation of Jan Palach. The next day they would be there again, and they would be set upon by police with dogs, tear gas and water cannons. These tactics would set off a six-day wave of violent demonstrations and riots, arrests and detentions.

On the following weekend, a pilgrimage of human rights activists, intent upon paying their respects at Palach's grave in Vsetaty, would be thwarted by a cordon of police cars blocking all the roads, by a heli-copter circling menacingly overhead, by commuter trains that ignored the scheduled stop at Vsetaty and – should they overcome all these obstacles – by a sign on the cemetery gate: "Closed for Technical Repairs.")

One night in November 1939, in Prague, police of the German occupying forces raided a committee meeting of the National Student Union where the Union budget was under discussion. Officials of the Union were arrested on the spot. In a simultaneous action, the university dormitories were raided; 1200 students were arrested and sent to forced labour camps. At dawn on November 17, nine students were executed by firing squad and their bodies burned.

This, in fact, is how Jan Palach died. At 3:30 P.M. on January 16, 1969, Palach, carrying a small can of gasoline, stepped out of a creaky Skoda in front of the National Museum in Wenceslas Square, took a seat on a block of masonry in its muddy forecourt, poured the contents of the gasoline can over his head and set himself on fire with a cigarette lighter.

The driver of a passing tram, seeing a man in flames from head to foot run into his path, jumped from the tram and threw his coat over the human torch. Palach suffered third-degree burns over 85 per cent of his body and died in hospital three days later. He left a letter. Imagine it as a poem.

> Our group consists of volunteers
> who are resolved
> to let themselves be burnt alive
> for the cause.
> I have the honour to draw the first lot
> and thus obtain the right
> to draft this first letter
> and become the first torch....
> If our demands are not met within five days
> by January 21, 1969,
> and if the public does not demonstrate
> adequate support,
> i.e., by an indefinite strike,
> further torches will burn.
> Remember August.
> Signed: Torch No. 1.

In his letter, Palach made two contradictory demands: that censorship be abolished immediately and that the scurrilous Soviet occupation broadsheet *Zpravy*, with its fabrications about "counterrevolutionaries" of the resistance, be banned.

Jan Zajic, a nineteen-year-old student from Moravia, died in Wenceslas Square a month later. He had drawn the second lot. He also left a message.

> In the name
> of your life
> I burn,
> Jan.

I want to accuse myself of shallowness, of having paid little attention in 1969 to anything but the tragic and pathetic. Did I learn of those *other* deeds – the committees and commissions and delegations and appointments during the Spring in student life? I did not. Of a Revolutionary Socialist Party that went underground and then to prison? Of the years they would spend in isolated cells, clipping hairpins to cards? In August 1969, 98 per cent of the employees of Prague walked off their jobs for five minutes, accompanied by the shrill fanfare of a hundred factory sirens. I wish I had imaginatively torn myself away from the brilliance of the human torch long enough to have studied what was happening modestly, in the unlighted corners of the occupied city.

In May 1963, in Saigon, religious riots led by Buddhist monks against the squalid regime of the American puppet Diem had resulted in the public suicides of men in saffron robes. Encircled by the pious and the merely curious, they had seated themselves in cobbled squares in the shade of trees in full leaf, soaked themselves with gasoline and lit themselves with cigarette lighters. No one stopped them, for they did not wish to be stopped. Arms upraised in surrender to the fire, they tipped ever so slowly sideways, down, down, towards the pavement until they had toppled right over, still seated in the lotus position, so much rubbish on fire. Had the two Jans seen a picture of this? Had the flames looked to them like the wings of an avenging angel travelling inside his own holy inferno?

But it is reported that Palach's last message, whispered from his deathbed, was that all the other would-be torches stay alive and struggle on. Perhaps he sensed that the image of the human torch, its limbs flapping like a scarecrow in a frantic wind, only frightened people. Who would want to be inside that idiot fire?

DOG DAYS

PRAGUE, 1968: In the spring and summer of 1968, they were swarming all over Wenceslas Square – the hippies and revolutionaries of the West. Martin invited one of them home, a West German New Leftist. Gave him his bed, cooked him meals. The guy was making a killing selling deutschemarks on the black market, and he was slaying the girls. When he left Prague, he lectured Martin about his petit bourgeois indifference to the misery of the proletariat under Capital.

Martin felt a vague sympathy with the protesting students of the West – and the slogans of solidarity of the young against the old – but only to a point. He didn't understand the hippies, never could. To "drop out" seemed hardly the point. Hardly the *revolutionary* point: Czechs did it all the time, just to get away from the din and blah-blah of the official environment. Anyway, in a society where the totalitarians and bureaucrats had weaseled their way into all the nooks, crannies and rat holes of society, where did you drop out to?

Petr thought western socialists were fools. Whenever he met one, he'd say: If you want to understand socialism, please stand in a food queue for a while.

TORONTO, AUGUST 21, 1968: In my second-floor room in a co-op house on Spadina Avenue it was unbearably hot. Breathless, I lay sprawled on my bed, tearing at my sticky clothing, ballpoint in my dangling hand. I was immobilized by the absurdity of what I was trying to do: write the concluding paragraphs to my thesis on the myth of Christian renewal in *The Brothers Karamazov* while the Russians were invading Czechoslovakia.

My brain seething, my heart in a flap, I stared out the window down onto Spadina. I imagined Yankee tanks rolling down the avenue to the lake, squads of FBI and CIA agents banging down the doors of the houses where my friends lived, smashing the machinery of the hippie press, escorting the staff of the Students' Union, arms in the air, to the windowless paddy wagon. I could see my own room being ransacked,

Che and Bob Dylan posters torn to shreds, diaries and address book confiscated. Down at the intersection of Spadina and Bloor, my lover, doused in gasoline, would become a human torch for the cause.

I stared out the window, seeing the melancholic mug of Alexander Dubcek floating in the shimmering air above the asphalt.

I tried to imagine myself in Czech shoes, rushing with other students to the centre of Prague, overturning buses, yelling "Ivan, go home!" at the Russians and lobbing Molotov cocktails into the herd of tanks when they didn't. Holding up a poster: "This is not Vietnam."

Vietnam was *ours*, in the West. "Amerika" was our problem. The behemoth in our neighbourhood wore a business suit; it wasn't bewildered Russkies in gun turrets who gave us nightmares but the guy with the briefcase in the war room, pointing at a map and calculating that month's draft call. "Create one, two, many Vietnams," we yelled, to give heart to the guerrillas in sandals creeping down the Ho Chi Minh Trail from Hanoi towards their engagement with the imperialists. When we heard about Molotov cocktails in Prague, we used that too. "Welcome to Czechago!"

Hey, hey, L.B.J., how many kids did you kill today? I remember reading later that L.B.J., who could hear the dull racket of the demonstrations wafting through the windows of the White House, felt hurt that we thought of him as a baby-killer.

We hurt his feelings.

Valka je vul. War is an ox. War is bullshit.

In the fall of 1967, kids in Prague had started at the Philosophy Faculty and ended at the American embassy, burning flags. The Czech authorities could hardly protest. The Ministry of Education had encouraged students to show solidarity with American students burning their draft cards and stomping all over the Stars and Stripes. The Union of Communist Youth had publicized the march among high-school students. These students turned up too, on a bit of a lark. When the marchers got there, the embassy was locked.

In 1968, students from Brno, on a Vietnam Peace March to Prague, had dropped in on the ambassador from North Vietnam. They said they wanted to go to his country not with rifles but with picks and shovels to help rebuild the devastated villages. You could call them the first *Gastarbeiter* – guest workers.

In Prague, in 1988, why won't they remember this?

PRAGUE, 1988: "Western support for us was important but you westerners are so fickle," Martin says. "One month it's one cause and the next month you're running off in another direction in pursuit of something else. What is it now? 1988? The Sandinistas in Nicaragua, right?"

"We saw there was a world imperial system," I say. "The U.S. was at its centre and the Vietnamese were resisting, not only for themselves but for all people who were in the process of becoming aware of that imperialism." That meant you, too, I don't say.

But the Czechs who were students in 1968 tell me, more in sorrow than in anger, that we western "revolutionaries" spoke with a wooden tongue that reminded them of the way the "politically correct" have always spoken. We repelled them. Vietnam was our obsession and the shooting and shouting of our demonstrations drowned out the tentative communications from behind the barricades of Prague where students were trying to communicate an obsession of their own: *Ivan, go home!*

They made exceptions: the German New Leftist "Red" Rudi Dutschke, for example, spoke with "clarity" about socialism as a *process*, wrote the Charter 77 militant Jaroslav Suk in *L'Alternative* in 1984, "but it seemed too often a one-way street.... It seemed our experience was incommunicable and that we were speaking to the deaf."

But, hey, they lost – the Russians stayed in Prague. The Americans left Saigon – we won.

Later that summer, I arrive at the Prague airport on a flight from Belgrade. There are a lot of passengers to go through Customs and Passport Control, so I take a seat in the lobby and wait for the lines to thin out. I look around. Green plastic furniture, the currency exchange booth, an old woman in a black head scarf mopping the stone floor. The flight board.

There is a flight departing soon for Hanoi.

It is very strange to see this word, "Hanoi," up on a flight board as though it were a normal word, a word like "Zurich" or "Paris." I haven't seen the word in years and, before that, I knew it mainly as a kind of conjuration. *Ho, Ho, Ho Chi Minh, Vietnam is gonna win.*

A large number of excited men move in a pack through the airport. They are small and skinny and wear cheap synthetic shirts and pants. They stagger under wondrous armloads of toys, packs of beer, boxes of sweets and portable televisions.

They are Vietnamese, the Gastarbeiter of the Eastern bloc. They have lived for years in Czechoslovakia, working at mean jobs for wages below the dignity of a socialist worker, living alone in workers' dormitories, snarled at and spat upon. Now they are laughing and happily jostling each other. They are going home. They have managed not only to pay back the airfare advanced to them before they left Vietnam but have also saved enough money to buy a ticket and a bicycle wheel, a plastic handbag, straw hats that they stack two and three high on their small, dark heads.

They are the fruits of the antiwar movement in North America in the 1960s and 1970s: indentured labour for the Czechoslovak Socialist People's Republic. If Hanoi had lost the war, these seedy Third World cowboys in cheap shoes and bellbottoms could be in Hamburg, swabbing dishes for deutschemarks.

But we won. We won.

THE WALL

PRAGUE, 1988: Rock is forever. What do they care that John Lennon would be old enough to be their father? It's the young John in long hair and round pink glasses that they draw on the "democracy wall," the "peace wall," a clean, cream-coloured surface that the municipal authorities periodically whitewash, erasing the inscriptions that have filled it up since the last time and leaving behind a brand-new canvas. They use pencils and coloured pens and crayons. "I'd love John Lennon even more if he was from Moravia." "Chapman, no!" (In English, like a shout just before the gun went off.) And, "How can I go forward when I don't know which way I'm facing?"

My Prague hosts and I stand together, looking at these disembodied cris de coeurs from young people who were not even born when the Beatles gave their last concert. We are worlds apart. It is *they* who now perform the obsequies and gather here on the anniversary of John's death, displaying his portrait, lighting candles, consoling one another with ragtags of lyrics they may not fully understand. I have all the Beatles' albums but never play them. I danced to the Rolling Stones.

I can smell the climbing roses curled around the gate and hear the giggle of children from the neighbouring yard. I take a picture of the Lennon Wall, but they can have it.

If they hear Chapman's gunshot as the judgement of this vile decade on sixties' dreams of love ("When will there be peace, John?"), then more power to them. But just where the hell do they think they are, the kids of the twentieth anniversary of the perfectly normal?

YUGOSLAVIA

1943: *Communist-led Partisans call for "brotherhood and unity" of the Yugoslav peoples; Marshal Tito declares provisional government* **1946:** *Constituent Assembly proclaims Federative People's Republic of Yugoslavia* **1948:** *Tito successfully defies political hegemony of* U.S.S.R. **1950:** *workers' self-management introduced* **1965:** *introduction of "socialist market"* **1968:** *student movement presses for more democracy* **1971:** *Croats protest Serbian dominance of federation* **1981:** *demonstrations by Albanians demanding republican status for autonomous province of Kosovo (southern Serbia) brutally suppressed* **1984:** *twenty-eight alleged dissidents arrested in Belgrade* **1987:** *Slobodan Milosevic gains leadership of Serbian League of Communists* **1988-89:** *Serbian Communists resist economic reform* **1990:** *opposition coalition wins free elections in Slovenia; election of ex-Communist nationalists in Croatia* **1991-92:** *secession of Slovenia, Croatia, Bosnia-Herzegovina and Macedonia from Yugoslav federation by popular referenda; pro-democracy student demonstrations in Belgrade; war in Croatia* **1992:** *war and "ethnic cleansing" in Bosnia-Herzegovina; Milosevic wins second term as president of Serbia on a platform of "greater Serbia"* **1993:** *Bosnian Serbs control 70 per cent of Bosnia; Croatia, nominally allied with Bosnian Muslims, begins attacks on Muslim territories; economic hardship in independent Macedonia; privatization of Slovene enterprises and rising unemployment; peace groups operate throughout ex-Yugoslavia*

CULTURAL WARS OFF MARX-ENGELS SQUARE

BELGRADE, SERBIA, 1984: How is it that this gritty and ramshackle city has become lovable to me? The site has been inhabited for seven thousand years, yet no structure is older than a hundred years and even the newer ones are dilapidated, falling away from their spines and disintegrating into clots of masonry as though reverting to a natural, more comfortable condition. A city sloughing itself off into the granular atmosphere. Stick out your tongue, lick this city... The slab-sided concrete apartment blocks are grimy, sooty, leached of all colour by the frigid autumnal rains. Their weedy yards are strewn with debris while inside the children run noisily along the soiled corridors.

Belgrade looks like a city that was once violently assaulted and never quite recovered or, on its way to recovery, was assaulted anew. Even the postwar politicians and architects, who dreamed of grandiose opera houses and parade squares, had to abandon their schemes: they didn't have the money.

Kalemegdan Park, approached from town centre along the old Stamboul road, was observed by Rebecca West in 1937 to be "the special glory of Belgrade": this now exhausted patch of greenery jutting out into the confluence of the Danube and Sava rivers over whose banks the Slavs poured in to settle down permanently in the seventh century. In 878 A.D., the Bulgars called the settlement Beligrad: the white fortress. Try to imagine this mediaeval glinting, this flashing – ivory? alabaster? whitewash on clay? – from within the palisades of a barbarian camp. The Byzantines held it until the eleventh century, and the Serbian kings made it their capital in the fourteenth. But it would be the Turks, seven hundred years later, who would build the baths, the fountains, the Bajrukli mosque, the tombs of the sheiks from which the sun bounced, lighting up the prize of the viziers. Then they too would be driven out. In 1984 ice-cream wrappers crackle in the bushes of Kalemegdan, teen-agers spray-paint graffiti on the shards of the Turkish fortress and I sit, the soft buzz of bees in my ear, drinking beer.

Thirty-seven times in the last two thousand years, Belgrade has been destroyed by invading armies. This works out to once every fifty-four years. Each generation of citizens lives in its own Belgrade, and this one too will vanish. There are dungeons in the fortress at Kalemegdan where the Romans kept slaves chained to the wall, and there are ram-parts where the Turks hoisted the heads of the executed. When the Serbs finally regained the city in 1815, they did not shut down the dungeons but turned them into a state prison and soon were sending their fellows underground, political prisoners fastened in the same chains to the same walls, turning fish-belly white and maggoty within the sunless prison pits.

In early May, the citizens of Belgrade turn their pale, winter-bleached faces to the sun like so many heliotropic plants. In August, we will all be wilting in the incinerating summer heat, our skin sizzling in the asphalt and cement stoves of the streets. The Turks loved water, loved the sound of it running out of the spouts of fountains. Where are the fountains now?

This city was so long Turkish that when Milos Obrenovic, first ruler of liberated Serbia, newly independent from the Ottoman Empire, bought a bed in 1834, he was reportedly only the second person to do so in Belgrade. There were no tables or chairs in his house, only divans, and he himself walked about in Turkish dress. When the great gram-marian and reformer of the Serbian language, Vuk Karadzic, began his work in 1815, there were only sixty Christian inhabitants of Belgrade, and of those the only literate ones were monks in the monasteries across the river in Austrian-held territory. In a flamboyant gesture, Obrenovic sent the head of his political rival Karadjorje, stuffed, as a tribute to the sultan in Istanbul. What exactly was Obrenovic, an illiterate pig dealer, the ruler of? Mean streets of caked mud, dark as a starless night, inhabi-tants shuttered indoors against the malevolent spirits prowling in the foul night air.

There has been violence visited upon Belgrade that is beyond my Canadian imagination still. I stroll along Terazije – shops and restau-rants, smells and shouts in the centre of the city – and will learn only later, in my reading (for no one brings this up in conversation), that the street lamps once were gibbets of the Nazi occupation, that the broken-necked bodies of partisans rotated slowly in the breeze just above the heads of jolly beer drinkers at their leisure in the sidewalk cafés.

Between 1941 and 1945 the Yugoslav dead numbered more than one million. The average age of the dead was twenty-two. Three and a half million people were left homeless.

Some say that, of the dead, one million were killed not in engagements with the Nazis but in fratricidal combat or crossfire. There were several sides: Serb Royalists, or Cetniks; Croat Fascists, or Ustase; and multi-ethnic Communists, or Partisans. In occupied Serbia, special Nazi military courts "tried" the men and women of the resistance and, working at fever pitch, carried out death sentences at intervals of five minutes. Out in the countryside, the peasants, with their own stubborn resistance, simply stopped tilling and sowing, and even Germans in the best restaurants found they were being served bread that was scarcely edible.

Viae Dolorosae: The routes of the occupying armies into Belgrade. The roads were lined with lindens charred from bombardments or fecund gallows or, in the case of the Turks, wreaking vengeance on rebellious Serbs in 1812, wooden stakes of impalement. The greased and sharpened head of a stake was hammered with great deliberation up the bowels of a wretched prisoner, skirting the vital organs and emerging from behind the left shoulder blade. Thus skewered, but not mortally injured, the victim hung along the highway, taking many days to die of thirst and madness, while the wild dogs of the deserted farms gnawed ravenously at his feet.

I stand at a bus stop while the gypsy families of the neighbourhood celebrate St. George's Day, roasting lamb on a spit, the odour of its melting fat and oregano mingling with the diesel fumes of the clattering green hulk of the bus. They are singing over top of it all.

It is this *easternness* – these pleasuring indolences, these nonchalant absences of the fastidious and the brisk, these cheerful dilapidations – that exasperated intellectuals will accuse Belgrade of: its too-long Ottoman interlude. (Four hundred years!) They will tell you that over the river in Zemun, incorporated into the Austrian empire in 1717, people know how to get things done. In Zemun the telephones work, you can get milk for your morning coffee and bureaucrats keep their files in alphabetical order. Ah, but do they, in Zemun, know how to marinate a lamb with garlic and fresh rosemary and roast it while turning, turning, turning the spit to the rhythm of their summer song?

On my first trip to Yugoslavia, in 1969, I skipped Belgrade. I was hitch-hiking along the Dalmatian coast and was prepared to tear myself off its hot beaches only to make the necessary detour around Albania through Titograd and down to Skopje, on my way to Greece. Belgrade was hundreds of miles inland. Besides, travellers' tales had it that Belgrade was not worth the visit: boring, Communist, uptight.

For me, as for so many other tourists, "Yugoslavia" consisted in the idea of sea water, dazzling silicate coves, plum brandy and the occasional, improbable Roman ruin. That certain rude events had intervened from time to time was obvious from the modest stone markers I noticed at points along the highway. I had many idle hours in which to observe the details of the roadside, and I remember being puzzled at the discrepancy between the message of these markers and the hilarity of the German tourists on the beach, for the markers told of the murder of local citizens at the hands of the Fascists and of the grief that still attended their loss. It would be years before I learned that the Fascists were other Yugoslavs.

Marshal Tito we had all heard about. War hero and giant slayer. After hounding the Nazis off his turf, he had arm-wrestled the Russians to the table, run up the Yugoslav flag (red, white and blue bars with a red star smack in the middle) and declared his socialist country open for (socialized) business, tourism included. It was one of the few guiltfree Mediterranean holidays my generation could take, Portugal and Spain and Greece all being held in dictatorial thrall by right-wing generals or juntas. That Tito himself was a dictator – the undisputed political and administrative chief of a one-party state – did not sink in. This wasn't what we meant by "dictator." We meant a fascist behind dark glasses, brandishing lethal weapons supplied by the CIA and arranging for the hideous torture of peasants or, at the other end of the scale, glum, overweight Stalinists so terrified of their own populations they didn't dare let them travel, not even to Yugoslavia.

Yugoslavia was welcoming, open, sexy. You could hear your favourite rock 'n' roll in the discos and swap reminiscences with students who had met Herbert Marcuse and Erich Fromm at an international summer school for philosophers of all tendencies held on the island of

Korcula. For a taste of something a little more exotic, all you had to do was take a bus from Titograd through the black mountains of Montenegro and share a seat with a wild man in long moustaches, his gorgeous waistband wrapped in thick woollen folds around his pistols. I thought of him as folkloric. I did not know he lived and breathed as everyday history, too – a warrior of the clans of South Slav brothers who killed each other with some regularity.

Yugoslavia. Literally, the place of the South Slavs. Intellectuals and visionaries trapped either in the Austro-Hungarian Empire or in the Ottoman Empire had proposed from time to time the ultimate union of the South Slavs – Slovenes, Croats, Montenegrins, Bosnians, Serbs and Macedonians – in a common state. Just before the First World War, twenty-six deputies of the parliament of newly independent Serbia declared, in the Resolution of Zara, that "Croats and Serbs are one nation by blood and language," anticipating the eventual liberation of their brothers and sisters from the Austrian yoke. In 1918, the Kingdom of Serbs, Croats and Slovenes, proclaimed over the ashes of empire, began a process of nation-building that was smashed in another world war. The kingdom, reconstituted as six republics within socialist Yugoslavia, would be smashed again in the wars of the 1990s.

We hitchhikers of the somnolent summers thought we were travelling through a single entity – the Socialist Federation of the Republics of Yugoslavia – a single country, a system. I must have registered the difference between the sunbathers of Pula on the Istrian peninsula near Italy and the wild man on the bus hurtling towards Macedonia as noteworthy but not crucial. That people spoke several different languages in this one country and employed two alphabets was "interesting," "multicultural." The twenty-some years the six republics had been hammered together in political and social union seemed quite long enough to me for them to have become "Yugoslavia." Only someone from the New World would think twenty years was a long time.

I do not visit Yugoslavia again until 1982. After that, I will visit over and over, starting in Belgrade and jumping off from that city to visit Ljubljana, Zagreb, Pristina, Skopje and Banja Luka as well. I will come to know that this is a state of dramatically different peoples who have shared a violent history when they have shared it at all. I will learn that there are polemics around languages and alphabets and heroic legends of long-past glories meant to define one people's separation from their neighbours. I will see that the people endured profoundly different imperialisms for hundreds of years – one has only to compare the Turkish coffee houses of Serbia with the Viennese cafés of Slovenia – and still live in different cultures in spite of a shared citizenship. I will know all this and yet feel that separateness has finally been superseded by the consciousness of a common Slavic ethnicity that embraces me along with them and an identity that transcends difference. In 1984, postwar generations, asked where they come from, answer, "Yugoslavia."

THE LAST OF THE PARTISANS

BELGRADE, SERBIA, 1987: In the winter, residents burn a cheap brown coal that deposits a greasy fog in the stinking air. You see the coal in large piles on the tilting sidewalks, left there to be shovelled through ground-level windows into basement furnaces. Pedestrians slip along the coal slopes. This is a nasty city in the winter. The cold, wet wind blows up my sleeves and slaps clammily around my neck.

Inside the Moskva Cafe Sonja and Milan beam broadly at me, cheering me up considerably even though there is no milk for our coffee, only the revolting *schlag* set afloat a bitter brew and served up as cappuccino. From here we move a few metres down the avenue to a pizza restaurant, huddling miserably in our coats under a naked light bulb, chewing with some gusto nevertheless the pizza crusts brushed parsimoniously with tomato paste. The conversation, naturally, is all about the economic crisis. There is only one economic crisis; it is permanent, endemic. You can drop in and out of Yugoslavia over the years and never miss a thing.

It is harder and harder for my friends to sustain themselves on their pitiable salaries from the Institute of Sociology. They've stopped answering the doorbell at bill-collection time. People are working second and third jobs, they are working seven days a week and at night, and still they keep sinking into the slough of their indebtedness. Sonja sees her neighbour, a grocery cashier, haul home a sack of potatoes once a month. These seem to be the sum total of her groceries. Where to find soap, cooking oil? Sonja tells us that most Yugoslav families are spending 50 to 70 per cent of their income on food. For the first time, she has seen old women and children scavenging in the big, verminous metal garbage bins that sit parked on Belgrade's sidewalks, squat and evil-smelling.

Later, at home, Sonja offers a concoction of hot tap water and instant coffee along with several glasses of schnapps. She has been getting rounder and rounder and refuses to eat the ambrosial Hungarian stew she ladles out for Milan and me – beef, sauerkraut, tomato sauce and sour cream; at her own place she sets an apple on a plate. Milan, too, is growing somehow larger, bulkier, his beard thicker and wilder, so that he seems, at each visit, to be turning before my very eyes into the Montenegrin mountain man he might have been had he never gone to university.

Milan is besotted with his computer. It hums insistently from the next room, and periodically he abandons the dinner table to rush over to it and punch something on the keyboard. For a whole week he has been writing a magazine article about desktop publishing that will earn him the equivalent of a local garage mechanic's hourly wage.

Sonja stares dolefully at her apple and smokes a cigarette. Her economic woes, she explains, are the least of her troubles. The true catastrophe of her life these days lies in the widening rift between her and her comrades in the opposition – their alarming recourse to nationalisms in the face of political impotence, their formulaic rejection of what they are pleased to call "socialism." Bonds formed in the heyday of the student movement in 1968 are dissolving as her erstwhile comrades argue that that experience "led to" totalitarianism and that only "market" and "democracy of property and political organization" can save Yugoslavia. They hold Sonja and her ilk responsible for the post-1968 reentrenchment of the apparatchiks who allied themselves with the students against the economic reforms of 1965. The students had worried the reforms would crush ordinary working-class families; the apparatchiks had worried they'd lose their limousines. These developments make Sonja fume and smoke too much. She is an activist of socialist democracy, by which she means political and cultural pluralism, independent trade unions, the rule of law and the emancipation of women.

Sonja feels the loneliness of the long-haul socialist; there is so little company these terrible days. Slovenian oppositionists declare themselves "for" John Stuart Mill and Thomas Jefferson as though this were revolutionary. Serbian intellectuals at public meetings lick their chops in response to the "masses" crying out for Albanian blood, as though they can now cease their wanderings in the postwar desert of internationalism and come home to Serbian chauvinism. A famous Hungarian critical thinker at a conference in Budapest declares with inestimable satisfaction that Ronald Reagan is the best American president since Eisenhower. The coherent, systematic, all-embracing, inspiriting worldview of multinational socialism that Sonja has been carrying in her mind and soul since her youth is becoming alarmingly tenantless; upright within it, she feels naked and exposed.

Years ago there had been other signposts, other possibilities. As early as the 1950s, the introduction of workers' self-management in the state-owned enterprises had seemed a brilliant idea – a refusal of bureaucracy and the cult of personality, a welcoming of direct democracy on the shop floor. Here surely was the beginning of a kind of pluralism in the body politic. Who could see then that the logic of the locally managed economy would produce not self-reliant workers but local elites, possessive enough of their power to play the nationalist card when necessary?

In the 1960s, a group of philosophy professors, loyal Marxists all, had had the vision to ask the Party if there was not room in the "socialist avant-garde" for "true, creative, non-dogmatic, non-apologetic Marxism" *after* the seizure of power? Never mind that they were sacked from their jobs; these were exhilarating questions. Still vivid is Sonja's own sense of having emancipated herself, in the course of the June Days of the student movement of 1968, from under the dead hand of the Party patriarchs. The whole point was to get somewhere you and all your neighbours had never been: a free and common home. As late as 1981, the national census showed a 450-per-cent increase in those who called themselves Yugoslavs. There were some who fretted that such a statistic bespoke the dilution of national identities: if you were calling yourself a Yugoslav, you were "lost" to the Croatian nation, or the Serbian nation, or the Slovenian. But for Sonja and other true believers, Yugoslavia was a house with many rooms. Its roof sheltered them all.

In 1972, Milan was held in solitary confinement in Belgrade's notorious central prison for thirteen months. He had been sentenced to two years of "rigorous imprisonment" for the criminal offence of having created "a group hostile to people and state," in this case a student group protesting unemployment. He lay in a cell, furnished with a bed, a toilet and a table, no wider than the span of his outstretched arms. There was no exterior window, only a pane of glass in the door so thick and grimy that on a cloudy day he could not manage to read. On a bright day he could read for an hour.

Perhaps this is the same prison that Milovan Djilas writes about in the opening paragraph of his memoirs, *Rise and Fall.* The brand-new jail of the bright new Communist regime was the brain child of the Minister of the Interior and his comrades, who remembered their own prewar prison experience in decrepit buildings that allowed them to tap messages on the walls, push notes through the sewer pipes and shout encouragement to their fellows in the torture chambers underground. They designed a prison with double walls, twisted sewer pipes and subterranean cells dark as crypts and silent as the centre of the earth.

Milan passed the months by arguing with himself about the questions bedevilling sociological theorists and by composing an entire science fiction novel in his head. Ten minutes after his release, the novel was erased irretrievably from his brain. He can't even remember the plot.

Milan's story begins with his pedigree, three hundred years ago, on his mother's side, in Kosovo. Rooted in the mediaeval heartland of Serbia, in the land of saints and kings, the family name is mentioned in the documents of the seventeenth century along with all those other families who, having fought the abominated Turk and lost, retreated north with the Austrian army. Milan's grandfather, a minor official in the municipal administration of Austrian-held territory west of Belgrade, was a founder of the Serbian Communist Party in 1919. His daughter Milka, Milan's mother, would become a Communist too. After the First World War, in the parliament of the new Kingdom of the Serbs, Croats and Slovenes, the Communists held third place. But in 1920 they organized strikes among miners and railway workers, and in 1921 they assassinated the Minister of the Interior; they were outlawed, and those who were not murdered by the police went underground. Some went south, to the poor villages of their supporters, the tobacco pickers and the railway men, and settled down to organize their own Communist villages in the dirt of the Kosovo farms their ancestors had abandoned centuries ago.

Milan's mother grew up in one of these Communist villages. The Party built irrigation works, machine shops, public baths, a co-operative mill, a school, a library, a clinic. Then came the Second World War. Milan's mother was arrested by the royalist Cetniks, who turned her over to the Italians, who turned her over to the Albanian Fascists, who turned her over to the Germans. Had her capture happened later in the war, Milan supposes, she would simply have been shot by the first to get their hands on her.

The Germans tortured her at Banjic, the concentration camp near Belgrade, then sent her to Ravensbruck. She was pulled from there to work at slave labour in the airplane factory in Dresden. Caught in an act of sabotage on the airplane assembly line, she was punished by immersion, for three days and three nights in December, in a hole filled with water up to her neck. She almost strangled as the ice coagulated around her throat. In the great bombing of Dresden, she escaped with some other prisoners and took a year to walk home, tramping across Czechoslovakia and Hungary. She claims to have arrived in Belgrade on board a Soviet tank, withered and feverish mascot of the liberators, but this is perhaps too colourful.

After the war, Milka was in love with her husband, a printer. She turned down all offers from the Party in order to stay at home and be housewife and mother. And so she was not present the night in 1949 when the comrades were asked to denounce Stalin. For overweening, unrepentant ambition in the Balkans – among other provocations, Tito had called for a Balkan Federation, to be convened, presumably, under his aegis – the Communist Party of Yugoslavia had been expelled from the Cominform (Communist Information Bureau) in 1948. And the curses of Soviet Foreign Minister Viacheslav Molotov rained down upon them. Tito-Fascist clique! Spies and provocateurs! Hired gang of criminals! Not backing down, the Titoists, in the name of a "Yugoslav Communism," hunted down the Stalinists in their own midst.

They were all lately Stalinists, of course, even the men running the meeting. A woman who arrived late, at the point where the chairman was asking the comrades, "All right, who's *for* this letter from Stalin?" naturally raised her hand. She disappeared to Goli Otok, a few acres of treeless, waterless rock. Over several years, twelve thousand Party members sentenced to "socially useful labour" were sent in scorching heat with sledge hammers to smash stone and haul it from one end of the island to the other and back again. After release, the survivors said nothing; they bit their tongues and trudged through the ditches of the "Yugoslav road" to socialism.

Milan's mother spent her last ten years in bed, immobilized by pain. It was an obsession of hers to live long enough to see her son come out of prison. Which she did. And then she died.

Eventually Milan would call himself a Communist too, "like my mother." Not just in honour of the intelligence engaged in the melioration of society as she found it but also – he doesn't say this but it's there – to keep faith with her courage. She had told him of the time she awoke from her sleep in the woods on the trek back to Belgrade from Dresden to discover she had taken her rest on soil littered with decomposing bodies. "She was very strong-willed," says Milan.

Milan's father was a printer and a typesetter. He was a Montenegrin of the tribe Bratonozici, Brothers of the Knife. From this Milan understood several things. That his forefathers had brought a printing press to Zeta (ancient Titograd) only twenty-five years after the death of Gutenberg. That they were warriors. That they had never paid tribute to the Turks but reserved their bloodletting for each other in endless feuds avenged by reciprocated murder.

A Montenegrin family tale from Milovan Djilas's autobiography, *Land without Justice*: Great-uncle Marko, lawless brigand in the hills, was murdered by a cowardly policeman who ambushed him at his cave. Marko's nephew then slew a nephew of the policeman's clan, cut out pieces of his heart and fled. In his turn, he died, hammered to death and left to rot in the field. And so on, down to the last male, and the daughter creeping out into the field to cut off the beloved head and wrap it in her apron and her kisses.

Before the Turkish invasion and occupation, Montenegro had been a principality in the realm of the Serbian czar. When the people lost their coast to the Venetians and their eastern territories to the Ottomans, they retreated into the mountain fastnesses where their clans became a little state unto themselves, "stubborn and bloodied," as Milovan Djilas describes them. Right into modern times, they would descend on Muslim villages and, in pogroms of the most appalling cruelty, harry their neighbours from their homes.

Milan's father told him that to be a Montenegrin was to be a thief of Turkish cattle.

In school, Milan was a natural rebel, the student who would not write an essay in composition class about why he loved President Tito and who would look for his own solutions in mathematics. The teachers found this irregular, except for the political science instructor who lent him books by Hegel and Kant. He was a political passion in search of a theory. It would be incorrect to call him a dissenter; he firmly believed that the Yugoslav road to socialism was correct, democratic and just. It only needed to be improved in some respects. For example, witness the circumstances of his own working-class family, whose father got up at 4:00 A.M. to go to the first of his two jobs, while the family of a university dean lived in a villa and owned a car.

In 1966, Milan decided to enter the Department of Sociology in the Faculty of Philosophy at the University of Belgrade. He read Latin American literature and, on a large wall map, kept track of the progress of the revolutionary guerrilla armies, dreaming of joining Che in Bolivia. The revolution, he reckoned, just might prove to be elsewhere. By 1968, he was an event waiting to happen.

JUNE DAYS

BELGRADE, SERBIA, 1987: I have set up my tape recorder on Sonja's kitchen table, moving aside the heaps of papers, leftover food and empty cigarette packages to make room for our conversation. This is the only time I will use a tape recorder in Eastern Europe. Having missed the Yugoslav student upheavals the first time around, I want to be sure I get them in detail now.

By 1968, students were dreaming of overthrowing the state. In the mid-1960s, the government had introduced economic reforms in the experimental "socialist market," proceeded to intensified borrowing from western banks to finance huge industrial facilities that would never go into production, and loosened border controls to encourage the unemployed to look for jobs in Austria and Switzerland. They dismissed an unpopular hard-line police chief but otherwise did not threaten the monopoly of the Party. They reassured the Party elite that its extravagant lifestyle, its villas and hunting lodges would not be threatened. Stipends to students were reduced, and no investments were made in student housing. The state was helpless before the predictable social crisis: unemployment, overcrowding in the cities, 30 per cent inflation, duplicated and triplicated bureaucracies, corruption. On the campuses, a generation of idealistic socialist "red diaper" kids, disgusted by the strangle hold of the Party on student organizations and the fetid air excreted by the sacred cows of Marxism-Leninism, were waiting for them to make a wrong move.

About six thousand students lived in school residences lined up like barracks in New Belgrade, across the river from the main campus. They were poor and they were bored. On June 3, infuriated by their exclusion from a Party-sponsored rock concert, the students decided to march to the centre of town. They got only as far as a viaduct defended by ranks of police. Beaten back, the students regrouped at their student centre and stayed up all night arguing about what to do next. They decided they would make the revolution where they stood, at the student centre, in the faculty buildings, in the auditoriums. They would assemble and stay in permanent session, talking. They renamed the campus Karl Marx Red University. "Down with the socialist bourgeoisie!"

In the early hours of June 3, Milan went around to the flat of his friend Sonja, and together they sneaked through the police barricades and made their way to the student sit-in at Red University. There was a great deal of indecisive milling about as yet more students, hearing the news over the radio, came down to join the occupation. A voice rose above the hubbub: "Let's organize an action committee!" They did, and elected Sonja to it. That night, a supporter approached her with a small donation of money. With some misgiving, she took it, thinking the occupation should be self-sufficient. But when a fellow student as round and plump as herself approached her in a whisper – "Look, *you* understand that we're going to have to eat. The skinny ones won't think of it." – Sonja put herself in charge of food procurements and sent Milan out for one hundred kilos of bread.

Sonja had thought herself unshakable in her faith. From the Central Committee of the Serbian Youth Organization of the League of Communists of Yugoslavia, she had arrived at the university still a Communist idealist – the system was "excellent," Tito was "excellent," only the incompleteness of people's actions dragged at the virtue of the state – and not even the anti–Vietnam war riots of 1966 in which she had been beaten by the Communist police had undermined her devotion. But the police of 1968 changed her thinking.

On the marches she saw students scraped across the streets by jets of water from the police water cannon, and she saw those wounded by gunfire from the windows of the apartments of military officers in New Belgrade. Unarmed, students were kicked and beaten to the ground; the girls had their blouses torn off first. There was even a rumour that a girl had died in hospital of police-inflicted wounds, that her body had been hastily removed and her family forced to move to another city.

The "people's police" were on the offensive against the students and in defence of Red fat cats. On the first night of the occupation, Sonja met an old revolutionary and veteran of the Spanish Civil War. The students poured out their hurt and grievances to him. He nodded in sympathy. He had never seen the police behave themselves so badly, not even the police of monarchist Serbia with whom he had skirmished before the war.

Sonja looked for a quiet corner. She wept as though to break open, letting go of that hot pith within that had been bound over and committed, with love, to the idea of Tito, the Father of the nation, Father of the revolution, more father to her than her own, the hero she had run after, waving broken-headed blossoms in her fist, when he came to visit her town. As a girl, she had become a Communist to please him. A locksmith from the labouring classes, son of a Croat and a Slovene, Tito could only be a revolutionary and a Yugoslav. As an escaped prisoner of war in Russia in 1917, he participated in Bolshevik demonstrations in St. Petersburg. Back in Yugoslavia, he climbed the ranks of the underground Communist Party. By spring 1942, the Liberation Army, or Partisans, he helped organize had 150,000 men and women under arms and was waging a struggle not just for the military defeat of the Nazi occupiers but for the political and social future of Yugoslavia as well.

It was the Partisans' victory on all fronts that consolidated the myth of pan-Yugoslav solidarity that would lie at the foundation of the new society's vision of itself – and in the hearts and minds of the boys and girls, like Sonja and Milan, growing up as its beneficiaries. *This* was Sonja's citizenship, and now the heroes were sending the police against their own children. The future was suddenly ambiguous.

While the police were burning copies of *Student* on bonfires in Terazije Street downtown, youths were burning *Politika* and *Borba (Struggle)* outside the doors of Red University. It was Milan's father and his co-workers at the printing plant, working overnight and without pay, who figured out how to print *Student* and smuggle it back to campus.

When rumours flew that the faculty building was about to be assaulted, Milan sprang into action, organizing teams of occupiers to barricade the doors and windows. But when that threat failed to materialize, the students subsided into discussion, and discussions based on discussion, about social inequality and economic reforms and French literature. They passed around the badge of the Red University – a blue circle around a red flag – and took heart from the public massed outside in the square.

Someone had sent his maid to deliver money anonymously to the occupation; it came in handy for yogurt and bread. A well-known actress arrived at four in the morning, victim of insomnia, to clean toilets.

Huddled shoulder to shoulder, the boys and girls of the political advance guard also talked about sex, the "sexual revolution" they had heard so much about from the West and "sexual freedom." Milan met a beautiful girl from Split. He would forget her name. But he would remember that it was "very nice" slipping away together to make love in the fire tower above Studenski Trg.

The Beatles. Some wine. Posters of Tito as a wartime partisan, in his prime, manly and potent with the desire for freedom and justice. The students ask: Now you are a marshal with forty villas and hunting lodges and many mistresses and sycophants, but why can't you be what you once were? Why can't you be like Che?

On June 9, the sixth day of the occupation, Tito preempted the air waves to make a conciliatory speech to the nation, reassuring the occupiers that he took seriously many of their grievances concerning the material situation of students and offering to resign if he could not effect improvements. But he would do nothing under the coercion of an illegal occupation in which the "bad apples" had manipulated the 90 per cent of the students who were serious about their studies. There was no more need for the occupation, he said. Now was the time for work, for final exams. Go home now, he advised, and study.

The occupiers poured out into the streets to dance the *kolo*, the circle dance of jubilation: "Oh, let our losses all be light." Sonja did not dance the kolo. She and her action committee of die-hard occupiers continued to meet for a few more weeks, prepared to take over the official student organization if need be. Instead, the Party dissolved it and merged its members with the official youth organization.

What was it that the students had wanted? The dismissal of the chief of police. More student funding. Democratization of the university administration and consultation with the students. The handing over of the villas of the Red bourgeoisie to orphans. Well, the state did do one thing for them: it turned over the club of the Secret Police for a cultural centre.

May Day, 1987. It has been raining all night and all day. People have carried their dripping umbrellas and coats, their squishy boots, into the cinema, so that only a few minutes into the film, the hall has the musty and steamy atmosphere of a public bathhouse. The moviegoers sit like duck hunters in a swamp, immobile, waiting watchfully to catch something in the moving picture that is fleeting, marginal, subtextual (blink and you'll miss it), as though not trusting the film to be what it says it is: an examination of the betrayal of the June Days, 1968.

How to talk about the Days of June without actually saying so: talk about an adolescent, a seventeen-year-old boy not in Belgrade but in the provinces, whose only sensation, the summer of '68, is his lust, undiscriminating and unappeasable, flaring at the sight of the librarian, the teacher, the shopgirl, in their miniskirts, their tight, busty blouses, until it finally lights on a girl his own age who, *mirabile dictu*, responds.

1968: the summer we got laid.

Subtext: the father hovering at the edge of the boy's concerns, a district judge and Party man, by all the signifiers a member of the Red bourgeoisie. The big house, the rose garden, the wine cellar, the wife into interior decorating. It is the father, not his snotty children, who watches the Belgrade fracas on television, but we know it is the Belgrade student ingrates, disrespectful and disorderly, we are meant to support when the father, this fat, Red sausage, ostentatiously removes the television set from the house and will not bring it back indoors. Our priapic hero has observed none of this; *we* have. He is in love with a girl from Czechoslovakia, a member of a school marching band touring Yugoslavia in a van. He is pedalling to her now, roses in the basket of his bicycle, the day after he has lain with her and unburdened himself of his irksome virginity. He is pedalling down the dusty road like a swain on his pretty pony to her camping site. It is the gilded, lissome morning of August 22, 1968. The campsite is deserted. No van. No girl. He stands transfixed by bewilderment.

Then he catches sight, far down the road and heading in the opposite direction, of the back of the van, vanishing in the cloud of yellow dust and solarized by the incandescent orb behind the haze: a brief flare off the chrome, and then nothing. The van is travelling north, to Prague, to Wenceslas Square and the summer tanks of Moscow.

WHERE DOES EUROPE END?

SLOVENIA, 1987: It is so pretty here, not far from Bohinj: round, green, plump. Cosy and furled. Peaceable. A narrow green river in a valley crimped out of the base of fuzzy green mountains. Willow trees trail their fronds in the slow, green water and bells toll solemnly up and down dale as we pick cherries in the rain. Old lilacs gone wild bloom at the doors of the ochre-stained Franciscan churches in the villages. Is this even Yugoslavia? I would have said Tyrol. Branko points northeast to a range of mountains crouching on the Austrian border. "That's as far west as the Slavs got." Why does he notice this? Why is this a demarcation, the point where the Slavs jammed up against the flank of European mountains after their rowdy, centuries-long dispersion from the broad Carpathian basin? Why is "west" the compass point of our desire?

Interviewed in the English weekly *Time Out,* the Slovenian rock group Laibach gives readers a history lesson: Europe has always been organized around the two poles of Catholic and Orthodox Christianity. After 1945, some nations (read: Slovenia, Croatia) who had always considered themselves to be in the West (read: Catholic) awoke one morning to discover they were now in the East (read: under Asiatic Communism).

How do you know you are a westerner, a European? You were subjugated by Romans, not Greeks; you received your alphabet from the Latin; you raised a mediaeval empire that was absorbed by Charlemagne of Gaul, not by Basil or Nicephorus of Byzantium, and you were Christianized by German princes. You lived six hundred years as a kind of afterthought of Hapsburgian estate managers – but you noticed, oh, you noticed, that German barons built their castles among your vineyards, German bishops supervised your Franciscan, Dominican and Cistercian priests and brothers, the German language was the first one published by your awakening writers. As far as you were concerned, you lived in Gosposvetsko Polje, but the Germans called it Klagenfurt, and when the map was drawn and finally redrawn Klagenfurt was *theirs.* You had a brief, thrilling brush with Napoleon – while your kinfolk to the east were run over by pashas in pantaloons – who incorporated you into a concoction known as Illyria. You had four years in which to master the arguments of the French Enlightenment.

This is as "western" as the Slovenes got: to have been colonized since the thirteenth century by Austria and treated like helots labouring on their own land for the enrichment of the *Übermenschen*. The Austrians did not love their little Slavs: back in the sixteenth century, when the peasant Matija Gubec dared to lead an uprising of Slovene and Croat peasants in the Krka Valley and was weak enough to lose, the German lords dragged him to the cathedral in Zagreb and crowned him King of the Peasants with a metal headband, molten hot, tightened by slow degrees around his skull. While he died they yelled at him, "Long live the peasant king!" Among their subject populations, the Austrians built barracks, brothels, inns and a handful of schools, as though to go further and build academies and hospitals and public parks would be to collaborate in their subjects' survival. And when the Austrians went to war against their subjects, in retaliation for the assassination of their archduke and countess in Sarajevo in 1914, they lynched peasants by the hundreds and mowed them down in the fields, where the furrows the peasants had overturned became their graves.

Are we still in Europe?

In Ljubljana, Meta takes me to the studio of her friend, the painter Karel Zelenko. I look at his pictures, but I want to talk about his name. "Your name is Ukrainian," I say. "Yes, yes," he nods, "but such a long time ago, from somewhere in the sub-Carpathians," and he waves his hand vaguely over his shoulder as though the sub-Carpathians were in the shadows outside the windows in the garden, among the pear trees. "Zelenko" means "green." Greenish. A little bit of green.

We are so far "west" that I feel marooned, cast among Slavs who are not Slavs. I grope for the shared familiar – certain sounds, certain words – but every other thing is empty of memento. There isn't a single reference I could evoke – the name of an important Ukrainian town, the name of a seventeenth-century Cossack hero, a poetic verse, the smell of the church, the wail of a sub-Carpathian love song – that would resonate among the Slovenes. This sudden and unexpected impossibility of solidarity leaves me rather confused, as though I were standing, holding the address to the house of relatives who had decamped, leaving the place to Bavarian vacationers.

Branko bristles at "creeping Cyrillization" – the westward advance, sneaky and unbidden, of the Cyrillic alphabet from Serbia into the ancient realm of the Latin. Unsurprisingly, this advance is known as the "Mongolization" of European script, even though an early version of it, Glagolitic, had been used liturgically in Catholic Zagreb, and even though it is perfectly obvious to anyone who visits Belgrade that it is the Cyrillic alphabet that is losing ground to the Latin system of signs, known as "international."

Mirek boasts he has been fifteen times to London and only once to Belgrade in the last twenty years.

There are no patriots of the Byzantine miraculous here, only cute Tyrolese who *yodel* their amazement. There is no comparison with the ineffable marvel of that moment in 1206, say, when consecrated oil flowed from the tomb of Saint Simeon in Kosovo. What ever did I care of miracle-working relics? But I have come to care, now that I am among Slavs who would rather be Teutonic and reasonable. I find myself too a sudden devotee of the Cyrillic sacral, an alphabet as a kind of revelation of the Slavic heart, like those ancients who adopted the Cyrillic in the first place because they judged the Latin alphabet inadequate to the tasks of faith.

FIELD OF BLACK CROWS

KOSOVO, SERBIA, 1988: I have joined a busload of Orthodox faithful on a trip south from Belgrade to the historic lands of Kosovo. This is not as peculiar as it might seem; I may be no Serb, but I was raised in an Orthodox church. I am offered a seat. In fact, I am offered several.

As we pass red-tiled villages squat on the red earth, their bare-footed youths whacking at the weeds in the field-strips of corn, wheat and beans, the crops gaily broadcast with red poppies, I am on the lookout for the first sight of a minaret. And when I see it, it is a shock. For the geography in my imagination does not site Islam so close to *here*. Here: Christian Europe. Mine. What I have inherited from the great treasure of European culture. *Here* is the place where everything *there* is not. What is Islam doing here, poking its minarets up from the humus of mediaeval Serbia, in brazen competition with Byzantine monasteries?

I am piqued. We press on.

Ah, the saints and martyrs thrown into the "blue abysses" of Byzantium ...

At the monastery of Zica, phalanxes of sputtering beeswax candles blaze in the shady narthex. As we passed through the main gate, suddenly the noisy little world just behind us in the road – young men on motor scooters, a wedding party – was extinguished, and we entered another acoustic world. The plash of water at the fountain, the birds in the convent garden and, inside the cool, dark nave, the bell-like voices of three nuns singing the serene responses of the Mass to the young priest lit up by dusty shafts of light so that he glitters in his vestments. Now we see that extravagance of the Serbian Orthodox church – the frescoes. But the saints disappear into the gloom under the dome, so severe, so unnatural, that they do not lure me away from my meditation but inhabit it, personifying in their speculative gaze and weightless limbs the very energy of the resting mind.

At Studenica we witness what I take to be a fertility ritual. Mass has been celebrated and the congregation has departed. A young couple stay behind. To the droning intonations of the priest, they fold themselves up on their hands and knees and crawl on their bellies – first the wife, her skirt riding up her thighs – under the silver and velvet casket holding the thirteenth-century bones of King Stephen the First-Crowned. Parishioners have left bunches of fresh basil and embroidered hand cloths as offerings on top of the casket, in thanks for the potency of the old bones that, in the time of the Ottomans, had been shunted hither and thither among the monasteries; in 1839 they finally came to rest here, in an independent Serbia.

We follow the priest out of the church. I watch him walk around a brand-new automobile parked at the bottom of the church steps. The owners stand by, looking proud and substantial, while the priest shakes his censer at the four open doors, chasing away, I suppose, the demons who torment the charioteers of the twentieth-century Yugoslav road.

We drive into Prizren at dusk and debouch at a hotel across a wide street from the stupendous hulk of a mosque. I am already getting used to this. I had better. The population here is almost 90 per cent Muslim. Just before the First World War, the Serbian Orthodox Metropolitan had confided in the English traveller Edith Durham that the Serbs were already in a "considerable minority." She herself had not expected to find them such a "mere drop in the ocean." I stroll down a cobble-stoned street lively with the animation of the evening promenade and stop to buy an ice cream. Assuming that the young man behind the counter is a Muslim, I order, loudly, in English, and am both ashamed of myself and satisfied that I have, in this way, let it be known I am not an Orthodox Serb. I am not alone in my subterfuge: one of our party, the monk from New Zealand, unmistakable in his black robe and beard, intermittently emits a hearty "Go with God!" in English as we walk along through the crowds.

Prizren lies on both sides of the Bistrica River, by whose gushing course a little upstream Czar Dushan had built the church of the Holy Archangel, intending it to be his mausoleum. To judge from the church's ruins, it was vast. It was not, however, long-lived, for soon after its completion the Turks were already masters of these terrains. They caused the cathedral to be demolished and its stones hauled into town for the building of the mosque of Sinan Pasha. The mosque is still here, conglomerated and intact, at the heart of the city. This is the hulk I see from my hotel window.

The story is told of Sinan Pasha that, on informing the sultan in Istanbul that Prizren's church of the Holy Archangel was succumbing to the attacks and lootings of local bandits, he received permission to tear it down all at once and build a mosque in his own honour with its stones. Later, however, the sultan received word that Sinan Pasha had misled him: there had been no bandits and no lootings; there had been only Sinan Pasha's hyperbolical vanity. The sultan sent Sinan Pasha the silk cord. Pasha knew what was expected of him, and hanged himself.

Next day, our group is ushered down a humpy dirt street to the four-teenth-century church of the Mother of God, and we stand in front of the narthex in the thin sunlight of the early May morning, admiring the frescoes that are emerging from behind the white plaster the Turks smeared all over the walls when they first took Prizren and turned the vaulted spaces of the churches into mosques. The pure white plaster – unadulterated, unadorned – is being washed off to reveal as though from behind a veil or screen the radiant faces of saints and angels in a riot of Byzantine colour. All of us in this group are members (or ex-members) of an Orthodox church, and we say to one another that these frescoes are beautiful. Even the redoubtable Dame Rebecca West had thought so, back in the 1930s, when she argued that the Byzantine had "preferred" the visual arts to literature and the "communal" form of the Mass to individual ideological correctness. We Orthodox, she wrote, were "drunken with exaltation."

Then I notice that there are others, at the very edge of our group, watching us – a Muslim Albanian and his young son. At first they are simply with us, passersby who have stopped to listen to the story. But then the man begins to smirk, an odd sort of lopsided curl of the lip that exposes his blackened teeth and red gums. He nudges his son, whispers in his ear. Then they both grin broadly, as though sharing a private joke, I assume at our expense. Their smiles are neither aggressive nor malicious but they are mocking and derisory, and I try to imagine myself from their vantage point. What I see is a group of grown-ups reverencing the faint and scoured and pock-marked faces of saints and angels and genuflecting before them, kissing the cool, white, gouged feet of the martyrs or brushing them with the tips of their fingers as though there were vulgar magic here in the paints. What I, and they, see is a group of Europeans worshipping images.

This Albanian would plaster the church all over again, washing away with cleansing white paste all our blasphemies.

KOSOVO POLJE, THE FIELD OF BLACK CROWS: According to the chronicles, Music Stefan paced his castle, watching for the rising morning star and the waning of the moon in the west, waiting to start his journey to the field at Kosovo, ancient inland sea soon to be the scene of battle. He carried out the silk banners embroidered with gold crosses and the icon of St. John, his holy patron saint, and as he did these things his sleeping wife had a dream. A flock of doves were in flight with two grey falcons flying on ahead to Kosovo; they alighted in Sultan Murad's encampment and did not rise again. She awoke and shrieked within the castle walls, "I fear that all of you are going to die!"

The chronicles also say that God spoke to Lazar, prince of the Serbian empire: "Choose, Lazar. The heavenly crown or the earthly crown. The Kingdom of God, or of Serbia. If you choose Serbia, you shall be victorious over the infidel, your enemy destroyed, your crown secure. But all such things pass. If you choose heaven, gather up your men, eat the bread and drink the wine, for you all shall perish utterly, entering the eternal skies."

We climb to the top of the bleak memorial tower to view the battlefield, the spacious plain between the Lab and the Sitnica rivers, the yawning Balkan entrance to Europe where two armies had encamped on the eve of St. Vitus's Day, June 15, 1389, the Serbs facing southeast, in the direction of their nemesis. There is an inscription on the stone: "Whoever is a Serb, of Serbian blood, and does not come to fight at Kosovo, may he never have the children his heart desires, neither son nor daughter; may his hand harvest nothing, neither the purple grape nor the golden wheat; let him rust away like iron in water until his name be lost." So Prince Lazar had spoken.

We look down on a panorama of belching industrial enterprises – the postwar boast of Communist government – spread across this field sacred to the memory of Serb and Turk. Sultan Murad is buried here, his tomb a martyr's shrine, for he was the first Ottoman sultan to die in battle. His army would win but he would die, stabbed to death by the Serbian hero Milos Obilic, who had cunningly infiltrated his tent. Milos too would die, and Lazar. Lazar's head would be taken to Istanbul as a prize of war, his body carried here and there by wandering kinsmen trying to find a place of rest for it and themselves.

On the one side had been forty thousand Turks and their janizaries, archers and cavalry in pointed helmets and light-fitting chainmail. Behind them, the wide sinister lip of a deep ditch studded with sharpened stakes and covered over with loose earth.

On the other side, twenty-five thousand Serbs, Bosnians, Wallachians and Albanians: archers in the front rows; heavily armoured cavalry behind them, bristling with knives, the two-edged sword, maces, their heads swaying under horned and feathered helmets. In the rear, the mob of untrained foot soldiers, sullen and frightened serfs dragooned by their lords off the fields and into this assembly of war where they stood waiting to die.

The battle began at sunrise with a Serbian offensive and a Turkish response by arrow, then a Turkish counteroffensive, and then, their lines breaking northward, the Serbian flight. It was over in four hours, and the dead were legion. A Turkish chronicler, viewing the dead and the unwinding folds of turbans of many colours, was reminded of a bed of tulips.

Music Stefan, who had fought and killed three pashas, was struck down by the scimitar of a fourth and died alongside the twelve thousand others. A peasant girl sent by her mother to the river for water waded through a lake of blood tossing up helmets and fezzes, broken swords and dying heroes. She reached down to snatch up a helmet of white silk intertwined with feathers: crown of the headless, homeless

Lazar. The chronicles again: "Great Tsar Lazar also perished on that day, and with him died a good and ancient Empire – with him died the Kingdom of this Earth."

We walk down to the bus to be met by a gaggle of clamouring Albanian boys who offer us fistfuls of blue-red flowers, sticky and heavy-petalled; this is the *kosovo bozur,* said to grow only here on Kosovo Polje, blooming as red as the blood that coagulated in the Kosovo dirt.

In a painting I have seen in the Belgrade art gallery, the kosovo bozur looks like a poppy, black-eyed and red-petalled, its stem crushed under the shoulder of a knight fallen face down in the grass. Already the dead are fading into the obscurity of the waning day, and the faint yellow light is being sucked westward over the blue hills at the edge of Kosovo Polje, "a field like no other … Heaven above it, Heaven below," wrote the poet Vasko Popa.

Not far off from the memorial tower stands the tomb of the sultan's standard-bearer, buried where he died. Rebecca West remarked in 1937 that it was unvisited except by gypsies who came on St. George's Day to sacrifice fowl, littering the desiccated earth with chicken heads. Now tourists tramp about who do not know the tale at all. This too is a kind of peace.

The light of day is disappearing behind the high, slender silhouette of the minarets as we make our way up a cobble-stoned path, away from the river bank, to the walled seminary of Prizren. We are greeted with great dignity, even reserve, by priests in tall black hats and invited to sit in the cool, watery garden as a respite from the hot day spent examining Byzantine frescoes in churches on the Kosovo plain.

We are served glasses of cold water from the well, thimbles of raki and chunks of Turkish delight, and our conversation becomes desultory and languorous, as though we really were travellers from afar, seeking hospitality at a caravanserai in this important town. The seminarian who serves us is wearing blue jeans and running shoes under his cassock and, as the lights go on in the dormitory in front of us, I can see the dilapidated doors and shutters of this complex, the stained and pitted walls, its meanness and shabbiness: a handful of country boys running to the cold water showers in ill-fitting trousers and thin white T-shirts. This institution once produced patriarchs and metropolitans of the Serbian Orthodox church and boasted an important library, but now it struggles along in "reduced circumstances," attracting almost no one to its classrooms and chapels except the sons of poor villagers who see in it an escape from labour on the land.

Lamentation of the Orator of Smederevo, mid-fifteenth century: "But we, your own folk, how You have left us. How shall we outlive this bitter and painful loss? How shall we survive this dark night, who will protect us, who heal the grievous wound of Your departure?"

We are invited to join the celebrants at Mass the next day. I take my place, standing, in an aisle on the left. A voluptuousness of candles sputtering in the candelabras, the smoke of incense on the shafts of tremulous sunshine, puckered kisses on the Mother of God under glass, the bone-rattling voices of the male choir, *Lord have mercy upon us,* and we are all down on our knees as the priest kneels in front of us to recite the prayers of the Pentecost. We are kneeling on fresh mown hay, and we scoop it up to make the grasses into wreaths, braiding into them our prayers for our loved ones. *Hear our petitions and the petitions of all Thy people and send down the multitude of Thy mercy.* Incense and clover and beeswax, knees aching against the cold slate floor, mournful and supplicating syllables, voices sending up a great cry to the dome, bells clanging at the end of a rope, the peals drifting off into a grey, dripping Sunday morning. I walk out to get a breath of air and I watch, from behind the great trees of the churchyard, how on Sunday the Albanians of Prizren take refreshment in noisy cafés inside the din of Turkish pop music. Students jog around the church square and women swarm around the tables of a bazaar laid out just across the street, outside the shadow of the domes.

I am not a believer, but I go to church all the same. If I have a church, it is this one: Orthodox. From Greek, *orthos,* straight, and *doxa,* opinion. This church, and all the nations that have embraced it, have been "eastern" since 285 A.D. when Diocletian, himself a Dalmatian, divided the Roman Empire into two administrative units, the western part governed from Rome, the eastern one from Constantinople. The historians remind us that this separation – Greek from Roman, Byzantine from Catholic, Cyrillic from Latin – has become permanent. It is one of the oldest features of European culture.

Pentecostal prayer of the Orthodox Church: "Hear us, Thy humble ones, who make our supplication unto Thee, and give rest to the souls of Thy ser-

vants who have fallen asleep, in a place of light, a place of verdure, a place
of refreshment whence all sickness, sorrow and sighing have fled away. And
establish Thou their souls in the mansions of the just."

I rejoin the congregation. We huddle together as though we had been driven here in a kind of roundup of the last of the Orthodox faithful, corralled into the last church. We gather up grasses so that we may say we have sown and reaped, therefore we cannot be torn away from here; we are on our knees, braiding prayers for the absent ones, ancestors and neighbours and kin who left long ago, on a great trek northward, away from the Turks, away from the green mountains, away from the ever-virgin and exceeding glorious Birth-giver of God who would disappear under the whitewash of the church's new inhabitants, be abandoned to the thousand indecencies of the infidel.

I am thinking that it has always been like this, peoples displaced and on the move, driving their flocks before them, loading oxen with pots and pans, slinging the old and dying onto stretchers, the babies into cradles, wrapping up the family icons, kissing the door stoop in farewell, and then leaving. Emigrating. Tossing up in a new place and beginning again. What, then, is this lamentation for a lost heartland when the rest of the world lies just beyond? But I suppose this is the jejune optimism of a daughter of the New World, whose story begins with kin who gratefully tore away from the ancient village and moved halfway around the world without once looking back. For these people here, kneeling on the cold slate, the trek is always a catastrophe, the way ahead always obscure. "Not even he who leads us knows / Whether the dawn will descend to us from there / Or whether a conflagration, in which we / Town by town, wheat field by wheat field / Shall burn," writes Ljubomir Simovic in *The Migration of Serbia.*

And so I say my prayers alongside theirs, trying, even, to insinuate myself, to feel what they are feeling: the grief of their abandonment, themselves a shrivelling minority in a Muslim world, the last to keep the faith, to fill the lamps and mix the bread and wine in the silver chalice of the patriarchs.

ARE WE STILL IN EUROPE?

BELGRADE, SERBIA, 1988: Igor, who will not speak English, happily speaks French. He is still grateful that the Parisians of 1389 "rang the bells of Notre Dame in alarm and grief at the news of the catastrophe at Kosovo Polje."

He's got this wrong. While the Serbs were burying their dead on the Field of Crows, a Te Deum was being sung in Notre Dame cathedral on the vainglorious assumption that the Serbs had *won* the battle against the Turks. Any other outcome was apparently unthinkable. The armies of Christ were considered so invincible that neither soldiers nor money were sent from the capitals of the West to succour them in their fateful encounter with the infidel armies of Mohammed.

Thus, they lost. But even this catastrophe was turned to good account in the West. More than five hundred years later, the French ambassador to the court of Serbia would convey his admiration to the Prime Minister on the "greatness of soul" the Serbian people demonstrated all those centuries ago when, sacrificing themselves on the plains of death, they had decided "once and for all for European civilization." Subtext: The Serbs were swallowed up in oriental empire so that the French could carry on, unmolested, with the great tasks of European culture. This is the *meaning* of the Balkans: the terrain where the dreadful East exhausted itself. This is the meaning of the Te Deum of thankfulness in Notre Dame.

It would be unseemly somehow to say this to Igor. We are celebrating Milos's seventh birthday, and we are all making exuberant pigs of ourselves with the roast lamb, pickled mushrooms, torte and plum brandy. Conversation is carried on in loud whoops and hee-haws, the guests are forever jumping up and down for more to eat, more to drink, the hot Belgrade night air slicks our skin like the lamb fat greasing our mouths and fingers, and Igor is in full flight clinking his glass of slivovitz all around the table.

When he bursts into French again, it is to talk inevitably of Kosovo: that there have been several murders recently of newborn Serbian babies at the hands of Albanian hospital staff – strangled in cribs, starved to death – a turn in the tone of the conversation so abruptly malignant that I shout in protest that this sort of report is hardly to be believed. That it reminds me of the cheap propaganda that nations at war have always unleashed against the enemy: The enemy disembowels pregnant women! The enemy uses babies for bayonet practice! Igor is indignant. "Ce n'est pas de la propagande, madame!" He looks right and left for confirmation. "C'est la génocide."

Igor comes from a Serbian family that traces its roots back to the sixteenth century in Kosovo; he tells me so himself. Some members of the family adapted to the new Turkish order while others – rebels – assaulted Turkish functionaries and fled to Bosnia. Igor's father is a partisan veteran with medals all up and down his Bosnian breast. Igor cares nothing for politics and keeps clear of the system by renting out a seaside apartment for deutschemarks.

The Serbs are tall and lean, of long leg, with facial features slightly askew. In speech they utter all the sibilants, including "sh" and "ch." Here in Belgrade, as in all the Balkan places, are the gypsies and their dancing bears and the old men with leathery faces and woollen leggings down from the mountains, Turkish coffee and cheese pies and wailing sopranos on the bus station loudspeakers. And here too are the stories of the resistance in the mountains – the hajduks, romantic freebooters in the hills, avenging the poor of the villages against the plundering Turks – and the references not to Istanbul but to Carski Grad, the King's City, Constantine's city, as though to refuse its Turkish name is to keep the thread intact that once linked Athens with Rome with Byzantium.

Those Serbs lucky enough to have lived across the river from Belgrade in Zemun were barely brushed by "the East." They had the great good fortune, to hear them tell it, to have fallen within the frontiers of the Austro-Hungarian empire.

In Zemun, Gina has portraits of her great-grandparents on the wall. I guess that the woman was a Viennese matron, the man a state official, and I am right, except that they lived in Zagreb, not Vienna. Never mind, at least it was in Europe.

Gina lives in a capacious turn-of-the-century flat with parquet floors and a large number of stately ceramic-tiled stoves throughout; large canvases by a renowned Serbian woman painter hang alongside small inherited oils: landscapes, dark and indecipherable. There is a great deal of clutter, a large colour television set and a boyfriend who orders Gina about. "Clear the clutter! Get me a beer! Light my cigarette! Come here, bitch!" And she offers him her neck and throat, the front of her shirt gaping open over white breasts the size of apricots. He nibbles at her while she feeds herself on apple cake. Her friends despise him.

They are artists. Europeans.

The Montenegrins come creeping: they have filtered into Belgrade, down onto the edges of the Pannonian plain from their harsh mountain perches. Every apartment building now has some; they are loud and bad-mannered and do not take out their garbage. They are spoken of as an infestation. This is very sad. It was the mountain fastnesses of unconquerable Montenegro that gave shelter and homeland to the Serbs still resisting the Ottomans. In 1861, three hundred Montenegrins, in a martyrdom even now evoked by their descendants, ploughed their way through Turkish lines to join up, bloodied and mangled, with their Serbian "brethren" in a war they would fight together again in 1912, along with Bulgaria and Greece on other fronts, to drive the Turks out of the Balkans.

Montenegro would be the first to attack. With fire and sword, they reinscribed themselves in "Europe." Now their neighbours call them "cockroaches" and draw a new frontier.

WHAT IS THIS OLD, OLD FEAR?

SKOPJE, MACEDONIA, 1988: I am taking lunch in the shady courtyard of what was once upon a time a caravanserai. My host is Vlado, from the university. He answers all my questions with the same gusto that he chops up the tomatoes and tosses them in the oil and oregano. Concerning the Albanians living in his midst, he is outraged that they have desecrated Christian cemeteries and put the torch to the refectory at Pec monastery, holy of holies. He complains they "breed like vermin." They sterilize the babies of Serbian women in the maternity hospitals of Kosovo, and they prey upon Serbian women out in the streets after dusk in Pristina. Violence is endemic to them, as though part of their ethnicity: this is what Albanian "means." My host is a man of refinement. He can quote from *Finnegan's Wake*. Just a few moments ago I watched him pick over a mound of tomatoes at the market with a fastidious eye. Strolling through the bazaar, he directed my attention to a certain bolt of cloth, a brass coffeepot. I am confused.

The Turks held Skopje from 1392 to 1912 (it was the *Austrians* who burned it down in 1689), and its glory from the eleventh century on was its great market near St. George's monastery, a cluster of tiny shops around the caravanserai: a seventeenth-century traveller says there were 2150 of them. Cotton and silk, veils, slippers, dyes, spices, brass and gold. I was here among their ramshackle remnants in 1969, seeking out a cobbler: the glare off the tin-sheeted roofs, the grizzled men in rags and tatters jostling me, the wail and whine of Turkish songs on the radio in the café, the stuffy mustiness inside the shoe repair shop. The market has been scrubbed clean since then and now seems airier and cooler. It is filled with large baskets of spices, ropes of hot peppers, canvas sacks of coffee beans, little sausages grilling over charcoal, hand-tooled sandals, embroidered village towels and a multitude of gold shops, for the people of Skopje, men and women, love to adorn themselves with jewellery. Vlado says that skeletons spangled with gold chains of exquisite delicacy have been unearthed from Illyrian graves.

Vlado leads me into the weightless interior of Mustafa Pasha's fifteenth-century mosque, an enormous, globular dome floating airily above threadbare Persian carpets and tendrils of blue, red and green plants in graceful riot on fading frescoes. Then he shows me the cool stone walls of a Turkish bathhouse, room after room filtered with light seeping through star-shaped holes carved out of the roof. Turks love the sound of running water, and so wherever they have governed they have built courtyards around fountains. They have planted flower gardens and run curved balustrades up the inner staircases to the harems but have left the street-facing walls blank and featureless: the stranger has no business here. The stranger is invited to the stroll, the bath: steam, tiny cups of thick coffee, conversation.

The slender spire of a minaret raised up from the untidy roofscape is so svelte and airy that it seems poised to lift off from earth and head for heaven.

Macedonians live here among Greeks, Albanians, Turks, Bulgarians. They live together on the Silk Route; they live with the ghosts of travellers on the Roman Via Egnatia who passed through en route from Dubrovnik and Ohrid to Constantinople. Polymorphs. Polyphonies. Who's afraid of the passageway?

The never-ending debate: what kind of people are we? We have wandered all over the southeast lands, scattering our bones, like our cold hearth ashes, in all directions. Austrian generals once measured off a wide swath of territory bordering on Serbia and Bosnia, marking the farthest extent of western Christianity into the Balkans, and called it the Bloody Frontier. That's where we lived: within the blood.

AND THERE WAS A DANCING GIRL CALLED MACEDONIA

OHRID, MACEDONIA, 1988: Goce takes me, under a full moon, to the church of St. Jovan, by Lake Ohrid, "the Macedonian sea." I sit on the ancient, scooped-out stoop of the little church like an audience for Goce's performance: he stands half-turned to the water, the winking lights of Ohrid at his back, as if unsure precisely who to address – me, or the shades of the dead, slaking their great thirst in the waves sloshing against the rock. He points to a modest headstone under a tree, all by itself on the rocky promontory jutting out from the churchyard. He tells me it is the grave of a priest who served all his life at St. Jovan and asked in return only that he should be buried exactly here, where he would lie forever in the heat and light of the Macedonian sun, feel the breath of the wind blowing in over Ohrid and hear the little song of the slapping Macedonian sea.

Goce is intoxicated with his birthplace. I have watched him here, the way he stands talking, unconsciously flexing the muscles of his arms under the denim sleeve, the way he rolls up his sleeves and unbuttons his shirt, unwrapping himself, brown-skinned, the way he tilts his face to the sun bouncing off the green swells of the lake; you would say the very skin and hair and sinew of him gloat upon the pleasures of his hometown. Whenever he goes abroad, the same thought occurs to him every day as he wakes up: "I wonder how it is today at Sveti Jovan?"

When we visit the church of Sveti Kliment, he yanks me by the hand up the pebbly path to see the tree in the forecourt, planted for the thousandth anniversary of Christianity here. A plaque underneath the tree reads, "We searched for you all day and almost didn't find you." The plaque promises that the tree will be watered and watched over "in honour of the thousandth jubilee of Methodius."

Methodius, a monk – some say Macedonian – was sent forth with his brother Cyril from Constantinople in the ninth century to evangelize among the heathen Slavs. According to some versions of the tale, in about 860 they created for the new converts an alphabet, known as the Glagolitic, on the base of the Greek cursive. But it was their second effort – or that of their disciples or even Bulgarian court scribes – an alphabet based on Greek uncials, that took root in Macedonia and Serbia and became the script with which some Slavs wrote themselves into European history: Cyrillic.

Labouring at Saturday School in the basement of the Ukrainian Orthodox Church of St. John, in Edmonton, I learned how to form the letters of an alphabet whose utter otherness – its weirdness, and the way it shows up as bits of cryptic text floating around the haloes of the saints on the church's icons or in the ferocious slogans of Bolshevik manifestos on posters in students' basement apartments – marks it as the peculiar acquisition of a separate race. Every time I write it out, I enter some other zone of awareness: I know this is so, because Cyril and Methodius, who invented it, were saints, lined up stiff and otherwordly in the pantheon of Orthodox afterlife, as though writing were a revelation and script writers the instruments of the mind of God.

And now this tree in Ohrid, this greening, rooting, flowering jubilation of the written word. First the alphabet, and then the books.

We walk down the slopes, pebbles rolling out from under our feet, the dry, reddish, granular earth rising in puffs of dust, the musk of pine resin released by the heat, and we are at the site of the monastery of St. Panteleimon. A few stones, a marble slab, a grassy indentation mark the great Ohrid School of Literature where, for some four hundred years, until the Turks came, monk-students copied and translated the texts of Christianity into the Slavonic and graduates were sent out on their liturgical missions: first the alphabet, then the books, then the libraries ...

In Ohrid the scriptorium was the work of Saints Kliment and Naum. They were canonized for their work among the Macedonians, for to bring to a community the gift of letters was to bring them self-consciousness; the people know themselves even to this day as Slavs and as Orthodox. And whosoever dares to remove the books – the psalters, the hymnals, the breviaries – from the heart of the community, which is to say from the church, "such is damned by God Almighty and by the Most Pure Virgin and by the holy 318 Godly Fathers and by our holy founders Simeon and St. Sava." So promises the psalter in the monastery in Hilendar at Mount Athos.

It is so still here, at the ghostly monastery of Panteleimon. The only sounds are the cicadas in the long grass and Goce's running shoe rubbing the sandy grit away from a Roman mosaic impressed upon a circle of flattened earth. The Romans were here before the Slavs, laying the Via Egnatia between the Adriatic and the Aegean seas. Goce motions for me to have a look: a little fawn, jumping between floral panels. It is a perfectly natural-looking creature, suspended in the natural world.

With the coming of the saints, serene and pensive and boneless in their vestments of the Byzantine court, the Macedonians will not see the likes of this little fawn again.

I stand for a long time, looking down at the shards of St. Panteleimon. I am imagining the incredible journey that began at this spot eleven hundred years ago. The nameless monk in the black cloak who, having finished his studies here in the cool, shadow-dappled scriptorium, filled a bag with bread and apples and some books wrapped in cloth, seized a walking stick and set out for Rus.

When he got there, and stepped on board a sturdy skiff that ploughed north up the river Dnipro, and alighted at the foot of the wooden palisades of Kiev, he showed the book to the princes there. In their amazement, they felt the scales fall away from their eyes, and they were saved. The old, black-robed Macedonian passed away, but in his place a hundred monks from Kiev and Chernihiv and Novgorod bent to their letters and books in the monasteries of St. Sophia of Rus, until one day each of them packed a bag and seized a stick and travelled throughout the Slavic settlements of the southwestern borderlands, *u-kraina*. Wherever they stopped, they left a church, a priest and a book. In the laying on of hands from bishop to bishop through many generations, an unbroken memory of the Macedonians passed down to the Galician village of my ancestors, who were adherents of the "Greek" church.

From this village at the opening of the twentieth century, my grandparents and their neighbours heaved themselves over to the New World, on the other side of the globe, and built themselves onion-domed churches on the corner of a quarter section of prairie bush and sent their children to them. Here my parents and then I took up the venerable, devout task of repeating the awesome hieroglyphs of St. Cyril.

And now I am standing here, Goce somnolent under the fumy pines, with my beginnings underfoot.

"Many go blind in Byzantium. It is the gold and the sea." – Maggie Helwig, "The Lost History of Byzantium"

We climb up the crag to the old gate and the relics of ramparts from the eleventh-century city of Samuilo.

The brilliant, unhappy Samuilo had welded a mishmash of peoples – Greeks, Bulgars, Turks, Albanians, Slavs, Vlahs – into an empire that for the brief, feverish span of a man's lifetime strutted its stuff from the Black Sea to the Adriatic and into Greece as far as the Peloponnesus. But Samuilo never was able to take the jewel, the Byzantine city of Thessalonike. It threw his forces back, for which providential deliverance the citizens gave thanks to St. Demetrius, the warrior saint.

In 1014, Samuilo's army was defeated at the Battle of Kleidon by Basil II, emperor of Byzantium. Basil took thousands of prisoners, then released them after blinding most of them, leaving one in every hundred with one eye. He sent them back to Ohrid, where their harrowed, ruined emperor is said to have died of shock to see them: the hobbling column of tatterdemalions mincing through the monumental portals, their arms waving in front of them like the unseeing tendrils of an underwater plant.

We stand at the base of the ravaged fortress at the summit of the town. It does not seem to me to stand at a very imposing height, nor did it intimidate the enemies of Samuilo. Four years after his victory at Kleidon, Basil II entered Ohrid and claimed the fortress – the walls, the ramparts, the gates – for Byzantium. The fortress had withstood the onslaught of Theodoric's Goths in the fifth century, but it could not expel the Greeks: they had it for the next 316 years. I can imagine the crackle of the stiff pleats of brocade and the breeze ruffling the thick fur turbans as the luminaries of the new order strolled, chatting of Herodotus and Maximus the Confessor, on their way to church and to the drones of the psalmodists, kicking at the dust blowing over the graves of the blinded ones.

"Our voices already fill the abyss above / and the smoke of the stake where our bones will burn / sinks with the sand into the abyss below." – Ivan Lalic, "Word of the Warrior on the Battlements"

Goce explains, with scribbles on the paper tablecloth of the outdoor café, that there are three Macedonias – Vardar, named for the river in Yugoslavia; Pirin, for the mountain in Bulgaria; Aegean, for the sea rimming the lost home harbours. The salt water once lapped at Macedonia but the Greeks threw off the Slavic mob and held onto Thessaloniki, which they have the temerity even today to call "theirs."

We were the barbarians. We, Slavs, were among that host of historical riffraff (Antae, Huns, Avars, Magyars, Pechenegs) who arrived into the light of the "known" (written-of) universe and dis/re/ordered it. With the Avars in the sixth century we overran mainland Greece, and in 807 A.D. the records speak of a combined Slav and Saracen attack on Patras in the Gulf of Corinth.

We are the barbarians, Goce and I. I watch him at the café table, recapitulating in the aggrieved look on his face the ancient disappointment: the Slav who was thrown back by Greeks from the salt sea at the mouth of the Vardar and contained with his back to the lake at Ohrid, where he comforts himself, calling it the Macedonian sea.

Goce was turned away at the Greek border. Other times they searched his car before letting him cross. What are they afraid of? "Write this down!" he shouts at me. "The Greeks force the Macedonians in the borderlands to write their tombstones in Greek!" I write it down, swallowing wine so as not to protest the obvious – that Macedonians write in Cyrillic, based on Greek – and risk an altercation, barbarian to barbarian.

"And this! Marshal Tito, super-partisan of partisans, scourge of fascists, ambassador of people's liberation – hallowed be his memory – directed the partisans at the end of the war to head *north* in pursuit of the retreating Germans instead of unleashing them to go south. South! South all the way to Thessaloniki … *to get it back.*"

Was it ever his? It may as well have been, so intensely can he taste the dust off the red Byzantine brick and the salt off the water of the gulf. It may as well be his.

A kind of drunkenness in Ohrid: I am disoriented in the streets as though in a swoon of confusion as to my whereabouts. I walk along a broad, stony seawalk and pass a string of fishing boats bobbing on the blue-green water of the lake as though moored up in the salty harbour of Cephallonia, say, or Hydra. Up on the scrubby hillsides stand Byzantine monasteries whose prototypes disintegrate on the slopes of Mistra near Sparta in the Peloponnesus. Down by the lakeside Goce holds a bottle of wine, and me, and sings the thousand-year-old song of the girl from Biljana who has come down to the water, waiting, waiting, under the wheeling flight of the gulls. *Biljana platno beleshe … Na Ohridskite izvori.* Starshine falls on stone, wave and rosebush. We sit at a table under a tree in the courtyard of a taverna, Goce's dark face disappearing into the shadow, and all around us dark men drink red wine and chew cubes of meat off the grill. Jasmine and garlic, lemon and salt.

The men begin to sing. I turn away from the shadow on the other side of the table and strain to catch some words. "Macedonia weeps for you, you who have gone away. Away to Canada, to America, to Australia. You who dream of coming back one day to Struga, to Ohrid, to Bitola ...," the song goes. Another narrative of displacement and nostalgia, of the emigrant's resentment – "I leave only because I have no choice" – and dream of returning, fat, rich and with many grandchildren, to open a café by the water's edge.

In Macedonia, this leaving the motherland to labour abroad, in a stranger's fields, is called *pechalba*. It is rooted in the word *pechal*, to earn money. The idea was to work a few months on the farms and construction sites and in the restaurants and bakeries of Turkey, Bulgaria, Canada, and then come home. Like Greeks, Macedonians have a horror of dying abroad.

THE DEAD COME BACK

ZAGREB, CROATIA, 1988: The street in Zagreb where Sonja and Emilio live has had four names in the course of Emilio's life: before World War I, it was named for a member of the Hapsburg royal family; between the wars, for a Serbian royal; during the Second World War, for Mussolini's brother, and now for a Communist partisan. Their flat – enormous, going on from room to room like a small ocean liner – used to be the property of a Jewish family. One by one, the family was taken away by the local Fascist authorities, right down to the last child hiding in the bedroom wardrobe. None came back.

After the Liberation, families in large flats, such as the neighbours of Sonja and Emilio, were ordered to house the homeless, no one having the right to more than one room for each two family members. The homeless had not, as in Belgrade, been bombed out of their homes, for Zagreb had not been bombed, but were arriving by the thousands from the mean and devastated countryside. Peasants swarming in the salons of the bourgeoisie. Only artists and professors, such as Sonja and Emilio, had the right to "protected" apartments where their space was their own.

One day, however, Sonja had a visitor. An old woman, or a middle-aged woman made old by the events of her life, identified herself as the former mistress of the flat. It was her family who had been taken away. She had come back. Not to claim anything but just to sit every now and then in the living room and look around, have a cup of tea and go. Sonja never knows when she'll show up. Still, they have become friends in their fashion, and Sonja is happy to put on the kettle for this woman who used to polish the heavy furniture with lemon oil, dust off the family portraits in the dark corridor and, to the sound of Ustase boots ringing against the cobble-stones under the shuttered windows, prepare the Sabbath meal. She sits down, folds her hands in her lap, looks around at the professors' flat and asks for one little kindness more: please never show her the bedroom.

Are we still in Europe? Will the Croats claim this Europe too, the Europe of genocide?

I remember a sculpture I saw in the Turkish bathhouse in Skopje that is now a civic art gallery, rooms yielding onto rooms, white, cool walls hung with framed paintings in a dramatic reversal of the Muslim practice of plastering over the polychromatic frescoes of the Orthodox church. The sculpture was called *The Pit*: a group of emaciated figures, nothing but boneracks, the orbs of their eyes blank, their gesturing limbs desperately flailing in space. My host told me the artist, a Macedonian, was inspired by a wartime atrocity in Croatia in which Serb villagers, scorned and reviled Orthodox minority in rich, Catholic Croatia, were seized by their neighbours, blinded and thrown into the pit, whether a natural abyss or a hole dug expressly for the purpose I neglected to ask.

After that, it became impossible not to hear all the terrible stories about Croatia. I took them down, not even recording their sources, as though the tales were generic and only in this case happened to be about Croats and Croatia because an enemy was telling the story. Did I not know that it was the Fascist puppet regime in Croatia that built Europe's first death camp, at Jasenovac, where mass murder took place? That it is said 500,000 Serbs died in that camp? Surely I was aware that the Ustase were committed to Croatia's "purification" from "alien" elements? Their victims were gypsies, Jews and Serbs, most particularly Serbs. Hadn't I heard that Monsignor Stepinac, Archbishop of Zagreb, made no protest when the Orthodox Metropolitan was tortured within the walls of a Zagreb dungeon? Nor the tale of Croatian thugs mowing down Serbian coal miners in the shafts of their mines, more deaths in a pit, blank eyes open in the deep? I hadn't known? Well, now I did.

There is a trial going on in Zagreb, in the summer of 1988, of an accused war criminal, a former member of the Ustase Fascist regime in Croatia. Friends in Belgrade tell me that a war crimes trial is a good thing: let the postwar generation of Croats learn about the nature of their parents' Croatian nationalism and their acts. Did I not know that Croats tore the hearts out of their Serbian neighbours, drank their blood and ripped their children to pieces? I hadn't known? I did now.

Serbian peasant lamentation: "Villages shall burn and the living shall cry unto the dead: arise, O dead, that we may lie down in your graves."

Of her husband, whom she otherwise detests, Viera boasts that he belongs to a family who has been in Zagreb, capital of Croatia, for five generations. The point she is making is that his family is well off the land and not to be confused with the peasantry whose members, though decamped to Zagreb since the war, still bear the mark of the soil, a certain humility, shall we say; an uncouthness.

Viera and her husband work in the media. Together with his parents they live in a Hapsburgian apartment downtown where, alongside the Swedish dining room furniture and the American bath towels (their brand-name labels faced outwards for the appreciation of the discerning house guest), one may admire the chandelier saved from the old summer house on the Dalmatian coast. The newer intelligentsia, those who are children and grandchildren of peasants, live in horrid phalanxes of featureless apartment blocks in the "new town."

The new town lies on the other side of the Sava River, eastward. It is said to be located "beyond Europe."

East from Zagreb: The mosque of Ferhad Pasha, built in 1579 in Banja Luka with monies raised by kidnapping Count Wolf Engelhard von Auersperg, son of an Austrian general, for 30,000 gold ducats, bears the glory of its minaret 41.4 metres into the sky. Ferhad Pasha, pious and observant, built it in the name of God and for the benefit of believers. In 1589, one of them, a slave in his household, murdered him. They say the slave was a Christian. The point is that both, master and helot, were Bosnian Slavs.

THE MEETING PLACE

BLED, SLOVENIA, 1988: Sonja and Stipe, professors of English literature, sing their Dalmatian songs. We have ordered one bottle after
another to distract us from the wet mist closing in on us from the lake.
Sonja sings in a high, clear soprano, but Stipe says that it should be a
wavering note, and he demonstrates the trilling, keening vibration that
comes out of the throats of singers from Pireaus to the Carpathians as
though they were drawing it down from the mountain air they breathe.

The two sing their songs and I recognize the words for "my darling,"
"to the water," "in the morning" and "white lamb." This isn't much, I
am thinking, for what are supposed to be sister tongues. And they have
words derived from the Turkish for the simplest things, like tavern and
gate, as though they had lost the habit of naming their own universe.
This, however, is a clue: the Dalmatians held the fort against the
Ottomans upriver from the coast while the Ukrainians held out against
the Mongols, picking up *their* words. *Kumys*, mare's milk. *Yasyr*, captiv-
ity in Turkey.

Stipko once lived awhile in New York City on Forty-Ninth Avenue,
among the Irish. He roasted lamb for Easter and his neighbours com-
plained of the stink.

We all laugh, superior Slavs mixing it up on the edges of the known
Western world. From the shadowy periphery of Mongol and Turkish
campfires, we learned the smell of roasting lamb's meat. We learned
eventually that it is good.

CATCHING UP WITH THE CRISIS

BELGRADE, SERBIA, 1988: Sonja has abandoned her diet, so we gorge
at a banquet of spaghetti and salads and cheesecake, washing it down
with local red wine and – because Milan has just come back from a
peace conference in Amsterdam – a bottle of duty-free cognac. He sits
monumentally at the dining room table and looks, in his large, benevo-
lent way, terribly aggrieved. It's those bloody-minded peaceniks from
Western Europe who have distressed him so, naïfs and opportunists
who cannot or will not understand why they should be very, very careful about working with the glib representatives of the official peace

groups from the Soviet Union. Everyone is gaga about Gorbachev, but please! Think! These groups are fronts for the Soviet state, and they should be challenged to meet certain minimum standards of conduct: to print and circulate, for instance, the texts coming out of the Soviet Union's *unofficial* peace groups. The official groups promise to do this but never follow through. Spaghetti sauce goes flying onto the newspapers from Slovenia: Milan is agitated and in a huff. Westerners can be so goddamned gullible.

You'd think the western Left had discovered "true" socialism, he says, like Columbus believing he had reached India when in fact he was only halfway there. "I read Trotsky for the first time while I was in prison. I have gone, in twenty years, from being a Guevarist to a Hegelian Marxist to a democratic socialist who believes in pluralism. If anyone knows this system, it's me!"

He struggles against one-party bureaucracy, intrusive censorship, poverty and jail in the name of that political and social normality westerners enjoy on a mundane basis at home. He dreams about legal aid, hard currency, photocopy machines and unlimited supplies of coffee beans. Westerners tell him he wouldn't want to live there – it's "militarized capitalism." But he would, he would.

Something's in the air, no doubt about it. Travellers in the Soviet Union report a shocking "normality" in everyday activities and conversations, as though the word were out that the plainclothesmen had been yanked back to barracks. The recent round of strikes in Gdansk, Poland, were a flop, as though the public no longer believes in the revolutionary potential of picket duty. And my friends in Prague, whom I said goodbye to just two weeks before the twentieth anniversary of the Soviet invasion, assured me that the only people interested in how Charter 77 was going to mark the occasion were "foreign correspondents and the secret police." One friend was going fishing. He gave no intimation of the thousands of young people who were going to show up in the streets in his place.

Sonja says she takes it for granted that their apartment is bugged and "absolutely for sure" that their telephone is tapped. She has used this situation to serve her own purposes: after her repeated complaints over the phone to her friends that she had been denied a visa to go to a conference in Vienna and her threat over the phone to make a human rights issue of it among her western activist friends, presto! A visa! A colleague of hers has exploited the fact that there are police engaged day and night without surcease in taping his phone calls; he enjoys ringing up a philosopher friend on a regular basis to discuss at great length, in German, problems of philosophy. In this way the men have been able to keep their "telephone minders" occupied with the transcription and translation of an argument about Essence.

The unrest in Kosovo is worrisome as always, the 78-per-cent Albanian majority demanding republic status for their province and the Serbian minority just as determined they should never have it. Yet the Serbs leave in droves, charging persecution by the Muslims. No amount of capital investment thrown into Kosovo enterprises – and it has been enormous – has closed the income gap between the poorest region and the richest. The only way to close it is the radical redistribution of income, the equalization of national incomes across the whole of Yugoslavia, but as Sonja points out, the decentralization of political authority to the republics from the federal centre since 1974 has stiffened the resistance of the more developed – Slovenia and Croatia – who see Kosovo and Macedonia, the poorest, as great black holes into which their hard-earned, well-deserved profits are sucked.

This financial tug of war between the republics is known as "economic nationalism"; *political* authorities tend to see themselves as bosses of autonomous *economic* units and play the regional cards of grievance and self-interest. Bosnia-Herzegovina, for example, has been complaining since 1967 that the allocation of federal funds is "unfair." In spite of twenty-three amendments to the constitution providing for devolution of powers to the republics, a massive student strike in 1971 in Zagreb had demanded, "Stop the plunder of Croatia!" The students were championed by local political bosses, who used the unrest to purge quietly their administrations of pro-federal (i.e., "Yugoslavist") officials.

Inevitably, the federal Party fought back, purging in its turn the Croatian "nationalists" and returning to Leninist norms of Party organization, leaving Sonja and Milan, for two, in despair. The universities became wastelands, fear filling the spaces vacated by the subdued activists of '68 while curricula remained unreformed and an alarming number of students failed their studies and withdrew.

Such are the sinister consequences – these violent swings between nationalist outbursts and Leninist norms – of the failure to allow for any development of political pluralism. Until there is some other political game allowed in town, Sonja and Milan argue, the Party and its army will have the monopoly on the idea of "Yugoslavia," and embittered and disenchanted citizens will have no alternative except in the idea of the "ethnos," the community of blood relations.

Sonja and Milan and their comrades across Yugoslavia are trying valiantly to build those political alternatives, in peace groups and nascent women's self-help groups and social democratic journals and Amnesty International and Helsinki Watch and environmental agitprop and street theatre. They want to create a civil society, a social space to which citizens can turn when the Party falls apart, as it surely will, and the ethnic warlords begin to beat their drums in the crash that follows.

It's very, very hot tonight. We are only half a kilometre away from the tree-covered riverbank, but nobody moves. We sit immobilized under the hot, bright lamp that hangs over the table in the hot, thick air.

TRIBUNES OF THE PEOPLE

BELGRADE, SERBIA, 1988: "Tell me what you notice most about my country." David's question comes out of the blue and startles me. Interviewer and interrogator from the West, I am rarely asked for my own opinion. I have got used to this, complacent even, manoeuvring in cruise control among my subjects.

Back and forth on the broad pavement in front of the Moskva Cafe's terrace, football fans parade the black and white colours of the Partizan team. It is Sunday morning; it is supposed to be quiet.

"I see the restaurants and cafés jammed," I begin, "the boutiques stuffed with expensive clothing, the colour televisions and vcrs in people's homes. The highways out of Belgrade are bumper to bumper with traffic getting away to the seaside, to mountain cottages and spas. Opera tickets to Placido Domingo's *Tosca* sell out in three hours at thirty dollars a hit. And yet the conversation, wherever I go, is about the wreck and ruin of the economy, the youth apathy amid the nasty, recrudescent nationalisms and political trials ..."

I trail off, sensing this set of observations is not somehow what is wanted, is too *journalistic*, if you will. I am meant, I think, to say something lyrical about the psychology of the country, to offer a comprehensive prognosis of its possibilities from the privileged point of view of one who drops in on the place only now and then. The big view; the long, speculative, haunted view of things. After all, the man who's asked the question is not a newspaper reporter. He's a writer of short fiction, "the greatest explorer of the possibilities of different narrative modes," to quote from the introduction to a collection of Serbian short stories.

David does not seem to hang out with other writers. I always meet him the same way – alone, at the Moskva. He's lean and pointed. Something in him seems pent-up, irritated. Smiling, he makes a wry face; delivering a witticism, he is astringent, peevish. Because he is not a political "joiner," he is beyond the consolations of group-think, and I am now used to his solitary opinions and do not seek him out for his representativeness but for his quirkiness. He always agrees to meet. Then we sit over Coca-Cola, pondering the fate of Yugoslavia. He could be a character out of one of his own stories. The narrator of "Stories We Tell Each Other," for example: "I told him I wasn't religious, but that once I really had believed. Believed what? asked Milosavljevic. Believed in people, I told him, which somehow didn't quite satisfy him. I told him that these nights I prayed, silently of course, and without following any rules."

The cultural situation becomes more grotesque by the day. David tells me of the hullabaloo that ensued in Slovenia when a commissioned poster for Youth Day turned out to be a deliberate imitation of a Hitler Youth poster from the era of the occupation. It took ages for the authorities to catch on that there was almost no difference and, when they did, the executive of the youth organization was dismissed. A magazine editor in Belgrade was fired for the temerity of having published an interview with the perennial dissident Milovan Djilas, compounding the error by announcing it *on the front cover*! An unholy ruckus was raised when a Belgrade student magazine ran a cover bearing the headline, "The Night of the Vampire," *on the same day as Tito's birthday*! Tito has been dead seven years. Who's going to stick around for a Party like this?

The West, says David, requires East European writers to be persecuted and disreputable. David's not disreputable. He's boring. He says so. Writing stories about family life and private conscience and domestic memory. Trying to find a place as a "Yugoslav" writer – not as a persecuted Jew, not as an insulted Serb, not as a dissident. Drinking Turkish coffee, translating Raymond Carver, making babies, strolling through Kalemegdan trying to catch a puff of river breeze in the furnace of the midday August heat ... not a bad life. But boring, okay?

Such a position puts David, born in 1948, in direct contention with an older, much more engaged generation, which regards the "aestheticist" argument as a kind of "moral co-operation" with the regime in its disinclination to be "summoned" to the urgent public issues of the day. Like the poet Stevan Raickovic in the 1960s, David would argue that "the only free territory for poetry is to be found in poetic creativity itself."

To witness tribunes of the people in action, David tells me, I need only go any Monday evening to the villa of the Writers' Union of Serbia, where week after week, month after month, the public packs itself into the main floor salon to eat up with terrifying appetite the testimonies offered by Serbian writers moved and inspired by the difficulties of their kinfolk in Kosovo.

David hates it. Serbia as collective noun, a prisoner of war groaning in chains forged by treacherous Albanians and pusillanimous politicians. The public adores this stuff, but David is disgusted by the spurious self-appointed vocation of the writer as the people's voice on issues of public import. Perhaps there was a time when the public *couldn't* speak for itself, but these Writers' Union meetings, he says, are shameful exhibitions where a thrill-seeking audience indulges writers in cheap displays of rhetorical vindictiveness.

These gatherings have been going on for some time. Back in 1986, the press had reported on "a meeting to discuss books written about Kosovo: influenced by numerous examples of the sufferings of Serb and other non-Albanian nationals in the province, which were described in great detail, M.B. came up with the pungent thesis that fascist-like characteristics on the Kosovo scene were of an oriental type. It was evident that not all participants in the discussion were always able to cope with the overheated atmosphere."

We are packed shoulder to shoulder and breathing down each other's necks in the hot, sodden, airless room; even those next to the open windows swab ineffectually at their sweating faces. We are all horribly uncomfortable, but no one gets up to leave. Indeed, more people arrive and jam themselves in at the doorway of the salon or heap themselves on the grand staircase in the foyer that, for those craning their necks, affords a view into the meeting room. The meeting – the last in the year-long series known as "Kosovo Meetings about and for Kosovo" –

features fifteen speakers (poets, journalists, dramatists, what have you) under the patronage of the Writers' Union of Serbia. There is an air of compacted excitement and expectation tonight. These meetings having become notorious, this may be the last time in a long while that writers and their fans may openly align themselves with demagogic appeals for vengeance upon the perfidious Albanians of Kosovo, a vengeance that the Party refuses to take. The writers have stepped smartly into the breach.

This militancy has been simmering since 1981, when Albanian student disturbances in Kosovo drew in workers and spilled over into violence against the Serb minority. The police retaliated with such force that eleven demonstrators were killed. Then came martial law, troops and Draconian prison sentences against "nationalists." The exodus of Serbs speeded up. In the summer of 1988, it has a terrible aspect, this aggrieved cry that "something" be done to stanch the flow of Serbs from their ancestral lands in Kosovo, to defend them from their "persecutors," the Muslim Albanians.

This is not one of my nightmares, this horror at the prospect of imminent de-Europeanization ("Islamization"), this "cry of anger and despair," as Arishi Pipa, a professor of Albanian origin put it, this "ancient ethnic phobia." Ensconced, white-skinned, in western Canada, secure in my numerical superiority over the aliens at my margins, buffeted within my majority by other white folks, cognates claiming ancestry from a democratized Europe, I sit sweating and perplexed beyond measure by the scene before me: a sea of cheerful faces alert to that odd pleasure of underdogs, the expectation of their own indignation.

The speakers speak. I strive mightily to catch the drift.

The land of one's faith, of the graves.... Prince Lazar chose the kingdom of heaven.... Only the priests of the Orthodox Church have behaved well.... The dark self of a nation.... Individuality, identity, genocide.... The crisis in Kosovo is the crisis of Yugoslav socialism.... If the Party can find no solution then it can no longer serve as a model for the future (sustained applause).... Orwell, disinformation, newspeak.... Albanian totalitarianism, Albanian fascism.... The two dangers of dogmatism and nationalism.... Pasha, sultan, Turk.... Coca-Cola, Zimbabwe.... The destruction of my tribe.

Tirelessly they declaim familiar themes, repeatedly deploy the same incantatory phrases and evoke that which is well known, yet the audi-

ence is not displeased: it is precisely in the repetition, the ritualistic for-
mulae, the familiarity of the narrative that they find their satisfaction.

I am now more than uncomfortable; I am distressed. As speaker after
speaker steps down from the podium and the crowd settles into its catechism of responses and shouts, I feel that I am witnessing a moment of
collective theatre in which the purpose is precisely *not* to resolve the
dilemma of the community's aggrieved helplessness before history but
to sustain it. *This* is what makes people feel good: their martyrdom.
And this is why they have come and the writers have come: to keep it
going.

LETTER FROM BELGRADE

July 23, 1989

Dear Myrna,

I have hard time now in Yugoslavia. I'm in depression and I think that I
will get neurosis pretty soon. Inflation is 1430% now and it will be more
than 2000% in December.

Cultural situation is as the political. Slovenian Writers' Union isn't
part of Yugoslav Writers' Union [any more]; they resigned from the
organization because of "Serbian nationalism." In fact we have here lots
of nationalism and it's our biggest problem. During family parties usually we are speaking about what Slovenians said about [Serbian presi-
dent] Milosevic and people refuse to buy Slovenian products. Similar
situation in Slovenia about Serbian products. Can you imagine our situation? People are rather buying products from abroad than from
another republic.

On June 28 we celebrated 600 years since the Kosovo battle and you
can imagine the political implications of it. People in Slovenia and
Croatia said this celebration was part of Serbian hegemony.... After the
ceremony (with 2 million participants), "His Royal Highness Crown
Prince Alexander of Yugoslavia" announced that monarchy is the best
option in present situation. Princess Jelena is learning Serbian. (They
live in England.) Everything is a soap opera.

We are calling our situation Catastroika.

Your friend,

Miki

CODA

In March 1991, I telephone Sonja and Milan in Belgrade. Huge anti-government demonstrations have been reported, with students once again trying to get past police barriers from their residences in New Belgrade to join the downtown masses, and news is circulating that activists are being rounded up. Milan is the chairman of the newly organized Social Democratic League and Sonja is prominent in the Helsinki Citizens' Assembly. In a state of high alarm, I want to know if my friends are under arrest.

They are all right. They are free and at home. They are laughing. "Listen to this," says Sonja, and holds her telephone receiver out to her radio. "This is what they've been playing all day long." It is John Lennon singing "Imagine."

The unimaginable has become imaginable: tens of thousands of Belgradians have broken the Titoist grip on their political mind and showed up in the streets to demonstrate that democracy is where *they* are. It has nothing to do with a parliament dominated by the Socialist Party – until very recently known as the Communist Party – which has played the nationalist card in a media they control. Sonja would write later in the summer that "civil society" had been blocked from developing while "national interests" consolidated themselves. Now, thanks to the demonstrations, there would be "an opportunity for the ... proliferation of pluralistic and democratic tendencies."

Instead, there is war.

BELGRADE, SERBIA, 1991: By fall, war is raging in Croatia, and so I am a little surprised that my Austrian Airlines flight to Belgrade holds a full complement of travellers from Vienna. The oppressive sense of a "queerness" will stay with me the whole month I am here – the result, I suppose, of a community of people going about their normal business, all the while aware of great violence being perpetrated offscreen, as it were, in their name.

Telephone lines with Zagreb have been cut. The Croatian government has shut the interrepublican gas pipeline from the Adriatic. There is no air traffic over Croatia, and it is madness on the ground. It is impossible to find Slovenian and Croatian newspapers and magazines. The media, with the exception of one heroic magazine and one tottering television station, trumpet the official government line. The claustrophobia is unbearable.

And yet, in the middle of Belgrade's urban blight, a family is growing grapes to make its own wine. Around the corner from the high-tech McDonald's, an old woman spreads her blanket out on the sidewalk and offers plastic trinkets and bubble gum for sale. On a bucolic Sunday, families take their coffee on the balcony, farmers sell gladioli at the bus stops, a tethered goat munches peaceably at a work site and, because this is melon season, all over Belgrade people are carrying melons home.

I meet Milan in the lobby of a fancy hotel in New Belgrade. We are awaiting the arrival from Novi Sad of the Peace Caravan, a bus convoy of peace activists from Europe and parts of ex-Yugoslavia with Sonja on board. It is a rather posh hotel, with boutiques called "Karmen" and "Dana" and a bar selling only imported beer. Why on earth would peaceniks pick this place? "We have connections with the manager," Milan explains. "We got a deal on the rooms."

We drink beer and wait and talk of the war. Milan says he feels he is a defeated man; he belongs to a generation defeated by nationalism. And indeed there is something deflated about him, this big, loquacious, tender, bearish man, now subdued and flattened by the utter failure to have avoided war.

The hopeful moments of the springtime, the "fifteen minutes" of the student rebellion, have proved ephemeral. His power shaken, the president of Serbia, Slobodan Milosevic, focusses public attention on the tensions with Croatia and, with every blundering move of the new Croatian state against its Serbian minority, the Milosevic government is able to portray itself the protector of Serbs, wherever they might find themselves. Where as a Communist he would once have argued for the "unity of the Party," Milosevic now calls for "Serbian solidarity." (The idea that the Serbian population in Croatia is not so much an alienated fragment of the motherland as a minority in a multicultural state is, I discover, quite literally unthinkable. Such minorities had been contained within the idea of multinational Yugoslavia; in ex-Yugoslavia, the new states seek not diversity but national homogeneity.)

Milan might have hoped that the public was too cynical to fall for such nationalist sloganeering. But the experience of long decades of Communism has been so ruinous to civil society, to the sense of community responsibility and of belonging to something bigger than family or tribe – what Toronto psychologist and peace activist Andrew Pakula calls "self-reference," all the different ways we can answer "Who am I?" – that the only structures left standing after the collapse of Communism are national. Who am I? A Serb, a Croat, etc., etc. This isn't nationalism as we understand it in Canada, Milan cautions me. "This is crazy stuff. It doesn't want peace. It wants to fight." Feverish and unquenchable. Even Milan confesses to moments of wanting to grab a machine gun and just blast away at buildings, shop windows, garbage cans …

Paranoia is rampant. Not that it isn't justified – Milan and Sonja have both received threatening telephone calls. On a radio phone-in show, a caller says that Sonja is "not one of ours." Sonja is a Jew. Twice a prisoner in Tito's jails (he was also incarcerated for a month in 1983 for his part in pro-Solidarity demonstrations), Milan is for the first time really afraid: "In the old days they threw you in prison. Now they shoot you at your front door." Unarmed, Sonja is beginning to feel freakish, vulnerable. Weapons are being sold on the black market. A friend's dentist offers to sell him a machine gun for deutschemarks. People are keeping guns in their homes.

The old comrades are comrades no longer; there have been vicious political splits over the question of the "progressive" and "pluralistic" aspects of the neonationalisms. Milan feels betrayed by the Slovene comrades who have deserted pan-Yugoslav initiatives in favour of Slovenian interests: "As if you pulled a nail out of a house and it fell apart, but you don't care. You've got your nail." And by the professor from the glory days of Belgrade University, 1968, who is regretting that he is too old to volunteer for the front. The environmentalists who say that questions of pollution are irrelevant in the life-and-death struggle of the nation. Mothers of soldiers who want their sons pulled out of the Yugoslav National Army so they can fight in the Croatian one.

Eventually, the buses arrive and we hop on for the drive downtown to the youth centre. A crowd of some two hundred Belgradians are amassed outside the centre, waiting. As the caravaners leave the buses, the crowd bursts into loud, sustained applause. Here and there someone tries to sing "We Shall Overcome," while others wave their hands in the V sign. Clearly startled by this reception, some caravaners are close to tears – old peace activists, suddenly with their cause returned, in a strange town, nonviolence mattering again. Sonja, ashen, exhausted, waves at friends, the notes for her speech crumpled in her fist.

Outside the centre I stand with one end of a banner – "Women of Berlin for Peace in Yugoslavia"; Dennis, a student from Rijeka, Croatia, holds the other. He has joined the caravan, he says, because he is trying mightily to be a "citizen of the world." He loves Croatia and he loves Yugoslavia but he wants to belong to the world.

My friend the university lecturer tells me that the "nationalist fanatic" Vojislav Seselj (not so long ago a political prisoner and a hero of democracy), said during a TV appearance that he looked forward to cutting the throats of Croats, preferably with the rusty shoehorn he was waving at the camera.

I repeat this to my friend the writer, who says that Seselj meant it sarcastically. As in: "See this shoehorn? I can hardly wait to use it on some Croatian throats. And for my next act, I'm sending submarines upriver to Zagreb." Seselj is not a monster, says my friend, but a "man of action."

I repeat this in turn to my friend the graduate student, who says Seselj was not being ironic; he meant it. My friend has heard that Seselj took a pistol to the television studio as well; he was waving it around and vowing to *shoot* Croats. It is said that Seselj's two years in prison have unhinged him. He is nuts. Who isn't?

David's wife has just given birth to a daughter, their second child. "If it gets any worse here," he tells me, over a glass of wine at the Slavija Hotel on the opening night of the annual meeting of the Serbian Writers' Association, "we're leaving." He means when it looks like the splintering of Yugoslavia is irreversible. "I'm not a *Serbian* writer; I belong to Yugoslav literature. Now you almost have to apologize for using that term. It's unbearable to me that I can no longer think of Slovenian and Croatian writers as colleagues in the same literary project."

It is already very difficult to find their books in Belgrade bookstores or their stories in the literary journals. When Slovenia declared independence, he says, Serbia slapped an import tax on Slovenian books, treating them as foreign. The only Serb the Croatian and Slovenian publishers are interested in is the one who takes an anti-government position.

David has always been impatient with the notion of the writer as dissident-by-definition. Now he finds himself in the ironic situation of being the dissident while staying in the same place. Those writers who had seen themselves as duty-bound to oppose the Titoist state are now with it in its "national" agony against Croatia. All those intellectuals who have felt their national identity squelched under the Communist Party have now been invited by the government to express it. Surprise! Their identity coincides with the state's! Do not look to them to denounce the war.

As for the groups you would expect to be at the forefront of a peace movement – artists, rock stars, Greens, feminists – they are dismal evidence that if you can't turn an issue into a "national" issue you can't pose it at all. How can you pose problems of the environment or poverty or the status of women as if they are only "Serbian" problems? The result then is silence.

That space in David's mind occupied by the sense of "country" is shrinking. As a Jew from Bosnia, he has no "nation" – he has a *country*. He isn't Jewish, Serbian or Bosnian. He is a citizen of Yugoslavia. Yugoslavia is the homeland. Now its borders have shrunk to within a few kilometres of where we are sitting. "Imagine a Yugoslavia in which I can no longer think of going to the sea?" In a way, he feels, living abroad might be easier if only because there he could keep intact the mental space called "country." Or perhaps he will move to New Guinea, in the middle of an ocean.

Or Israel. David, who has never lived "as a Jew," has suddenly discovered the one place that is "home" now that home has become unlivable.

Speakers at the plenary session of the Writers' Association of Serbia:

"This is a war where children, poets and priests are being killed on the same terrain where their mothers and fathers died. It is a domestic continuation of World War Two – a war against the Fascists. We Serbs are the new Jews. The world public seeks to rehabilitate the evil of fascism and deny the Serbian nation's right to exist."

"It is grotesque to portray this war as an act of Serbian aggression on the emerging democracy of Croatia – as if Croatia were a western-style democracy. This is one more example of Germanic-Catholic Europe expelling Slavic-Orthodox Europe from its concerns."

The Serbs of Croatia, Sonja understands, are fighting from fear and a suppressed need to avenge their dead in the death camps of the fascist Croatia of 1941-45. "Nothing is more powerful" than these motives.

Beware the creation of a purely Serbian army, then, she warns. Serbs have a militant tradition of ferocious war-making against the Turks and the Nazis. "They would eat the grass if they had to, and carry on one more day."

Sonja is dark with fatigue and disappointment but keeps a relentless pace of activity. Her flat has become a warehouse of papers and documents, and it looks as though no one has cooked or eaten a meal there in weeks. Our conversation is interrupted by a stream of international calls having to do with her frenzied schedule: the fallout from the Peace Caravan, the Labour Party conference in Brighton, the meeting with the Italian peace activists and then the trip to Budapest... She admits that she stays busy so as not to register emotionally the reality of the breakup of Yugoslavia and her life's work. At times she even feels suicidal. She goes to a movie, the first one in months, Milan *dragging* her there, and all she can do is weep through the whole thing.

Discussion has become problematic as people lose confidence in their own analysis of events, old intellectual systems no longer being adequate to the madness. Discourse has become monolithic and reductionist. If you can't talk about "ethnos" and its "memory" you can't talk at all; there is no other way to identify yourself as a citizen.

Suddenly Sonja is on her own. She has sought shelter with comrades across Yugoslavia who are now calling, from their respective independent republics, for an "anti-Serb struggle." Is that her? Is she a Serb? Does she have to be "struggled against," she who has lost most of her family to the Nazi gas chambers yet never said she is anti-German? What the hell is going on?

"When we were all in the democratic opposition together, we were held together by the politics of being against the system. In retrospect I can see that it's much easier to stand against a system than against a nation, especially your own. The pressure to conform to nationalist agendas is practically irresistible because it is so terrible to be alone."

But she and Milan are carrying on. One night I join them at the nightly peace vigil on Marshal Tito Boulevard behind the Serbian parliament. A drizzly rain, a handful of sodden peaceniks, a banner held in memory of *all* the war dead and a ring of candles sputtering on the pavement. No speeches, just quiet tête-à-têtes under the umbrellas, and then everyone goes home.

After twenty-five years as a socialist, Sonja confesses that perhaps the only way out of this nightmare of murderous nationalisms is the nurturing of a capitalist economy and a liberal democratic state. After all, it was these two forces in tandem that produced civil society and the idea of the inherent dignity of the individual citizen. In other words, the capitalist pluralist state has made it possible for a person to be defined first as a member of a civil polity – a citizen with rights and an autonomous consciousness – and then of a group or nation or sex. Without this individuation, it is very difficult for the person to emerge from the tribe and identify his or her interests separately from it, not to mention opening up civil space to the "stranger," the "other."

If there once had been the possibility that such a person would emerge from Yugoslavia, it is now rendered void. Whether or not such a person will emerge from the separate states is difficult to see, amid the blood.

POLAND

1944: *Red Army installs pro-Communist administration as (unelected) government of liberated Poland* 1948: *Polish United Workers' Party (*PUWP*) monopolizes political and economic power* 1950: *Stalinist industrialization drive* 1956: *strikes in Poznan against the centralized, planned command economy; intellectuals call for democratic socialism; artists create the new "post-socialist realist" movies, novels, plays* 1968: *student demonstrations* 1970: *strikes* 1976: *more strikes* 1980: *founding of free trade movement, Solidarity, under charismatic leadership of electrician Lech Walesa* 1981: *martial law declared by General Jaruzelski and Solidarity suppressed* 1981-1988: *Solidarity operates underground; strikes, massive economic failure* 1989: PUWP *agrees to power-sharing with re-legalized Solidarity; partially free elections held* 1990: *austerity program of pro-Solidarity government; falling living standards, collapse of cultural subsidies, strikes* 1991: *first free national elections elect Lech Walesa to presidency; feminists protest anti-abortion legislation* 1992-1993: *agonizing recovery of the economy with growing disparity between rich and poor; ban on abortion; collapse of Solidarity as a political movement*

AND A WIND BLEW IN FROM THE SEA

NAFPLION, GREECE, 1981: I am the only woman in the *kafenion*. We are all staring at the television screen. The television is very loud. I do not understand a word. My eyes bulge out of my head in my effort to dredge some meaning out of these images in black and white: the falling snow webbing the air of Warsaw, black figures engulfed in thick, shapeless coats, tanks rolling past bus stops.

I run out into the square. It is dark and wet, on the Peloponnesus. People are having their soup. They shake their heads. Men pull at their moustaches.

We will all learn later that, even while the executive of Solidarity was meeting in Gdansk on December 12 to endorse resolutions calling for a general strike, the telephone lines to the city had been cut and armoured convoys of troops were fanning out along the highways all over Poland. On December 13, almost the entire leadership of Solidarity was arrested and the union's offices were occupied by security forces. The Military Council of National Salvation under General Jaruzelski proclaimed the existence of a "state of war" and suspended civil liberties, claiming they acted to forestall a plot to overthrow the socialist order. On December 17, seven miners were shot and killed at the minehead near Wujek. I am days and days late getting the news.

It seems to me, in this Greek town, that I am enduring a particular form of exile. I have been in Greece for a month, arriving in November to watch the election of a socialist government here. After a year and a half of following the sensational news concerning the rise and triumph of the independent Polish trade union Solidarity, culminating in massive strikes and negotiations with the Communist government, I am now trapped in a language I do not understand while history unrolls in Poland.

I think of it as History with a capital H. Poland and its people have produced and lived through some of the most traumatic historical events in recent memory: reemergence onto the geopolitical map of Europe in the 1920s, invasion and occupation by German troops in 1939, the Warsaw Ghetto uprising in 1943 and the murder of the Jewish population in the extermination camps on Polish soil, the Warsaw uprising in 1944 while the "liberating" Red Army bided its time on the opposite bank of the Vistula, the rebuilding stone by stone of the shattered city of Warsaw ... and now this monumental confrontation between Polish workers and the Communists and their army.

More often than not, in these showdowns with History, the Poles have lost, but this does not seem to have diminished their ardour. If anything, the *meaning* of Polishness seems to reside in this combination of challenge and failure. Often the combination has had lethal consequences, and every thrilling episode of Polish resistance to the historical forces marshalled against the people has produced its dead. Indeed, it has sometimes seemed to me that death is the point. I think of Chopin's heart reverently buried in the marble column of a Warsaw church (his body in a Parisian grave), of the mounted Hussars charging Hitler's tanks on horseback, of Solidarity down on its knees in prayer for the memory of the proletarian dead in the strikes of the 1970s and, because it is a Catholic country, of the Mother of God, Queen of Poland, raising up the souls of the dead from the battlefields and gibbets and crematoria to join the pantheon of Polish martyrs in Polish heaven.

Inside my Greek limbo I think about all this. Naturally, I had wanted Solidarity to win, but the next best thing is to imagine the ongoing resistance of the heroes and heroines of the movement in the underground, clandestinity and peril being if anything more congenial to the Polish spirit than the bright glare of parliaments and television studios. One can almost envy them their sure-footedness in the face of national catastrophe and their sense of mission as they go about their martyrdom, as though the mission (Poland Is Not Yet Dead!) is precisely to be accomplished against impossible odds in outbursts of extraordinary courage. But, then, this is the envy of a citizen of a "normal" country.

Somewhere in the back of my mind there is the memory of another kind of Pole, the one my baba had called "*Pan.*" In a drawer I had come across a bundle of old documents in a foreign language that my father explained to me was Polish. They were a school report card and a baptismal certificate. I wondered briefly why they were in Polish, Baba being a Ukrainian, but when it was explained to me that her village had "belonged" to Poland I was satisfied and had no more questions. I learned, too, that "pan" meant landlord and that it was the Polish pan who had held sway in her village. Since the English word "landlord" is benign enough I thought no more about that either. But I had absorbed important information: in the old country, Poles and Ukrainians were neighbours.

My baba's story is not the one I will be tracking when I finally visit Poland for the first time in 1984. I will go in search of the stories that make Poland Polish, beginning with the one that galvanized *my* generation, the birth and convulsions of Solidarity in the shipyards of the Baltic coast, and continuing back through the generations of partisans and poets, priests, kings and Hussars who erupted into European history, were beaten down and reared up again. Unlike the single issue that will haunt me in Prague – the travail of the generation of 1968 – the question I will have of Poles is panoramic.

How, I will wonder, as I go to pay my respects, can a people bear so much History?

IN THE NAME OF LENIN

GDANSK, 1984: Four years ago, at one of the gates of the Lenin Shipyard, in the heat of the August strike, a wooden cross was embedded in the ground on the spot where four striking workers had died in December 1970. This humble memorial instantly became a shrine. Now, three crucifixes, each thirty metres high with a bronze anchor impaled on its crossbar, rear up from a concrete burial mound not far from the looming, stately cranes that supervise the shipyard. Words from Psalm 29, "The Lord will give strength unto his people, the Lord will bless his people with peace," are written in large cement letters on a cement wall flanking the gates. The great exiled poet Czeslaw Milosz is quoted too: "The poet remembers. You can slay one, but another is born. The words are written down." There is also a bronze sculpture of a worker in a hard-hat, his head tilted back, his mouth slightly open, his hands raised up in front of his face as though to ward off the blows of his tormentors and to show us the stigmata of his martyrdom. Those who have come to visit the monument have draped the worker's hands with red and white ribbons (the Polish national colours), with rosaries, with holy para-phernalia. He does not make a fist. He is not resolute, he is not enraged. He's not even very big. He's about to die.

As the workers marched, they picked up thousands more, swelling their ranks with sympathizers, students, pensioners and fellow workers who up to now had been reluctant to desert their assembly lines. They lobbed the tear gas grenades that had bombed down on them from army helicopters at the police, torched Party headquarters and stormed police cars in a search for weapons and loud-speakers. They looted shops, dragging away refriger-ators and television sets and throwing them into the sludgy waters of Radunia Creek, which ran by the offices of the regional Party committee. Then they marched back to their shipyards and occupied them. The local partocrats, refusing to negotiate, sent soldiers, tanks and more armoured cars to surround the stricken sites.

Early the next day, Petro was hurrying to the gates of the Lenin Shipyard in a snowfall, the darkness of the December morning lightened by the flat snowflakes whirling in thick profusion around the street lamps. From all directions, fifteen thousand men and women were streaming to the ship-yard to join the workers in a general strike, their footfalls muffled by the soft, wet snow underfoot. Petro heard nothing until he turned the corner and saw the tanks and heard the loud, metallic snickering of a machine gun in the breathless air.

"Shoot to kill" orders came from Warsaw and, at No. 2 Gate of the Lenin Shipyard, armed militia fired directly into a crowd of strikers, killing four. Over the next two days, many more strikers were slaughtered (forty-five? sixty-nine? four hundred?); hundreds were wounded and hundreds more arrested. They would die all up and down the coast, at the railway stations getting off commuter trains, on railway bridges crossing the tracks, in the streets as they ran away from the sounds of trampling militia and whizzing bullets. In Gdansk, the dead lay under the snow until refrigerated trucks, normally used to transport meat, crept through the darkened town and culled their corpses from the streets.

The strikes would eventually die down and the government be replaced. The new political boss, Edward Gierek, a former coal miner who had ripped out coal with his bare hands from the super-exploited pits of France and Belgium, opened his arms before the strikers and said, "Help us, help me. I'm only a worker like you." And the people bought that, for a couple of years. But they kept demanding a list of all those who had died (thirty-

four? sixty-two? five hundred and twelve?). They became obsessed with this.

One morning in 1980, a schoolteacher friend of Petro's came across a newspaper containing individual accounts of what happened that day in the snowstorm, stories of bereaved families driven late at night to open graves and given five minutes to make their obsequies over plywood coffins. The schoolteacher read all about this at 6:00 A.M. When he went back to the kiosk later to get another copy, the vendor told him the police had beat him to it. They had bought up all the copies.

I share the monument square with two plainclothes policemen who eye me eying them. I have been warned not to take any photographs directly of the shipyard gates and so I snap around them from every possible angle and perspective, focussing on stone, blossom, water stain, glint. The policemen have effectively banished most human activity from the square, yet people have managed to slip by to lay bundles of red and white carnations at the base of the crucifixes and to jab the flowers into niches in the cement wall, then to slip away again, board a gassy, bawling bus and scrawl on the back of the bus seat, where I will read it: "Solidarity lives!"

The square was filled with the sounds of a shipyard on strike: eight thousand workers milling about in meetings and arguments, their supporters at the gates yelling encouragement and handing over food; hammers on corrugated iron, banging "hotel rooms" together; eggs frying in an iron pan; a squealing pig, a gift from a farmer; the whir of a camera, the backfiring of a news van, the clamour of a news conference. Slogans, shouts, anthems, prayers. Our Lady of the Strike, the Madonna of Czestochowa, her image heaped with flowers, called to serve her chosen people yet another time. It was October 1980, and they had been there since August.

They had many demands. "Our union sprang from the people's needs," they declared, and they demanded the right to establish independent and self-governing trade unions and the right to strike. They demanded constitutional guarantees of freedom of speech and increased maternity leave. They demanded improved supplies of meat to the public. And they demanded the erection of a monument in the memory of the dead of 1970.

By the end of 1981, their solidarity had been declared illegal and they were rooted out of their factories, their mines and their sanctuaries.

I will visit the monument again in 1987. By then, even the plainclothes policemen will have deserted the square, leaving it to courting couples on the benches, the chilly Baltic wind swirling at their ankles and whistling through the shipyard gates that are flung wide open, as though nothing out of the ordinary is expected, least of all a strike.

In 1980, Pawel tells me, he was a happy man. Solidarity had him running around the country, factory to factory (him, professor of the history of political thought, short-sighted, nervous, twitchy like a rabbit), meeting the strikers.

"It was a very happy time. Not just a personal domestic happiness but a 'public' happiness. An excitement. A time when words *meant* something and were useful to people."

Now, in 1984, conversation has gone underground. You can debate in underground publications but it all takes place pseudonymously, without context. You don't know where your interlocutor is "coming from" or what has happened to him/her. You can't refer to your own writings, because they languish in a desk drawer.

A parish priest invites Pawel to his village. People know that something new has happened to them – the Solidarity movement and its discontents – and they know that the old categories of right/left, reactionary/progressive, bourgeois/proletariat cannot explain it, or not all of it, anyway. On the other hand, in this chilly climate, they are not free to discuss which categories *could* explain their experience. It is very frustrating.

When I ask Pawel if westerners are in danger of mythologizing Solidarity, he replies that we can't mythologize it. It all happened. It was real.

THE BIRTH OF POETRY

Full of questions about the opposition in Poland, I am at Harvard University interviewing Stanislaw Baranczak, professor of Polish literature and culture. I know he is a poet who was involved in clandestine publishing in pre-Solidarity Poland.

In June 1956, Stanislaw was ten years old. His parents' apartment in Poznan was situated precisely above the spot where the most important workers' protests took place. Although he was forbidden to leave the apartment, he watched from the windows. He saw workers march to the nearby prison, then march back in the direction of the police headquarters. He saw their weapons (probably taken out of hiding for the first time since the end of the war) and then heard the shouting and the shooting. He was watching for his friend, a schoolmate who had made it to the streets.

The striking workers had abandoned their factory, the giant ZiSPO engineering plant. They had torn down the plaque reading "Joseph Stalin Factory" at the plant's entrance and marched now in this direction, now in that, brandishing placards for "Higher Wages! Lower Prices!" and "Bread and Freedom!" Troops were being gathered as the factory workers, whose ranks now swelled with communications and tram workers, descended upon the prison and released its 198 inmates, burning public records before continuing to the headquarters of the secret police. The armoured cars of the army opened fire and strew the dead about – some say thirty-eight, others say fifty-four, or eighty – and injured hundreds more. The day came to be known as Black Thursday.

The schoolmate was rounded up with dozens of others and disappeared into a police station. He never reappeared. It was said later he had been shot in one of the cells.

Fifty-four workers were held responsible for the riots of June. The court proceedings were broadcast and, standing outside the open windows of apartments, Stanislaw could see how everyone was at home, listening. For the next twenty-five years the workers of Poznan were a cautious class.

But Stanislaw would go to a different school. The embryonic poets in 1960s Poland had their own lessons to learn. Stalin had died in 1953, and in the discreet relaxation that followed in Poland – the release of political prisoners, veiled criticism in the press, better food supplies – ideological orthodoxy began to crack. Stanislaw recalls the exhilaration of finding something new to read: some translations of Sartre and Kafka, a fragment of *1984*, the rehabilitated Polish avant-garde, three books by Witold Gombrowicz, abroad since 1939, stranded in Argentina but sending back irreverent and bilious salvos to the "fawning ninnies" of Polish literary circles. It was too good to last.

In late 1957, the Party, feeling secured against its own citizens after the repressions in Poznan, condemned workers' councils as "anarchistic utopianism" and abolished the right to strike. The magazine *Po Postru*, which in 1956 had spoken up for the rioting workers of Poznan, was banned. The closure provoked a brief, flaring protest by students in Lodz, Cracow and Warsaw who were scattered by the police and heard from no more.

A literary journal, *Europa,* was shut down before it had even published its first issue. *Nowa Kultura* lost almost its entire editorial board in 1958 when its editor-in-chief moved to impose the Party line. Liberals vanished from the Ministry of Education, the Institute of International Affairs, the Writers' Union. In 1963, a weekly, *Przeglad Kulturalny,* was shut down for editorial unreliability, and a discussion club at the University of Warsaw, together with a group of high school students calling themselves "The Contradiction Seekers Club," was dissolved. Stanislaw, now a university student of Polish literature at Poznan, learned that, although a 1945 collection of poems by the exiled Czeslaw Milosz was on the reading list, the book was nowhere to be found.

He remembers the slogans – *Hands off Cuba!* – painted on walls with deliberate misspellings, misshapen letters, so as to seem spontaneous, and the anti-American propaganda that informed the public that the plague of potato beetles destroying the crops had been dropped into Poland by American low-flying bombers. There was the whole question of language in this regime of falsifications and lies. A worker could defend himself with hand-printed manifestos and the concrete demand for meat for Christmas; what were the weapons of a budding poet?

As a student of history or literature or philosophy, Stanislaw explains, you knew that there would be no decent way for you to make your living after graduation, not just in the sense of a decent salary but in the sense of living decently among fellows. As a history graduate, for example, you knew you'd be working as a censor, either literally, in the press offices, or indirectly, in the classroom. As a published writer, you could be sure of tailoring your text to meet the needs of the Ministry of Public Security. Whatever you did in the way of protest would be considered foolhardy by some, evidence of complicity by others.

Leszek Kolakowski, writing in Po Postru: *"What is socialism? A state which doesn't like to see its citizens read back numbers of newspapers."*

This is how Stanislaw entered the 1970s: dumbfounded by the din of falsehood and hyperbole that represented public speech. He had no idea how he was going to grow up to be a poet. Then in 1971 a new party secretary introduced another little thaw in cultural life, and Stanislaw was invited to a meeting.

Here he is in Warsaw with a group of writers at the offices of the

Central Committee of the Party, of all places. The Secretary for Culture, after the polite chitchat, the clinking of glasses of mineral water and tea, admonishes the young writers to quit writing all the time of blood: "Blood is all over your poetry." It is a shrewd observation.

The young writers arrived in Polish literature, in the early 1970s, dragging in new themes, new topics, new characters with them like tramps off the street. If the official poetry of socialist realism could not look History in the eye, then these poets would write socialist surrealism. Here were the lives of the new Poland, the peasants storming the emptied, postwar cities to live in hostels, whoring and drinking to the background screeches of railway cars shunted onto the siding under the hostel window. They doled themselves out ten cigarettes a day and ten zlotys on pay day for a drink with the boys in the open air, just to get away from the foul grit of the factory and to forestall the moment of reckoning with the wife who was waiting for the pay packet. They brought pride with them, big, leathery, calloused hands and the cult of the Madonna. "A feather pillow, a gallon of vodka, and the lust for girls.... Un-human Poland, howling with boredom on December nights," writes Adam Wazyk in "Poem for Adults."

The Party Secretary, too, appears in the poems, sleek and fleshy, presiding over local corruption, principally his own.

To tell these tales, the poets created a new language by imploding the jargon of officialese – the *mowa trawa*, grass language, in which nothing is "for real," is not even expected to be, and words have lost their original meaning. "To speak a language in which the word 'safety' awakens a shudder of terror," Stanislaw would write, "the word 'truth' is the title of a newspaper, the words 'freedom' and 'democracy' are under the jurisdiction of the chief-of-police."

In 1975, Stanislaw signed a letter protesting censorship and found that some of his work was suddenly deemed unpublishable. He could still publish translations and book reviews, but his poems were blacklisted. A year later, he joined KOR (Committee for the Defence of Workers' Rights – intellectuals in support of arrested strikers in the labour unrest of 1976), and then it was a total blacklist, to the point that, if his name were quoted, it had to be deleted or erased. He contributed to literary magazines under a pseudonym. A book review would pay for two good dinners.

In the autumn of 1976, at the invitation of friends in Warsaw,

Stanislaw became the first poet to appear at what would be regular meetings of students and poets "whose works were not readily available." Having travelled three hundred kilometres to keep this appointment, he learned on arrival that the suburban community centre rented for the occasion had cancelled the booking. The company simply trooped over to a private apartment. Stanislaw read his poems, then read them again, and promised to make copies that his audience could pass on.

The next poet in the series, Adam Zagajewski, submitted his poems in advance of his appearance so they could be copied on a typewriter in an edition of fifty. A friendly artist agreed to make cardboard "covers" and to bind each copy. These sold out at the reading and netted the group 2500 zlotys. A group of writers began working on the first issue of a literary review called *Zapis*, breaking the state monopoly on publishing and spawning an industry that would produce more than 100,000 copies of books and pamphlets in three years. Their publisher was NOWA, and Stanislaw joined up.

Underground activity was maniacal. Duplicators, which could not be sold to individuals, had to be handmade from wringer washers. Stencils, ink and paper had to be purloined from state supplies or purchased from sympathetic salespeople. Volunteers laboured long and odd hours in basements, prepared to transfer operations to a safe house the moment their hide-out was known to the police. They typed and duplicated two hundred copies of individual books and seven thousand copies of monthly journals. Books were sold out of suitcases in private apartments. The underground publishers had the satisfaction of hearing excerpts from their books routinely read over Radio Free Europe (17 million listeners a week), Voice of America (9 million) and the BBC Polish language service (7 million). For this privilege, they were under constant threat of surveillance, detention, assault, imprisonment. Most of their profits were lost through confiscations and fines. They were, naturally, completely banned from public media. All the better. Those writers who continued to be published by the state-owned houses were increasingly viewed by readers as "collaborators" with the regime. Underground activity was dangerous. But the alternative was silence, and a privacy so complete that the spoken word arrived as an indecency.

The striker and the poet: two Poles who remember, who make speeches, who dream of a new Poland. They do not seem to be suspicious of each other's intentions nor are they indifferent to each other, as they are in my country. It seems they have agreed that they are both essential to the mission of the liberation of Poland, the one for the courage of the body, the other for the courage of the tongue.

Although it was to honour the memory of the strikers of Gdansk that I first went to Poland, it is the Stanislaws who are familiar to me. Polish poets and workers may have felt continuous with each other on the spectrum of resistance, but to me the strikers were strange – their Masses in the littered shipyards, their flags unfurled over their committees, their evocation of a primal motherland that had been kidnapped by its enemies and to which the redemptive acts of their solidarity would return them. I can lay flowers at their shrines but I cannot join them, even in spirit. My motherland is elsewhere.

But Stanislaw, I think, has a more open-ended view of things. The point of poetry is not to return to some historical chastity that is only Polish and only Catholic and of one mind about things but to imagine a future that is, at long last, ambiguous. Not programmed or determined but left open to the vagaries of individual conscience and private speech and spontaneous movement. Is this Polish, too – the liberal gentleman who lives and lets live?

WHAT THE TOURIST DOESN'T KNOW WON'T HURT HER

PRZEMYSL, 1984: Chestnut trees. Yellow plastered walls. Yapping dogs. We walk through a perfectly normal residential neighbourhood to the home of an elderly Ukrainian couple who have invited us for tea. My host says something about a Ukrainian cathedral, a seminary, perhaps even something about libraries, newspapers, parliamentarians. I am not paying close attention. As far as I am concerned, we are in Poland, in the middle of nowhere. Much later I will learn that this town was an important railway centre fought over by Ukrainian and Polish armies as they struggled for control of the Ukrainian lands while the Austro-Hungarian empire was noisily collapsing in World War I. The Poles won, of course.

We sit quietly, drinking tea. My hosts are modest people who do not shout or make flamboyant gestures. Perhaps it is more correct to say they are repressed, or unnerved, for I note that, at the sound of the front door opening to let in their upstairs neighbour, they fall suddenly silent, their faces twitching with unease until we all hear the sound of his footfalls above our heads. When our conversation resumes it is if anything more subdued.

"He's a very fine man, and a good neighbour, but the fact is, perhaps he suspects ... well, which is to say he never sees us at his church or celebrating his holidays, but as long as he never hears us speaking Ukrainian... So far, he's said nothing."

The churches that once belonged to the Greek-Catholic parishes of the Ukrainians have been pointed out to me. There are still families here with Ukrainian names and there are cemeteries, bearing gravestones inscribed with the Cyrillic genealogy, that disintegrate among the wild chamomile and nettle. But this is what happens to minorities, I think: they become overwhelmed. The only attitude I could think of taking to this provincial settlement is nostalgia, but nostalgia requires an object of remembrance: one has to have a memory of something in order to regret it, but I do not know yet that anything has happened in Przemysl.

"After the war, when Ukrainians were being deported out of the area ...," my host continues.

He had lain low, hidden by Polish neighbours. But a friend of his who lost everything in the deportation made his way back after twenty-five years and managed to buy back his own house! The exclamation is mine; in the past I have attributed such disorderly events to the vagaries of war. Uprootings, transfers, scenes from black-and-white movies glimpsed on television on a Saturday afternoon – mobs of stunned refugees in oversized tweed coats being shunted across smouldering countryside in cattle cars open to the wind. I did not know that such scenes were possible in peacetime.

The only story that had mattered in my childhood was the story of the arrival of my Ukrainian grandparents in Canada: everything that preceded it was a folktale, and everything that happened in Galicia after *they* had abandoned the place was hearsay.

If, in the fall of 1930, armed units of the Polish Army and the police terrorized some eight hundred Ukrainian villages in Polish-held Galicia and called it the Pacificacija – demolishing the community halls and reading rooms, putting books and newspapers to the torch, confiscating property and arresting more than two thousand "nationalist" troublemakers – this had happened elsewhere to somebody else. If Polonophile intellectuals in the West found the concentration camp in Bereza Kartuska – which had held two thousand political prisoners in 1934, most of them Ukrainians – "a minor aberration," I was in no position to argue. It was the vaguest of stories.

Later I will see I have missed the point of everything: that this town in the middle of "nowhere," once known as Peremyshl in Ukrainian, had been a scintillating hub of politics and culture in the Austro-Hungarian Empire – seat of the Greek Catholic bishops, site of libraries and schools – the westernmost city on Ukrainian-speaking territory. Now it has become Polish. It has suffered and declined; its people have been violently dispersed, its language and faith made relentlessly private. But I have not yet absorbed this. In 1984, I am not in Galicia, I am in Poland. They speak Polish in Przemysl and this is as it should be.

WHAT IS A POET FOR?

WARSAW, 1984: It is Ryszard's "constantly recurring dream" to live in an ordinary country. I meet him in a café in downtown Warsaw not far from the concert hall. I have just spent three weeks in Soviet Ukraine, and it makes me nervous how we are meeting openly in a popular café to speak in normal voices, in English, about ourselves. The clatter of dishes and glasses comes from the kitchen; the air is filled with pungent cigarette smoke and the snuffling and wheezing of the customers. Desiccated layers of torte detach themselves from the glutinous smears of raspberry jam, and clots of yellow cream float on the tarry coffee. Ryszard seems relaxed, unhurried. This is, I decide, Warsaw café life. Almost normal.

My contact in London had advised me to memorize all addresses before going into Poland, to have nothing written down. Memorizing Ryszard's address was easy. He lives on Shakespeare Street. It is in the flat in Ulice Szekspira that we have most of our conversations. We sit at a little table by a window while he smokes unfiltered cigarettes and speaks readily, if tersely. He has longish hair curling around his ears and a long nose I think aristocratic, even "Polish," and he wears a T-shirt with the logo of the New Orleans Jazz Festival.

I have made several assumptions about Ryszard. One is that, as a university student in 1968, he was formed by the uproar that year on the campuses of Warsaw and by the savage official anti-Semitic purges of Party and university that followed it. I am right. "I didn't then acknowledge myself as a Jew but when your friends are attacked that identification becomes inevitable." He pauses. "Many people felt more Jewish than they wanted to." There is no further conversation about it.

The second assumption is that, as a child of remarkable times and heroic peoples, he will not be one of those writers who has gone into "internal exile" – or Kazimierz Brandys's "circumvolution" – to "save" literature and himself by slithery, evasive manoeuvres around the pedestals of History, whether Polish or Proletarian. He will, I assume, have turned to meet them. How could a writer in our times refuse the subjects provided by violent social change? What a gift! It is the wrong assumption. Ryszard does not think like that.

"History," writes Czeslaw Milosz, "is a curse." He means for the poet, who discovers that poetry is not an autonomous activity in Poland but a historic enterprise charged with the responsibility of saving the nation, as though within poetry's codes were another government. Milosz reminds us that the voice of the poet should be "purer" than the "noise" of history.

There is something miraculous in this special burden of history on the poet – the miracle of reconstituting the life of the nation in mere language. Truth. Meaning. Purpose. Memory. The martyred priest Jerzy Popieluszko believed this. In one of his sermons, two years after the imposition of martial law, he preached that the only alternative to collective memory – "recollection" – is silence, that the "everything" that lies between them is the speech of "enemies of the fatherland."

But it is precisely this "everything" that lies between that the poem is *for*: the "private exultation, unnecessary talents, surplus curiosity, short-range sorrows and fears," in the cri de coeur of the philosophical poet Wislawa Szymborska. The extra-literary requirements of Polish Historical Romance forget this as easily as does Socialist Realism, and both are dangerous to the poet. "The hunger of the public is unappeasable," says Ryszard. "It makes you feel more important than you are. You aren't important. The apparatchiks treat you any way they like."

Ryszard's situation is full of ambiguities. Unlike the two extremes that faced writers in the Soviet Union in the late 1970s – inanity in the Writers' Union or starvation in the gulag – Ryszard has choices. At one end of the spectrum (this is always present), speechlessness. If, as the

French post-Maoist philosopher Bernard-Henri Levy argues in *Barbarism with a Human Face*, totalitarianism forces citizens to "chatter," to "tell all" in defence of their loyalty, then obviously the anti-totalitarian shuts up.

There are other possibilities. The writer can seek refuge in "art for art's sake," in the belief that, stripped of all public obligation, he or she has only one task: to write the perfect sentence. It is immaterial whether this is published. A circle of close friends, to whom one will read this sentence, is sufficient. More dramatically, the poet can go underground and put the poems in the service of the revolution or the Polish people or the national mission. This has its attractions: there is an insatiable desire on the part of the Polish public for uncensored books. In this scenario, though, the poet takes all the risks – poverty and clandestinity – while the regime remains aloof and unaffected. ("Come to think of it," a friend says in passing, "who *was* that old writer found half-dead from hunger and grain alcohol, alone in an unheated flat, who was 'boycotting' official literature?")

Or the poet can move right across the spectrum, choosing full co-operation with the authorities, risking the soul but gaining a career, with the bonus of feeling summoned by Dialectic and Historical Materialism to recall to the reading public, in editions of 100,000, the glories of the People's Army, the savage heroism of war and the writer's own modest contribution to the defeat of Fascism. In interviews granted to "semijournalists," expressing "semitruths to … semireaders," in Kazimierz Brandys's formulation, the writer purveys self-inflated reminiscences of his or her first years as a "struggling" young artist.

Ryszard has made none of these "pure" choices but lives and works in the interstices between them. He is employed as an editor at an uncontroversial literary magazine that specializes in translations from world literature. He concerns himself with the short stories of Frank O'Hara. In 1982, he submitted a collection of his poems to an official publisher. He still has no contract but has been assured the book is in the publishing plan for 1986. Even then, he won't know if it is going to make it to the printer's: on its way there, the censor will have a look. Ryszard has included some poems about the experience of martial law. (As it turns out, it is these very poems, some "three or four," which will be found to be "antisocial" and which will immediately make the entire collection "interesting" to an underground publisher and Ryszard "indispensable" to the public weal.)

"It's easy to think you are more important than you are," Ryszard repeats, like a salutary catechism. "Some people think that just writing about what your countrymen and countrywomen live through every day is a political act." Ryszard, though, doesn't kid himself. He has no illusions – despite the admiration of tourists from countries with more easy-going literatures – that by writing poems about martial law he has joined the underground. The whole country is in opposition, and sometimes it seems that the underground is the real publishing industry.

In Poland, even under martial law, the total number of uncensored publications is several times greater than the sum of samizdat publications produced in all the other Soviet bloc countries put together. From duplicated typescripts banged out at odd hours of the morning to stencil and spirit duplicators toiling undetected in cobwebby cellars to offset printing on glossy paper financed by monies smuggled in from sympathizers abroad: who was it pointed out that in Polish the word "people" rhymes with "miracle"?

Why should the poet take special credit? And I catch the whiff of admonishment – gentle, yet pointed – that we sympathizers from the West make too much of such modest gestures – the antisocial poem, say – and are indignant out of all proportion on behalf of the semi-repressed writer whose work is tied up five years at the publisher's. The idea that this experience should qualify one as a "dissident" is absurd to Ryszard. The "dissident" is the only sane person around. It is the Communists who are crazy.

We westerners would do better to reserve our indignation for the real heroes: the students crippled by exorbitant fines for keeping typewriters, broken-down copiers and underground leaflets in their garrets, the Solidarity activists made to forfeit their cars for having transported illegal literature, the three women in Lublin fined a full month's salary each for hiding tape recorders and cassettes, the teachers jailed for distributing illegal publications. Not to mention the man near Warsaw, who was assaulted by police when they found him reading an underground novel while waiting for a haircut in a barber's shop. They beat the shit out of the barber, too.

You want romance? Here's romance: The printing press is in the cellar, hidden by sacks of potatoes, but nothing can mask the fumes of printing ink blotted up by the curtains, the laundry, the blankets. You can't trust anybody, not even your sister-in-law, who drops in for a cup of coffee and unwittingly sits a few inches away from an illegal manuscript shoved into a bread basket. The "publisher" hasn't slept for days, hasn't even left the cellar; his arms up to the elbows in printing ink, he waits for the midnight raid. Actually, they usually come about six in the morning.

You want romance? Daring young writers in the "hole"? Herewith the testimony Dr. Zofia Kuratowska of the relief committee for political prisoners and their families will give in 1986. Solitary confinement in a frigid cell, sleep on bare planks. Consequences: degenerative changes of the spine and gynecological disorders. No fresh fruit or vegetables in prison, food parcels only for "good behaviour." Consequences: vitamin deficiency. Lack of hot water, acute shortage of cotton wool and sanitary towels, parasitic fungi. The prison rules forbid lying down during the day, so you spend the hours sitting on a tiny stool with no back support or pacing a small, overcrowded cell. Consequences: stomach and duodenal ulcers, skin disease and poor blood circulation. If you are in prison longer than three months, you lose your outside job, and no employer will willingly hire on a former political prisoner.

"What," asks Ryszard, "has any of this drama, this tragedy to do with literature?" A writer writing is not a citizen and has no obligation to confront anything except language itself. To do this, he requires tranquillity and privacy. History is clamorous and populous and its obligations better left to politicians and revolutionaries. If he lived in a normal country, History would take care of itself and send him to his blank pages in the typewriter. "In the West," he argues, "it is said that writers are not 'socially necessary.' This is perhaps as it should be."

All you need is three good friends. This poignant refrain, which I am to hear so often in one version or another in Eastern Europe, always seems to me somehow limp and inadequate to the situation I face as a writer in the open contests of the West's political life. I want to protest that there is no perfect privacy and no pristine page. "I have arrived at the page in the company of ancestors and comrades and neighbours," I want to point out. "Why would I want to shut them out?"

I *want* to be necessary, as necessary to the well-being of my community as the hammering skill of the men who fix the road bed outside my house, as the woman who stands at the blackboard, showing my neighbours' children how long division is done. I want to be a citizen, not the solitary, misunderstood and antisocial "genius" of western imagination. I want to be available, like the Polish writer, in public.

But I have not lived my life in the middle of an uproar of slogans. I have not had to burrow like a rodent for a little dark peace and quiet away from the floodlit, queuing throngs. In a young country with an emerging voice, I stand more in danger of loneliness and reticence than of the brouhaha of History. In Poland, on the other hand, the Party is the sole proprietor of the collective, and Social Necessity has sent the dead to their untimely graves.

Ryszard is gagging on history. Leave him alone.

THE MOTHER OF KINGS: A FILM

WARSAW, 1987: Matka Krolow is forever writing a letter. No matter the decade, it is always the same letter. She appeals to: the Marshal, the Reichskommandant, the Commissar, the President, for some help. Not for herself, heavens no, but for her dear boys, the future of the country! Some consideration, please, in: getting a job in a better sort of establishment, finding a flat with a bath, seeing to it that her local milk shop receives fresh butter once a month. Perhaps the Greatly Honourable Sir could also look into the case – please forgive her presumption – of her imprisoned son: a good boy, sincere, hard-working, whose only mistake was to trust an informer.

This is not History by revolution, by eruption. This is the never-endingness of events, history as life as usual, meatless Sundays and soapless washdays, far from the shimmering masculine realm of political spectacle.

The Mother of Kings gives birth on the plank floor of her dreary basement flat just before the war, then trudges out with soapy bucket and brush to scrub the floors, down on her knees, in the offices of: a lawyer, a Nazi, a Communist big shot. You know this is Iron Curtain country, for she is transporting a package to her imprisoned son but cannot gain admittance from the expressionless gatekeeper. She slides to the ground, banging helplessly at the unyielding iron door. Inside, her son is being tortured. Not to be discouraged, she perks up during the Thaw after 1956 and marches enthusiastically in the May Day parade, passing over to the leaders' rostrum her latest pleading letter to the authorities. A bodyguard promptly pockets it. She doesn't see this. She keeps scrubbing while waiting for the mail.

PRIVATIZATION

WARSAW, 1987: Barbara floats from room to room on the parquet floors, trailing cigarette smoke, the strains of a Dvorak quartet approaching and receding from the enormous AM-FM radio machine in the kitchen as she moves among wardrobes, bookcases, china cabinets: a kind of domestic wraith. It is an old-fashioned flat with very high ceilings that seem to shrink her. The dark, glossy furniture is pushed to the walls of the rooms, leaving the uncovered parquet open like a ballroom floor. This is a whole world, somewhere in Europe.

She supervises this flat as though defending it against the encroachments of a state that says she has no right to it, or at least not to all of it. It was where her parents lived and it is they who have left the watercolours high up on the stained, greyish walls. In the living room is a portrait of them from the photography studio of L. S. Klebanovsky: a young couple in stylized peasant dress, amusing themselves – now that they are securely established in the city – in the masquerade of the class they had not so long ago escaped. Standing in front of velvet drapes, they glance back laughingly over their shoulders at the peasants of Mazovia hoeing rows of beets and potatoes just outside the frame. The young madame extends a pretty foot in a leather boot out from under a frothy skirt.

Barbara's parents are dead now, and she has no siblings. She has friends – expatriate teachers at the university, Polonophile scholars and writers on British Council exchanges, journalists from the BBC. They're the ones who get excited, raise their voices. She crosses her legs and smokes.

She once lived in England, working as an au pair and studying English at the Institute of Modern Languages. She came back, perhaps to consolidate her hold on this flat. She confesses that sometimes she wishes she had stayed on in Sussex and evaded History. She could have escaped the necessity of stoic survival during the period of the strikes in 1980–81. She admits, though, that it grew no worse for her than running out of cigarettes.

She works for a state-owned publishing company that produces glossy books for the tourist trade on the art and treasures of Old Poland. At her office during the Solidarity strikes there had been an uproar when the translators refused to edit any material that boosted the Party. Barbara had seen this as a kind of objective correlative to the empty shelves of her neighbourhood grocery where, in July 1981, the only thing for sale was plastic jugs of vinegar. She had lost heart and thought Solidarity could not win. She was right. The best place to live is inside her head.

The bookcases hold very old editions of Mickiewicz and new Penguins. Her desk is strewn with the blue-pencilled galley sheets of a book about Polish castles. She judges herself uncompromised by the theme. She sits smoking and looking out the kitchen window onto the backsides of apartment blocks, dun-coloured and scabby, their court-yards full of mud under the autumn rain. Dried flowers in clay pots and a box of sprouted onions sit on the broad marble window sill, arranged as though in readiness for the state apartment snoops who are intent upon her flat. She will throw clay pots and putrifying onions down upon their heads.

MASS FOR THE FATHERLAND

WARSAW, 1987: Professor Maria Byrdy, the pathologist who performed the autopsy on the body of Father Jerzy Popieluszko, spoke in court of two gags in the inventory of the case – a cloth glued together with blood and vomit and disordered from the victim's obvious efforts to dislodge it with his tongue, and a wrinkled, blood-stained wad of gauze secured with tape that ran around the priest's neck and covered his nose. A loop of rope had been wound around his neck and tied to a rope around his ankles in such a way that any movement of his legs forced the noose to tighten. Trussed up in this manner, he had been transported, in October of 1984, in the trunk of a police car, a Fiat 125P, from Gorsk in the province of Torun to a causeway on the Vistula River not far from Wloclawek where, weighted down with a sack of rocks, he had been thrown into the river.

Captain Piotrowski: "We turned right on the dam. We crossed the dam. We stopped the car by the outlet. I said, 'We have to get rid of him here.' "

Lieutenant Chmielewski: "The body went in vertically. We simply shifted it over the railings."

I ask my friend to stop the car. I run down the green slope of the dam to the little lookout point over the river. I know exactly where it happened: bunches of flowers, poked into the wire of the fence, hang desiccating in the breeze blowing in from the Vistula. I imagine the black backside of a police car, the red flags of its official status flapping in the wind, as red as the stains on the chrome bumper and the carpet lining the trunk. But that's not right. Father Jerzy wasn't bleeding. He choked to death. He didn't even mess up the trunk: the vomit stayed in his lungs and drowned him there.

The priest's biography: born in 1947 of farmers in eastern Poland; entered seminary at 18; assigned first parish in Warsaw, working with student groups in 1968; came under surveillance; sent to Warsaw steelworks in 1980 as chaplain for strikers. He stayed for five hundred days. He wondered, in the chaos of the first day, where he would celebrate Mass, who would read the text. The workers, who had given some thought to this, led him through the cheering crowd to his altar, a box covered with flowers, and brought him their blue-and-white flag inscribed with the logo of Solidarity and bearing the likeness of St. Florian, patron saint of steelworkers and firemen, so that he might consecrate it. He bent over to hear confessions, leaning away from the bellowing heat of the smelters at his back.

In December 1981, after the declaration of martial law and the outlawing of Solidarity, the priest was transferred to the church of St. Stanislaw Kostka in the Zoliborz neighbourhood of Warsaw. There would be no more parishes. Fished out of the Vistula, he would be buried here. He died at thirty-seven and has become, three years later, something of a saint. So it seems to me, joining the peaceniks ringing his grave to lay flowers, one more bouquet among the hundreds: there are always mourners here. They kneel at a prie-dieu, murmuring the verses of the rosary and meditating upon the flickering candles stuck among the bouquets or, eyes raised, upon the wooden effigy of Christ crucified to the tree that shelters the grave.

Until October 19, 1984, when he disappeared on his way back to Warsaw from Torun, Father Jerzy had preached a mass for the homeland on the last Sunday of every month at seven o'clock in the evening. Thousands of worshippers attended his services. "I receive many letters," he wrote in 1983, "from people saying that these monthly Masses for Poland help them live in hope, help them cleanse themselves of the hatred which, despite all, grows in them. This is a great reward for a priest, who really has no life of his own."

In 1987, the worshippers still come at seven o'clock on the last Sunday of every month to celebrate a Mass for the Fatherland in honour of Father Jerzy's memory. On this cold, damp evening in May, half an hour before the Mass is scheduled to begin, the churchyard and forecourt are already jammed. Everyone is very quiet. They do not drink or smoke or jostle each other. They stand, holding up crucifixes and the only Solidarity banner I have seen in Warsaw in 1987. "Our right to freedom and peace!" it says.

This is a Catholic Mass. The priests intone, the worshippers respond and genuflect, the boys' choir sings angelically. The old women, hugging themselves in their thin coats, their lacklustre hair escaping from dark head scarves, slide off the benches to crouch as best they can on their knees when the priest passes by bearing what I take to be the Eucharist.

The priest preaches of the sorrows and indignities suffered by the working people – one of Father Jerzy's favourite topics – and of the salvation promised in the sacrament of the Eucharist. Men with furrowed faces hold up stained and stubby fingers in a V salute and sing that Poland is not yet dead. There is no restlessness, impatience or display of bad temper. I suppose there is a relief in congregating at a public place to say and hear said, under the open sky, that one is suffering, that there is a reason for it and that one can imagine an end to it. It is almost as though, in the act of coming together to remember, their immediate past has been erased and what is left in the collective memory bank are the old, old forms of Polish communion: on their knees in front of the tortured Son of God.

MOTHER POLAND

WARSAW, 1987: I meet her, as I have met so many other Poles, in a haze of cigarette smoke trapped under the ceiling of a murky café. She is very thin and very passionate. She invites me to meet her friends, a handful of Warsaw feminists. The little circle of friends has been meeting for seven years and has never grown larger. Sometimes they mind. But mostly they are patient.

They met one another while they were students in the first year of Solidarity's "revolution," but the raucous, belligerent male proletarian elite hunkered down in the shipyards along the Baltic didn't suit their still thin-skinned, tentative women's politics.

Over the years that followed, the small circle of friends, meeting regularly in Teresa's flat, biding their time (reading, arguing, translating, confessing), watched the better part of the underground disappear into the maw of the church, and they gave up the idea that Polish feminism would ever find its champions in Solidarity. It would find its champions in ordinary Polish women or not at all.

Teresa says: "To take up the cause of Polish women is to take up the issue of abortion." A freelance journalist from Paris interviews her. Teresa says that the availability of abortions remains one of the few aspects of Communism that has not been discredited. Ready access to abortion is important as long as abortion remains the most common means of contraception. Women are afraid of the pill, the locally manufactured IUD is unreliable and the condom, produced by a rubber tire manufacturer, is dismissed as "a compromise between Catholicism and Communism."

Women tend to keep their first two or three pregnancies and then start aborting. Teresa's mother has had seven abortions. Teresa has no children at all. Posing as the friend of a pregnant woman, Teresa phoned up a crisis telephone number operated by a Catholic family counselling agency. She was told that the pregnant friend would be offered shelter at a convent and that negotiations on behalf of the fetus would be undertaken between a priest and the pregnant woman's father.

These women do not expect Solidarity to intervene in the dismal scenario at the convent. The opposition has no wish to confront its ally, the church, and the church's implacable hostility to Polish women's historic right to abortion; perhaps, the women suggest, the male leadership of the opposition even agrees with the church. Two years later, in post-Communist Poland, a Solidarity senator will sponsor a bill to outlaw abortion, introducing it with the argument that "at the moment of conception a woman becomes a mother."

Mother. *Matka*. Mother Poland. *Matka Polska*. Genuflect, genuflect, genuflect.

A year later, the small circle of women will be busy at a new project, collecting and translating important feminist documents from the West for a university journal. Progress! They've drawn up the proposed table of contents, including texts by Kate Millett, Nancy Chodorow, Adrienne Rich and Dorothy Dinnerstein. They have not all had the chance to read these writers in the original but they have read, here and there, that these women are the important ones.

Shulamith Firestone's book *Dialectic of Sex*, now, is a bit problematic. All the references say this book was very important in the United States for its pioneering effort to unite disparate strands of feminist analysis. On the other hand, what do you do with Firestone's vocabulary – "dialectic," "oppression" – which reeks of Marxism? Just try to get a Polish woman to read it!

"Because there is only getting up at dawn, drudgery, queues and the television news and maybe also queuing in front of the shop overnight, a shop where once upon a time they were selling fridges, or washing machines, and later, inevitably the first time you feel the fist of your drunken husband in your face; those women would eat the carpet for a wee bit of love."
Janusz Anderman, *Poland under Black Light*

Teresa has been married for fifteen years to a man she met as a student and with whom – staying up until all hours, singing, drinking, arguing – she enjoyed until recently a relationship of friendship and "absolute equality." Now, feeling the pressure of the social and economic crisis (as he explains it), he renounces such egalitarian notions of marriage and demands that his wife be at home to cook his suppers, wash his socks, stroke his poor, embattled head. Teresa's not the type.

Those friends of hers, those feminist buddies she goes gallivanting around town with, are a bad example, he shouts. They are frigid, disappointed and, well, unattractive. They are no longer really women. Unsexed by their anger and their independence, and deeply unhappy in their repression of a woman's real desires (marriage, motherhood), they should seek their satisfaction among husband and children. In serving the happiness of others, a woman ensures her own.

Oh, Matka! Genuflect, genuflect, genuflect.

From across their renovated apartment under the eaves, separated by a pile of feminist newspapers that a visiting Dutch feminist left behind, Teresa and her husband glare at each other and no longer invite each other to bed.

Portrait of the average Polish woman, taken from data published in

1985 by the Chief Bureau of Statistics: The "average" Polish woman is keen to marry and does so at an increasingly younger age, seeks a divorce earlier, has more than one child, interrupts her career to look after her children, frequently becomes pregnant, very often has a miscarriage or an abortion, spends more time on housework than the "average" Polish man (by about 3.5 hours a day), has less free time than the "average" man, which she spends, as he does, watching television and seeing friends.

From a letter to a Polish magazine: "My husband looks after himself only – he has breakfast and we don't see him again. My husband very rarely collects the child.... My husband wanted a child. When I asked him at the beginning of my pregnancy if I should terminate it, he was very indignant, but now he doesn't help me at all."

Teresa and her friends say there are two sorts of female destinies in Poland: the devoted wife and mother, selfless and speechless in the family, and the nun, likewise effaced in the church. Then they add a third: the streetwalkers near the socialist train stations, fucking for vodka.

"AND THERE WAS TOO MUCH OF LVOV, AND NOW THERE ISN'T ANY . . ."

WARSAW, 1987: It is from Tomasz, a young theatre critic, that I first hear the lament of the Polish artist for Galicia, the lost territories of the East.

Tomasz was born after the war and has never known the Poland of his forebears, that gorgeous, polyphonic, many-stranded Poland that lay sprawled all over the lands of the Lithuanians, the Byelorussians and the Ukrainians. It resonates within him nevertheless through the poetry of poets who did know it and who sucked sustenance from the song and fable and dance of the local folk. The Polish spirit, cast down by too many failures of "civilization," replenished itself at the wells of nature and in the villages, among the simple, labouring peasants. Now this old Poland is gone, all gone, within the redrawn frontiers of the Soviet Union.

Something very new in European culture had been created in the East, Tomasz tells me, something *fused* and conjunctive, at the "crossroads of East and West." In salons and libraries and studios in the city the Polish called Lwow, the Ukrainians Lviv, the Polish genius had inscribed into Europe the eastern Slav it dominated: thanks to Roman Catholicism and the Latin alphabet, what had been "Asiatic" was shoved westward.

The Poles had snatched Galicia away from "Asia" only to have the Soviet Union lop it off as a prize from Hitler in 1939 and definitively reoccupy the territory in 1945, violently incorporating into "Russia" the native soil of the Polish poets. Thus the poets speak of it: native realm, native soil, the lost homelands; and they regard with embittered cynicism the reunification of Ukrainian lands under the red flag. In the poets' lamentations, there is no Ukrainian desire; there is only Polish, and, obversely, Russian.

But something is obscured in this nostalgia of the artist for the birthright of which he has been robbed. It was a "native soil" on which the vast majority of Poles were colonists, pure and simple, awarded latifundia confiscated as recently as the 1930s from the Greek Catholic church and distributed among veterans of the Polish officer corps. For all of Galicia, that lost territory on the other bank of the San River, that generative soil of the Polish imagination, that vanished world of "white napkins and a bucket full of raspberries," of Galician peasant-servants doing the laundry in the great houses of the Polish gentry while the little master of the house sticks his finger in the cream jug – for all of Galicia, there was one Pole for every seven Ukrainians in the population.

THEY HAVE A HOME AND IT IS HERE

USTRZYKI DOLNE, 1987: The low-slung heap of the country taxi pulls uncertainly into the farm yard and comes to a stop in muddy ruts a few metres from the side door of the brick house. I can see Anastasia in the kitchen window, watching discreetly from behind thin, white nylon drapes. I pay the driver, step gingerly into the mud. Then, the door flapping noisily behind her, Anastasia comes scurrying across the yard, wringing her hands in her apron.

"Welcome, welcome. My husband and I welcome you," she starts her little speech. "You may wander all over God's green earth but when you come here you have come onto your own lands."

I had met Anastasia in Greece, just a few months earlier, when she had come to visit her daughter, Maria. She had seemed haggard to me and distracted. Now she is soft, and weeping.

Most of our time together we spend in the kitchen, cosy with heat from the wood-burning, ceramic-tiled stove and from the yolky sunshine in whose pools we loll like cats on a windowsill. We munch on young cucumbers, boiled eggs and rye bread, sip black tea from glasses and toast each other with great gaiety with Russian champagne. From the window, close by as though next door, I can see the neighbouring furniture factory, which never shuts down. Soporifically I watch the drift of its kaleidoscopic plume of noxious discharges as it cruises over the landscape, over this house and farmstead and out beyond over the fields of hay, of turnips and sugar beets, over the pastures holding cattle. Each colour of the plume represents a different chemical.

Anastasia's sister, Elizabeth, runs the village bookshop. As a state employee, she is expected to fulfil a monthly "norm," a quota of sales of books. Recently, says Anastasia, a Polish neighbour saw Elizabeth go to Mass in the Ukrainian church and reported this sedition to the local authorities. This, at least, is how Anastasia accounts for the fact that the screws have been tightened on her sister: she's been warned that if she has one more month of unfulfilled norms, she'll lose her job. But how is she to fulfil them? The shelves are empty because the powers-that-be in Warsaw refuse to fill her orders.

Anastasia is the secretary of the Ukrainian cultural club in her village. It has been only since 1956 that the Ukrainian minority in Poland has been officially permitted to engage in cultural activity, and then only under the auspices of the Ministry of the Interior. With enormous circumspection, they have organized branches, published a newspaper, marked jubilees and collected membership fees. During Solidarity's heyday, Anastasia's husband, Vasyl, will tell me, the activists up there in Gdansk wondered aloud what good an officially subsidized Ukrainian-language newspaper was when the paper it used up could be used to publish something "important." In Przemysl there had been a unanimous decision by Solidarity not to return to the Ukrainian community three Ukrainian churches taken away from them in 1947. The Tamka Street printers in Warsaw had refused to print the Ukrainian club's newspaper because it was "Russian." The Ukrainians were very cagey about openly supporting Solidarity. Suppose Solidarity failed? The Ukrainians risked losing what little they had in the backlash: an office, a bit of a library, a newspaper.

And if Solidarity won? A Warsaw journalist, 1987: "During the legal existence of Solidarity, most Byelorussians and Ukrainians were frightened. They feared that once the Poles freed themselves from communism, they would start oppressing them."

Anastasia's daughter, Maria, is still in Greece, picking oranges near Argos, waiting for papers that will take her and her child, Hanna, to Canada. Anastasia's son remains in Poland, working as a "highway technician," meaning roadworks labourer. Only Poles are engineers, says Anastasia. Maria had wanted to study medicine but was diverted to training as an agricultural chemical lab technician. The committee overseeing admissions to the faculty of medicine in Cracow discovered her Ukrainian origins; this, says Anastasia, is why Maria is not studying medicine. Only Poles are doctors – or only those who admissions committees believe to be Poles. It is, for Anastasia, an explanation.

Poles call Ukrainians "black palates," meaning "dogs." Anastasia recalls Maria teasing her Polish boyfriends: "Wanna see my black palate?" Maria grew up in schools where she learned that she belonged to a tribe of rogues and fascists, in a village where the only monument to the dead is to those Poles killed at the hands of the Ukrainian "bandits," in a home where only the vaguest stories reached them, third- and fourth-hand, from across the border with Soviet Ukraine, of catastrophes among their kinfolk. Rumour, insult, bitten tongues. Where do such people go to utter their own lives?

There are other women in Anastasia's village whose children have moved away. These women all go together, the mothers of the departed, to pray for the souls of their children and to tend the candles and the icons in their abominated church, in a parish where it will be the task of the old to bury each other.

"We'd barely crossed the stoop, outside the house, all our belongings in a few bags, when they burned the house down behind us and sent us west in the trains." Anastasia speaks as though she were wringing her hands, which are, in fact, playing agitatedly with the bread on the table between us. She is speaking of 1947. The army had come to their village and summoned the farmers. The roundup didn't take long. The Polish officer said he was giving each of the inhabitants half an hour to pack up. No one supposed they were leaving forever.

How much can you gather together in half an hour? And what? What can you take when you don't know where you're going or for how long? Anastasia's parents didn't have a horse. They could only creep along with their cart the nine kilometres to the train station. Anastasia looked back just once. Their house was on fire.

The army had prepared a camp near the station. The deportees slept on the ground, enclosed like prisoners by barbed wire and watched over by guards. In mud and dung, in April rains, nothing to cook on, children sick.

Ahead of Anastasia and her family were nine days in a railway car travelling across the bombarded face of Poland – God alone knew where they were headed: to a concentration camp? – and then assignment to a large stone farmhouse without a roof. There they made their home, three generations under the open sky. "We had been deported because in the hills behind our villages the boys of UPA (Ukrainian Insurgent Army) had made their camps and we gave them some help."

At fifteen, Vasyl had run off from his father's farm to join the UPA hiding out in the Bieszczady hills behind the Ukrainian villages. The forests were swarming with men from these villages, on the lam from the Polish People's Army. Vasyl claims that it was difficult to separate the UPA out from the villagers themselves since they were often one and the same: farmer and combatant. Even the women were mobilized, sewing uniforms and bringing out food, medical supplies, information and news to the men and boys in the woods, as though the partisans were some kind of extension of the farm hands in the fields at harvest time. It is true that UPA sometimes killed civilians, especially Polish ones, but there was always a reason, says Vasyl. You'd find the body hanging among the branches with a note pinned scrupulously to the chest: "He died because he was an informer."

The UPA I know something about. I remember them as another group of unhappy Ukrainians tossed up in Canada after the war, refugees from who knew what, exactly? On the one hand, I heard glorious accounts of hopeless battle in the Carpathians, the UPA trapped between the pitiless troops of the Soviet and German armies, then the Czech and the Polish too – self-sacrifice on the rocks for their belief in "neither Hitler nor Stalin." On the other hand, there were dark and gruesome tales of UPA atrocities upon the Polish villages, sinister suggestions about their being on the Nazi payroll, queries as to just how voluntarily the luckless Ukrainian villagers had pitched in to succour them.

Here is the official Polish view of things, in the foreword to a 1985 edition of a photo book showing views of the "wild, unpopulated Bieszczady": "The Ukrainian Insurgent Army, armed and equipped by the Germans, waged a cruel and uncompromising campaign … terrorizing mountain villages and settlements, threatening small towns.

Murder, armed incursions and arson became everyday occurrences. UPA started a civilian network in the villages, hoping to establish a kind of Bieszczady state ruled by fear and death."

And the roosters of two contradictory villages crowed noon and evening at once. – Julian Przybos, "Mother"

The Ukrainians, for having tried to wrest themselves from Poland, would never be forgiven. For having incubated the "bacillus of nationalism" in their villages and taken up arms against the Polish People's Army, they were punished with the principle of collective responsibility. Whole villages having been labelled collaborationist with the "terrorists" in the mountains, the residents were condemned to the "social surgery" of mass deportation from their ancestral lands and resettled in bits and pieces – never forming more than 10 per cent of the local population – in lands won from Germany at the end of the war. People's Poland got its wish: when *Akcja Wisla* and *Akcja Przesiedlienie* (Operation Vistula and Operation Resettlement) were over, 150,000 "Lemko" villagers and farmers had been moved out of Lemkowszczyna, leaving behind mere husks of community that incoming Polish settlers would obliterate or supplant with Roman Catholic churches and Polish schools. People's Poland would be *Polish*. That which had been Ukrainian would pass into a dream dreamed by the next generation, growing up on the frigid shores of the northern sea, who would remember who they were – whose sons and whose daughters – if only because Polish hatred had named them.

Some three hundred Ukrainian churches were destroyed – burned or dismantled or vandalized – and their graveyards levelled with the blade of a bulldozer. Sometimes one or two stones were left standing, but their Cyrillic names were erased with a smudge of cement to render them blank, as though no one rested here, as though this soil were unfertilized.

Those Ukrainian churches that remain in the Carpathians are magnificent sculptures in wood, arc and dome and stave piled up in a gorgeous heap of hand-carved timber. When not used as barns and granaries, they have been restored as "state monuments" and delivered to Roman Catholic parishes, their original sanctification as the house of the Greek Catholic rite all but smothered by the prayer and genuflection of a Polish country church. The Mother of God has become the Queen of Poland, festooned with the gold chains of the faithful.

From a story in a Polish Ukrainian-language newspaper: "And so the Poles arrived, tore us away from our homes, burned them to the ground, desecrated our churches, and then went up into the hills to clean up the 'bandits,' murdering our boys in their bunkers with grenades and gas. And then they invited Polish farmers to come onto our land. But the Poles were in no hurry. They were afraid of us, afraid that we would come back at any time and slit their throats."

Anastasia buried her mother and father near the Baltic Sea, then, with her sister and brother, her husband and children, she returned to her village – now called in Polish Ustrzyki Dolne – and bought up a farm unclaimed by the Polish newcomers. The returning Ukrainians rebuilt the church and crept to Mass.

Ustriki Dolishni. Anastasia's hand over her mouth. Stewed gooseberries in a glass. Vasyl's flatbed truck grinding ancient gears as we go into town, down from "our" Ukrainian hills.

I am not prepared for how witheringly the Poles hate the Ukrainians in their midst. (It is *Ukrainians* who hate, I have always thought.) The Ukrainian people of southeast Poland have been sentenced to endure the loss of public memory. Nothing that belongs to public discourse as a whole – monuments, names, liturgies, nomenclature – refers to them or their view of things. And so the names of the Ukrainian dead, the boys from the curved San River valley, rest uninscribed, their exploits and engagements evoked only as "banditry" and then sunk once more into oblivion. In this word "banditry," meaning perverse and unmotivated lawlessness, meaning murder of women and children and attacks on peace-loving Polish villages, there is no record of the grievance that lay behind the passion of the fifteen-year-old boy who crept out to the forest, in bare feet, to handle a rifle.

We visit an open air museum in Sanok, a recreation of a typical sub-Carpathian village: thatched roofs, woven willow branch fences, straw-filled embroidered cushions, family icons exhibited in a row high up on the wall near the ceiling. It's intensely familiar to me; I've seen it all a hundred times in museums in Alberta. The Sanok museum catalogue notes that the "Lemki were very conservative in their culture and reluctant towards novelties." It says also that their ancestors "belonged to Ruthenian and Walachian tribes with a dominating share of Balcan [*sic*] ethnic groups, mixed however with shepherds from Hungary." The Lemki are, in face, a branch of the Ukrainian people who live near the mountains. The Poles have seized upon this nomenclature to call them anything but Ukrainians.

Vasyl says that before the war the Polish authorities, in an excess of crusading zeal, foisted upon the villagers of the San valley a great number of Lemko dialect textbooks for their schools. The villagers threw the books in the fire. They were *Ukrainian* people, they said; they were of the *narod* who dominated the earth from the San to the farthest stretches eastward of the steppes, and they wanted textbooks in their own language. The language they spoke, they said, was Ukrainian.

During 1980–81, the time of Solidarity, Vasyl allowed himself to hope that the truth of history could be told. It wasn't just the sudden and invigorating activity – farmers taking over public buildings in Ustrzyki Dolne; shepherds pouring out their grievances against the pampered apparatchiks who had set up a recreational estate known as the Red Principate on sixty thousand hectares of the shepherds' own mountain pasture. It was also the remarkable fact that the inhabitants of the Bieszczady Mountains, Poles as well as Ukrainians, demanded that the villages be restored to their original, Ukrainian names. In the room where they met, Solidarity's headquarters in Ustrzyki Dolne, someone had scrawled an inspirational "We don't care about life. The pig also lives. We want a life of dignity."

Here, perhaps, was the beginning of a chance: a chance to correct the public record, to utter, in Ukrainian, what had happened and why, to uplift the young people. And so Vasyl went to all the local meetings and came home with his pockets and hands stuffed with pamphlets and leaflets to show to Anastasia, who had been left at home in charge of the pigs and calves. There was some initial progress: local maps were issued with all the village names restored to Ukrainian; Kazimierzowo, for instance, named for a loathsome bodyguard at the Red Principate, became Muczne again. But then came martial law and the restoration of "order." By the summer of 1987, when I visit them, Vasyl and Anastasia once again live in a Polish town.

Now we stand at the side of the highway and look out across a little valley crumpled with green hillocks. I follow Vasyl's finger to a distant yellow smear in the green; these are the walls of the church that stood in his village. The village no longer exists, vanished even from the regional maps. I have only Vasyl's word for it that this was once a place, a community, a home. It is situated now only in his memory and makes no noise there.

So I name it here, on this page, and bring it back from the void: Kryve nad Sianom. The curved place on the San.

These are not just hills. These are "our" hills. "We" populated them. "We" danced and sang and married. "We" walked up and down the bushy slopes and called for "our" cows and sheep. Generations of "us" were buried alongside the timbered walls of "our" church. "We," meaning of this place, coming from here. Not a single Pole lived here. Meaning: all these Poles you see here now, these farmers and government men, are interlopers and infiltrators. They are from another place, from beyond, outside the scope of the wave of Vasyl's arm. They don't even speak "our" language. *They* live in Ustrzyki Dolne. *We* live in Ustriki Dolishni. Because that's what it was called. We were the first ones. We gave it a name.

Grassy banks sliding at a gentle angle down to the bright, narrow river San. Here stood house upon house, here were whole villages! Hummocks roll down from the hills, covered in a soft green weft of young deciduous trees. These once were fields, cleared, cultivated and fertile. Further on we can still make out the ground under an orderly plantation of pine where a church once stood, destroyed utterly when the Poles came to take the timber away for the purposes of erecting a machine shed and a pig barn.

Coming across one of the abandoned churches, Ukrainian-Polish journalist T. Karabovich wrote: "It's a hallowed day when, passing through the demolished church gate, you approach a boarded-up, sometimes even nameless church to look upon, in meditation and peace, the closest, best-known things of your own. Here, burned out by savage time, is a sanctuary. It doesn't die; it just isn't there anymore.... I felt the sun-burned sky and the wild, grassy green which endless memory held wrapped in her hands."

I am shifting my focus away from the heroic Poles of the perpetual uprising – the heroes of the conspiracies and cellblocks – away even from the Poles of the "lost" Galician territories where they once ruled splendidly in their chateaux, glittering in winter season in Lwow, extracting wealth from the faceless Ukrainian serfs on their estates. Ukrainians who are *always* peasants, sans literature, sans philosophy, sans destiny, sans everything, breaking through into historical specificity – *named* – as bandits, traitors, rogues, murderers, pillaging through the Polish patrimony only to be cut down by the sword and cannon shot of Polish heroes and to subside again into glum, uncouth servitude.

And if it is this point of view I am now attentive to, then the Poles become the "other" and I am wrenched away from the Poles of my imagination – the freedom fighters – and towards the Poles of my baba's stories – landlords and rapists. I remember only fragments, anecdotes lacking context, unassimilable into what was my 1950s girl-child's mind. The stories didn't fit anywhere. They didn't make me feel anything. Who were Poles? Where did they come from? Where could I see one? Why should I hate them?

LIVING AS A FREE HUMAN BEING

"The whole trip to Sopot smacked of a great adventure. On the main Monte Cassino Street you could get ice cream from an Italian machine and eat a hamburger some five years before the rest of the country caught up with these Western inventions." – Marek Garztecki, "The Rise and Fall of Polish Rock and Roll"

SOPOT, 1988: Julia is in charge of the large and ramshackle flat. It is a crash pad, a sanctuary and liberated zone. The floor boards warp and heave; mattresses are thrown into the living room alongside bulky pre-war cabinets with ornate façades. But the greasy, discoloured wallpaper is slowly disappearing under white paint, and those who stay overnight are asked to help strip old paint off the window frames in preparation for clear varnish. In the kitchen, odds and ends of crockery pile up in a stained and pitted sink while vegetables rot in the bottom of the fridge. Wooden matches that have failed to ignite are heaped under the stove burners. This is the nerve centre of Freedom and Peace, Sopot branch.

In the water closet, with its old and uncertain plumbing, someone has prepared a small stack of newspaper squares that serve as toilet paper, an innovation I have not seen since the 1950s when I used to visit my baba on her acreage. Suddenly, it's here again, her tottering and malodorous outhouse, the large, thick nail on which were impaled scraps of Ukrainian-language newspapers, left- and right-wing.

There are cassette tapes strewn over the sideboard. Talking Heads, Van Morrison, Polish rock. Over all the furniture and underfoot are alternative journals and peace newsletters from everywhere in Europe, dictionaries and lots of books.

People drift in and out, kindred souls from the peace movement in Hungary and Germany, and in Poznan and Warsaw and Katowice, and the phone rings without cease, for this is the weekend of the peace festival and Julia has spray-painted the phone number all over town – at the train station, at the bus station, on kiosks. Eventually the authorities will disconnect her phone and the kindred spirits will arrive unannounced at the door, looking hopeful.

Anatol, wiry and with the caved-in belly of the vegetarian (he refuses even eggs), is stabbing zealously at the window frame. Chips of paint go flying down onto the floor and into the cuffs and pockets of the oversized army jacket he's wearing open over his bare chest. He is a Buddhist and has no plans: "I could die tomorrow and nothing would be lost."

Anatol has been in this flat for many weeks. Freedom and Peace is taking care of him because he's a stateless man, though a Pole by nationality, or so he claims. He arrived in Poland from the U.S.S.R. on an invitation from Freedom and Peace and has no intention of going back. He is demanding Polish citizenship from the authorities in Warsaw. He speaks Polish, Russian, Ukrainian and some English. He has an earring in his left ear. He is unremittingly cheerful.

Anatol tells us that he was born in Kazakhstan of Poles deported from Poland in 1939 by the newly installed Soviet authority in eastern Poland (now western Ukraine). He has never been employed, he says, preferring to take his chances with odd jobs on the run, moving around the Soviet Union as the local authorities closed in on him, demanding to see documents. He calls this "taking the hippie ideology."

I come in and out of the flat many times. Always he is there, flailing at the window frame. Each time I enter, he pauses in his work to say to me, in Ukrainian, with smiling gravity: "I welcome you to Polish soil. How does it please you, our Polish land?"

There is lots of tea in the flat but no dope, and no booze except what westerners purchase from the Pewex (hard currency) shop. I am a sugar daddy, bringing the girls and boys treats from the West. Being older and richer, I accept this assignment. From Pewex I bring cans and cans of Austrian beer, brandy, orange juice, chocolate bars and peanuts, enough to last a week. It lasts one day.

At eighteen years of age, Anatol had walked across the border from Ukraine to Czechoslovakia and across Slovakia to the Austrian border where he was apprehended, sent packing to the u.s.s.r. and then detained in a cell of the psychiatric hospital in Dnipropetrovsk. Or so he says. He's telling this story, over bottles of beer, to Gabor and Judit and me. We are seated on bits of sofa cushions in the living room.

"Oh!" says Judit. She tells us about her mother, who worked in a pharmaceutical factory near Budapest in the 1970s and always wondered about the extravagant orders to fill from the Soviet Union: "A whole nation of lunatics!" We pause to consider the possibility that Anatol had been tortured with drugs packaged by the deft hands of Judit's mum.

I have another role. Julia's comrade Ule is at the dining room table, in a flurry of flying paint chips from Anatol's furious scraping at the window frame; she is doggedly at work on a translation of the lyrics from *Jesus Christ Superstar*. I am the only anglophone in the vicinity. I am asked to explain the meaning of "That's all right by me" and "scripture-thumping hack." You try it.

We had met a year earlier, Julia, her friends and I, in the courtyard of a Warsaw church where we were all attending an illegal peace meeting. I had felt a little lost and at loose ends, representing as I was nobody but myself. The organizers had given me a badge all the same: CANADA. Julia was the first to speak to me, in English. Two sentences later I had an invitation to visit her group in Gdansk and Sopot. They were *Wolnosc i Pokoj* (WiP): Freedom and Peace.

It is Julia's intention to live as though she were a free human being. To this end, she eschews all regular employment, the better to obscure the traces of her activity, and has declined as compromising an invitation to join the rest of her family in Miami. Miami, of all places. Twenty years earlier, Julia's father had got away to America. His mother, wife and children stayed behind in Sopot, just in case life got better next month, next year, and the patriarch could come home. Last winter they all left too, except for Julia. Julia stayed behind, as she wished, in the Polish house of cards.

The wind from the Baltic Sea blows in the kitchen window. The sea is grey and roiling, swans huddled miserably at its shore, its waters so polluted that Julia hasn't swum in them since 1980, the first summer of

Solidarity and the summer that thousands of dead eels, thrown up out of the stink, rotted in putrid ardour on the Sopot beaches.

According to tradition surrounding the hallowing of Midsummer Night's Eve, an effigy of an old woman, representing all that is infertile and used up of the old year, is thrown out to sea. With her goes all the spiritual and psychological debris of the community.

In 1985, Freedom and Peace dreamed up the more appropriate idea of making an effigy of General Jaruzelski, president of Poland, and then summoning the public to the seaside, where they would be presented arguments from defence and prosecution alike as to the redeemability of the old man in uniform. The fate of the effigy would lie in the public's vote, aye or nay.

Two days before the scheduled event, which by now had been widely publicized on WiP flyers, Julia and her friend Konrad were awakened by an ungodly hammering at their door. Guessing that this was the police and that the flat was surrounded, blocking off egress from the French windows, they resolved prudently to stay where they were, cuddled in bed.

A neighbour, thinking a crime was taking place, phoned the police.

With the arrival of more cops, the racket became untenable, and so Julia and Konrad decided to let them in. Because pregnant women may not be arrested in People's Poland, Julia claimed to be pregnant. But Konrad was taken away in handcuffs to his former flat, where suspicious flyers and newsletters were seized along with his anthropology notes which, being illegible, were deemed subversive. Also arrested was his refrigerator. It was hauled off by removers as the single item of any value that could be sold to make good state losses in the very likely event that Konrad would refuse to pay his highly probable fine.

Konrad was taken to the police station, charged with attempting to provoke public disorder – the Midsummer Night's Eve happening – and with "spreading false ideas about reality," presumably on the basis of the confounded anthropology notes. At his comrade Krzysztof's flat, a commando squad brandishing axes and brand-new, fast-repeating Spanish revolvers burst through the door and arrested everyone present, including some hapless foreigners spending the night on the floor. Not overlooked were the dinner pots caked with a "suspicious substance" (the dregs of a vegetarian stew) and two female wigs. (Aha!)

Konrad was fined fifty thousand zlotys, more than a month's wages. He refused to pay it, reasoning there would be nothing to confiscate.

Being a free man, he owned no television, no computer, no car – and now, no fridge.

Back at the seaside on Midsummer's Eve, only the police showed up for the show. All would-be spectators had been scared away. The defence and prosecuting "attorneys" were unavailable, having been arrested. So Julia was left alone, to toss gamely the bewigged effigy of Jaruzelski upon the foul waters and to watch as a resolute cop strode manfully into the waves and rescued the General from the deep.

We are speaking of Gorbachev and *perestroika*, and Julia sticks to her principles. For her, the traditional political process, no matter where and how it takes place, is just another means for the professional politician to seize power and manipulate those caught in his net. If you play this game – as in Solidarity's behind-the-scenes round-table negotiations with the Jaruzelski government – you will inevitably be corrupted into making trade-offs, betrayals and false speech.

At first I find her rigorousness rather alarming; it seems deterministic and ahistorical, admitting of no exceptions or modifications within the dialectic of real life. But when she adds that to live as though one were a free human being means also to try not to be afraid, I think I understand the uncompromising rigour. It serves to shield against the thousand perils – grotesque, enervating, sinister – of the uncircumscribed oppositional life. And so she will resist the blandishments to "work from within." She will resist them even from a dear old friend who's on the road this very day from Gdansk to Gdynia and Sopot, bearing proposals that Freedom and Peace join the Socialist Party and work within the parliament – along with the Communists, to be sure, but with its own agenda, boring through the pulpy organs of the state to let in the oxygen of democracy.

Boycott! Julia will say. And pass out WiP flyers: "Crazies of all countries unite!"

Surveying the life of her compatriots, lives dribbling out in the inanity of labour that gets you nowhere, in the hoarding of emotional currency and in the useless exercise of cynicism, Julia would not live any life but her own.

A year later, on the eve of Solidarity's formation of a government, she will write me: "Today it comprises expressions like 'the spirit of the round table,' 'new thinking,' and so on. I suppose that Poland is in a situation where we have to be tactical but too often these tactics are in bad taste. Like [Solidarity leader Lech] Walesa becoming the honourable leader of the communist Peace Council of Poland ... or [dissident Adam] Michnik participating in Catholic ceremonies on TV, while the church is doing so much harm to Polish society, in terms of intolerance, for example, or its attitude to women."

Konrad works in a jewellery shop in Gdansk in the heart of the (restored) historic quarter. From here, I imagine, mediaeval traders first made their excursions all the way down to the Black Sea along the so-called Amber Route, selling the honeyed stone that made Gdansk/Danzig famous and that still provides a living, even for anarchists in Poland in 1988.

Konrad, in fact, is gloomy. It is very, very difficult to mobilize public opinion. He refers to the public's "ghetto mentality," that phenomenon of Jews who, having managed to escape the ghetto during the Nazi occupation, returned to it voluntarily because they so much missed their home and neighbourhood. It's the same with today's Poles, he argues. Despite being subjected to the world's worst environment, they continue to live in it without protest, drinking untreated water, growing their veggies in sewers, living uncomplainingly next door to factories that turn their filters off at night to save electricity costs because no one can see the fumes in the dark.

Freedom and Peace members lay flowers in Kielce, the site of Poland's last pogrom in 1946, and are fined thirty thousand zlotys for disturbing the peace. They collect signatures to protest the plan to build a nuclear power plant in Zarnowiec. Just as Chornobyl was a devastation of the people of Ukraine, these activists see the program of nuclear plant construction as a plot against the physical integrity of the Polish people. They champion the conscientious objector on hunger strike for the last nine months for the absolute right not to serve in the military forces: he is force-fed every second day and they say his throat is a raw and bleeding mess from the feeding tubes. His black-and-white photograph hangs in Julia's living room like an icon.

Julia tells me that the Freedom and Peace group, Sopot branch, smuggled a very primitive printing press into the shipyards in Gdansk during the strikes of May that year and printed up newsletters in their inimitable anarcho-gonzo style, linking up the workers' strike with workers' traditional pacifism and calling on the militia to throw down their weapons and join WiP – a variation on the image of the American peaceniks plugging up the rifles of the National Guard with flowers.

The women students of the philology department of Gdansk University make a passive boycott of military training on campus: they refuse to take notes, answer questions or participate in drill. Naturally WiP supports them.

On the other hand, with no apparent awareness of contradicting themselves, the men of Freedom and Peace recently enjoyed the televising of the Miss Polonia beauty contest. Julia tells me she pointed out in disgust that this was a spectacle not unlike the army boot camp – a zone of manipulation and compulsion, the one sexual, the other militaristic. What, she wanted to know, was the difference?

She's not normally so forthright, at least not when I'm around. When I'm around, I am invited to play the role of the jackbooted feminist from the West, letting the Polish women off the hook. Thus I sweep Julia and Ule out of the flat to a nearby café, leaving behind the male comrades to do the dishes and to puzzle out why I would not want their company at all times. This could only be a western idea.

And when some boys from WiP arrive with a handwritten petition to Ronald Reagan and ask Julia to type it up, I ask the obvious question: is there no Polish male capable of doing his own typing? Konrad retorts that of course there are such men, himself, for example, but Julia types the best. I say: "Naturally, she's had the most experience." Julia soothingly intervenes: "But only I can handle this ridiculous machine." And takes her place in front of a small and sticky Remington of uncertain provenance.

Julia tells me she first began to hate the church because the parish priest, at the annual blessing of her parents' home, never failed to address some hectoring remarks to her about her obligation to get married and bear children. When she grew older, she argued with him, saying she wanted to be educated, she wanted to travel, she wanted interesting work. The priest would sneer at her, warning that girls who have "big ideas" are always punished. This didn't stop her, but it has stopped others.

Women activists are a rare presence in Freedom and Peace – Julia counts two in Gdansk, two in Poznan, one in Warsaw – although women can be found hanging back in the wings, applauding their daring boyfriends and offering to make coffee and sandwiches if pressed to "do" something in the movement. There are women saddled with babies and shiftless husbands who envy Julia her freedom. And young women who, fearing the disapproval of men, dress up in lots of make-up and tarty little skirts so as not to be confused with the likes of Julia – Julia in blue jeans and with a thing or two to say at a student gathering. And women fed up to *here* with kowtowing to western feminists who have big houses and refrigerators stuffed with meat, and who dash about in their cute Japanese cars, bringing enlightenment to their oppressed Polish sisters. What the hell would *they* know about oppression?

Some months ago, Julia says, a couple from Germany came to Gdansk to conduct a workshop on nonviolence for Julia and her friends. The male visitor took the men aside and advised them that, since feminism was "inevitable" within their peace movement, the men had better get used to the idea and adjust themselves to the growing confidence and expression of women. His admonition did not, alas, have the desired chastening effect. The Polish men took it as a challenge to their Polish manhood. Relations between men and women in Poland would develop in a specifically *Polish* direction, they argued. Meaning: Polish patriarchal. The implication was clear: In "allowing" women to identify and act as feminists, the man from the West had lost his balls.

THE MASSES RETURN TO THE CROSS

GDANSK, 1988: It is my third visit to the Solidarity monument. A crowd of Polish tourists huddle together, heads strained forward, to catch the words of their tour guide, a young man in a tight brown suit. He presses his hands against his chest but the wind snatches his words out of his mouth. The old women in cardigans turn away from him, lay their cellophane-wrapped bouquets all in a heap and begin to walk, arm in arm, in the direction of the old town.

They have piled their flowers at the base of the crucifixes. The concrete slabs of the memorial mound have cracked and laid bare the soil, in which coarse grasses and the stems of wild chamomile have taken root. The bouquets lie beside a puddle of cement into which Pope Jan Pawel II stepped, one foot at a time but quickly, quickly, before the glossy material stiffened around his soles. So now, pointing away from the crucifixes as though their owner had stood here to view the traffic, is the broad, smooth imprint of a pair of men's shoes.

SHE HOLDS HER TONGUE

"One should sing village courtships, peasant bridals, / Flocks, hillsides, shady trees. / We Slavs love idylls." – Adam Mickiewicz, "Forefathers' Eve"

CRACOW, 1988: Her name is Kateryna. She is short, wiry, vehement. She is about sixty years old, a widow, the mother of a daughter who has moved to Canada. She lives tenaciously, battling prying neighbours and tattling tenants for the right to live on in her vast, ancient and slovenly apartment within the mediaeval walls of Cracow now that her daughter has absconded. She shares her kitchen and bath with a tenant, in whose company she is very careful to speak only Polish.

I too am getting used to this charade: Kateryna and I in Ukrainian conversation until the outside door opens and the tenant enters – an imposing, broad-shouldered middle-aged woman carrying a bag of onions. I shut up; Kateryna natters at me in Polish. The tenant, after throwing an inquisitorial glare into the kitchen, passes on magisterially down the corridor to her room. Now Kateryna and I, speaking once more in Ukrainian, whisper nose to nose over the teacups.

At the age of fourteen, Kateryna was transported to Germany to work at forced labour in a munitions factory. She says it was the best time of her life.

She holds up her left hand. The fingers are bent forward in a para-lyzed claw. In 1949, the Security Police hauled her into their office (there, that corner window on the second floor of a splendid, cream-coloured renaissance building on the square) and, in an effort to make her talk, held her hand inside a door jamb and slammed the door shut. Where are so-and-so and so-and-so hiding? they wanted to know, of the Ukrainians of Cracow. Bandits and nationalist scum! But she said nothing. Sucked on her broken fingers and swallowed her own blood. She was threatened with more torture and then released. Her priest advised her to leave town immediately and hide out in the countryside with a family she could trust. Which she did, until the roundup of the bandits and scum was over.

She married, bore two children and was widowed within five years. She went out to work, leaving the babies alone at home, in the care of a cat. "You had two kids, no man, no mother. How could you go out to work?" "I had a cat."

She lived stealthily, passing herself off as Polish, afraid even to contact other Ukrainians who, like her, had hidden themselves and were now creeping back into daylight. She did find out, though, about the Ukrainian church services held in a side chapel of the Roman Catholic cathedral, and she would slip in among other women and bow her covered head into the bowl of her hands. She still goes there, daily. She calls the church "Mother."

She is the lucky one, after all. Thousands of parishioners were arrested back in '49 by police standing just inside the doors of the churches, picked off one by one as they entered for Mass. They were sent by cattle car eastward, to Kazakhstan and Siberia. Kateryna talks of a woman who threw her baby out of the moving train to "save" it and of another who went mad from beatings. But it is the story of the priest that obsesses her, and now me. Savagely assaulted, his teeth knocked out and his ribs broken, he was turned over to the Soviets and then shipped out to a Siberian labour camp where he laboured ten years. At the end of his sentence he hobbled, broken, to Lviv, where he lived "like a beggar," says Kateryna, who became active in collecting money in Cracow to ease his circumstances. Then he lost both legs and died of gangrene, just like that.

There is a large market square in this city with an impressive bell tower, the famous one where the bugler at the top, noticing the arrival of the Mongols on the eastern horizon, blew one last blast and died, a Mongol arrow through his throat. It was here, says Kateryna, at the base of the tower, that a young man sat down in gas-soaked rags one afternoon and set himself alight. This was 1981, and as he died he screamed, "They're coming! They're coming!"

REVISIONISM

SOPOT, 1988: Out of the blue Julia asks me: "If there were a free Ukraine, would you go 'back' there?" The question throws me off balance. It has never occurred to me that I am a Ukrainian in exile, doomed to fret about the goings on "back home" from the temporary margins of North America. I explain that I am Ukrainian-Canadian and that the hyphen is essential – the juncture of sources. She remains puzzled. She has never met a hyphenated Pole. Poles in North America are Poles "abroad." One is a Pole or not a Pole. A Ukrainian or not a Ukrainian. Thus: I am the first "Ukrainian" she has met. She has yet to meet a Jew.

Before this summer, Julia had never met a Soviet citizen. Poles who travelled to Rumania or Bulgaria through the territory of the Ukrainian Soviet Socialist Republic found themselves passengers on a sealed train, the carriage doors having been bolted from the outside to prevent escape at the Polish-Ukrainian border. (Why would anyone want to escape *into* the Soviet Union?)

But she has no national prejudices. It is against her principles of non-violence to harbour ill will towards any nation, including the German, even though her grandfather died in a Nazi concentration camp. Thus it follows that the "Freedom and Peace movement considers striving for national independence to be just. National oppression is an evil and eliminating it will lead to freedom for nations and will bring peace among them."

The members of Freedom and Peace have reviewed all they learned from official sources as they were growing up about the history of Poland in relation to other nations. They have, for example, taken another look at what happened between Poles and Ukrainians in the villages and countryside of southeastern Poland right after the war. They now know that this was a state-run campaign called Operation Vistula. They did not know that in school. It was not in the books.

From the Polish school calendar for 1980–81, this list of special events to be commemorated during the year: 41st anniversary of the outbreak of the Second World War, Polish Army Day, 63rd anniversary of the Great Socialist October Revolution, Miners' Day, 36th anniversary of the Liberation of Warsaw, month of National Remembrance, Victory Day.

With their new sense of responsibility towards history as Freedom and Peace activists, a group travelled southeast to the Przemysl area in 1986. Introducing themselves to older Ukrainians as Poles of the postwar generation who wished to inform themselves about what had *really* happened, they asked to hear the stories.

Then they went back to their homes and in 1987 issued a declaration that says, in part: "We, members of the Freedom and Peace movement, think that even the greatest atrocities committed by the [Ukrainian] guerrillas cannot justify the use of collective responsibility towards civilians. The repressions that began with the resettlement continue today. In connection with this, we demand that it be made possible for Ukrainians and Lemkos to be given the right to return to the historical lands of their forefathers. We demand the return of their real estates seized by the state."

I am touched by this, as though reconciliation of Ukrainian with Pole had suddenly become thinkable through this generation's willingness to rewrite the history of their country.

WHERE DOES EUROPE END?

WARSAW, 1988: Just beyond Father Popieluszko's burial mound I can see a row of small placards on stakes – a kind of Stations of the Cross marshalled like pickets in a fence – each one inscribed with the date of an uprising or act of resistance from 1794 to 1981. Alongside the last one in the series stands a simple red granite pillar supporting the carving of a woman's head tilted back, her eyes and lips closed and a smile pulling at the corners of her mouth. I read that this is a memorial to the women who died in the Warsaw uprising in 1944.

To the left of the memorial, at the base of the eastern wall of the church, a workman on his knees is deftly but painstakingly painting in the fading inscriptions on a series of plaques fixed to the church wall: name upon name upon name of men and women killed one way or another during the Nazi occupation – gassed, shot down, executed, incinerated – heroes of the courier networks, the convoys and the Red Cross, heroes of the camps, the cellars and the sewers, heroes of the torture chambers and the shower rooms.

Krysia Gorska. Jozef Weber. Jerzy Falkowski. Jan Kornas. Kazimiera Falkowska. Sobibor: 250,000. Plaszow: 150,000. Oswiecim-Brzezinka: 3,840,000.

The Martyrology. The word is inscribed right into the church wall. The wall is a meeting place for the living to come together in public rituals of unforgetting what has not completely unhappened.

Magda is small as a bird with tiny thin hands that shake as she lights up a succession of foul Polish cigarettes. I have been telling her about my visit to the museum of Pawiak prison. The prison was built in 1863 to hold political prisoners seized after the uprising against the Russians. "Pawiak is a very dark place," she says. Prisoners of the Gestapo – men and women of the resistance – were held there and so savagely tortured that their families could recognize nothing in the rags and bones delivered them for burial. She works for a publisher; she's seen the photographs from the prison's archives. They have never been published, and Polish parents do not tell their children about Pawiak.

It is about the only secret they keep to themselves. Poles forget nothing, she says.

It's true, says Magda, that Poles know how to run in the streets in displays of bravado, but they do not seem to know how to live in the time between uprisings. The first strikes of Solidarity were "superb," she says, but after the strikes you still had to go home to the greyish life of food line-ups, bus line-ups, smudged newspapers. There seems no life in common, no collaborative project, only shabbiness outside and, at home, privacy and the recitations of historic grievances.

Poles learn within the bosom of the family what it is to be Polish – this hot, hard, obsidian hatred of the Nazis and the Russians, this high-minded pride in an unbroken history of resistance and defeat. Magda learned it within hers from an uncle who had fought in the Home Army. After the war, the Communists put him in prison and held him there until 1956 as though he were a traitor or, worse, a criminal, soiled and reprobate. They tortured him by chopping all his fingers off at the first joint.

I had not noticed the sewer the first few times I crossed the street. When I did, I went back to the curb and read the plaque fastened to the wall of the building on the street corner. I learned that out there in the middle of the intersection, under a black disk of asphalt, lay the mouth of the last sewer through which the last of the resistance warriors had tried to escape on the last days of the Warsaw uprising in 1944.

They worried most about their rifles which they had to hold high above their heads, clear of the raw sewage through which they waded, sometimes on their hands and knees.... From time to time a German would lift a manhole cover and throw down hand grenades and the dead air of the small tunnel amplified the detonations and the shrieks of the dying as though inside a diabolical kettledrum. This continued for the whole of September 1 ... [some], maddened and suffocating in the foul air, ... slipped and disappeared under the sewage, their bodies a foothold for their comrades in the rear. Finally, the Germans poured fire from a flame-thrower directly into the sewers. The Old Town was completely abandoned. By September 2 the Warsaw uprising was over.

September 2, 1944: the day I was born.

There is another memorial not far from the sewer. The names are inscribed on marble walls that are blindingly white from the sun bouncing off their flanks. The inscribed walls surround an inner court, as if to give shelter there, but just beyond them runs the asphalt road and the strip of embedded railway tracks of the place called Umschlagplatz. This is where the cattle cars stood and where they were loaded with their cargo from the ghetto. It was the end. These are some of the names: *Tauba. Tema. Teodor. Teresa. Trajna. Tymna. Tysa. Talia. Zakkaj. Zelman. Zenon. Zachariasz.*

"Along this path of suffering and death over 300,000 Jews were driven in 1942–43 from the Warsaw ghetto to the gas chambers of the Nazi extermination camps," reads the memorial. The gravestones of their ancient cemeteries were broken up by forced labour gangs and the rubble distributed with stones to make up the cobbled streets of the towns of Terespol and Podlasie. They say that if you walk with your eyes cast down to the road you can still catch sight here and there of a letter or two of the Hebrew alphabet swept suddenly clean by rain or wind. They say that at the camp at Majdanek there stood a small hill composed entirely of human ash. Majdanek was on the outskirts of Lublin. I've walked through modern-day Lublin. The old centre is a zone of utter dilapidation: crumbling brick walls exposed under plaster that has fallen away, steps disintegrating and windows retreating from their frames, all surfaces soiled with soot and grease. A cold, dry, raspy sort of wind blew around all the corners lifting up the dirt of the ages. It was an ashy wind.

ARE WE STILL IN EUROPE?

Go to the National Museum, my friend had said, and have a look at Jan Matejko's painting of the battle of Grunwald. Why should I do that? I asked. You will see, he said, a picture of the last time that the Polish nation felt it belonged to the East.

In 1410, the Polish armies, in alliance with the Grand Duchy of Lithuania (on Poland's eastern frontier), routed the Teutonic Order of the Knights of the Cross. The Teutons were Germans in white capes with flashing black crosses; they had subjugated Prussians and Letts and penetrated eastward to Latvia and Estonia as far as Peipus Lake before being unhorsed by the noble savages of the eastern marshes and their allies at the battle of Grunwald.

I stand in front of the gigantic painting and have a look at them, these Teutonic "civilizers." Effete Europeans in silk stockings, tiaras, whirls of damask cloak, their emblazoned black crosses and glinting silver blades are mere dross in the mud and blood of the field disintegrating before my eyes under the bloodied axes of the Slav and Baltic hosts.

The victors are bare-chested supermen, rampant and triumphant in gaudy costumes of peacock feathers, leopard skins and furry caps, sitting astride snorting steeds. Supervising everything in an aureole of blue and gold, the Virgin Mary, Mother of God, sends out rays of salvation and sanction. Almost exactly three hundred years later, in 1717, she will be ceremoniously crowned Queen of Poland, as though, among all the Christian nations of Europe, she has made her choice of subjects: the Roman Catholic Poles. Through Her, the Poles will belong to the West, marrying into the royal houses of western Europe, breeding saints, cardinals and poets who will die in Paris. They will be a vanguard nation, the flank of the Christian Occident, holding back the Hun, the Mongol, of whom they have a fearful memory.

In the thirteenth century the Mongol hordes had surged out of the steppes all the way to Czestochowa, where in 1280 they were finally smitten at the gates of the monastery of St. Paul of the Desert: fiery Tatars confounded by the miraculous image of the Black Madonna. It is said She was painted by St. Luke on a table crafted by the carpenter of Nazareth and thence taken to Constantinople and venerated there until the eighth century, when She found Herself hidden in a forest in eastern Poland (or Ukraine, depending on your point of view). The princeling of these parts, having had a miraculous dream, took Her cradled in his arms to the monastery in Czestochowa, and there She was when the hordes arrived, intent upon irruption into Europe.

Seven hundred years later I see Her image, reproduced on glossy paper, tacked to a kilim on the wall of a Polish worker's flat, the two sabre scars across her right cheek faithfully reproduced from the original. The infuriated Tatars had hacked and slashed with their knives on the gilded, Byzantine limewood board in their vain effort to overthrow the Lady and press on. She prevailed, they withdrew and Europe danced on, never knowing the miracle that had saved them for their minuet.

A prayer by J. Olechowski, 1944: "At the hour of the final battle, between the walls of Warsaw in flames, one sole prayer remains: give us the grace to resist, O crowned Queen of Poland, with the scarred face."

In 1980, Her image appeared on the suit lapel of Lech Walesa, the strikers' leader. In 1982, by decree of the military government, She appeared on a postage stamp.

The evening light is going down over the Plac Zamkowy in old Warsaw and the twittering birds of dusk flutter noisily outside my window, which is medallion-shaped, and through which I can see the long, clean, Gothic lines of the Cathedral of St. John with its sharply pitched slate roof. The solid Teutonic form not far from the banks of the Vistula, laid out so stoutly, so trimly, seems a kind of statement that here the West holds, under the sign of the Roman cross.

We meet in front of the concert hall, stride past drunks passed out on the sidewalks or propped up against the walls of the department stores on Marszalkowska Street, and emerge from the alleyways of the old city onto the ramparts of the Barbican. We turn to face the Vistula, looking eastward to the suburb of Praga. Here the Red Army crouched for long indolent weeks while the Nazis mopped up the partisans of the Warsaw uprising before retreating to Berlin. My guide is a historian and the son of a historian. He draws my attention to the domes of a Russian Orthodox church in Praga, and I see their characteristic onion shapes protruding above the banal postwar skyline. "There," he says, "is the frontier of Europe. There is where Asia begins."

"There" is where I come from. A moment earlier, we were colleagues. Now I am an Oriental deportee.

I am at the National Museum again, this time looking at a painting called "View of Ujazdow and Lazienki." There are two focal points of light in this picture. The first is a foregrounded group of Polish gentry astride their horses, looking very much like English gentlemen in plush riding coats with gold braid looping around their shoulders. Even the animals – the horses and hunting dogs – are noble of countenance. In the background, the villa – the dwelling place and property of these gentlemen – glows warmly in its own spotlight. Between these two points of illumination, as though lurking in the shadows of after-thought, is the remainder of the landlords' property: cattle, sheep, a low, dark, windowless, thatched-roof cottage and some peasants. Shreds of clothing, a muscled arm, the white head scarf of a woman like a pale moon faintly reflecting the magnificence of her master's estate. And in the sallow luminescence the face of a young man – his moustache, his forelock – looking out at us as though the picture were about him: his youth, his strength, his audacious dream of liberation.

Into this pastoral in 1648 had come crashing the Ukrainian Cossacks, the spoilers of the wealthy and brilliant Polish community huddled in the "granary of Europe." The Poles never got over it. They had seen the sons of Cossack chieftains come to study in Cracow, take Polish brides, convert. They themselves had taken up land endowments in Zaporoze (now Zaporozhia) on the Dniepr (now Dnipro) bordering on Cossack fortresses. But when those same Cossacks, freebooters at the rim of Europe, rose up in bloody massacre, leading hosts of peasants who cut swathes among the landlords and priests with scythes and sickles, it was as if "Asia" had erupted within Polish order, threatening to overwhelm it. Suddenly, the peaceable Ukrainian serf, tilling the immemorial earth in the repetitive rhythms of the seasons, had become monstrous and unpredictable, no longer the pan's Galician, no longer "ours" but "*theirs*," Mongol progeny stampeding out of war camps and over the parcelled estates, upsetting everything. The Poles were so frightened that, when they had captured the Cossack chiefs and dragged them in chains to the market squares of Cracow and Warsaw and Lwow, they subjected them to the torments of the damned, tortured them hideously and then quartered their corpses and left them putrifying at the city gates. Who then was the Mongol?

The Lost Territories: an equation. On the Polish side, nostalgia, fear and regret. On the Ukrainian side, resentment, bitterness and vengefulness. In Czeslaw Milosz's noval *The Seizure of Power*, I come across a last, lingering whiff of Polish proprietorship. It is 1944. The (pro-Communist) Polish divisions of the Red Army are dragging their mutilated brigades back across the Ukrainian territories towards Poland in the scorched wake of the German retreat. Peter Kwinto, political education officer, and his sidekick, Ivan, an illiterate peasant from the Carpathians, are with them. Together they wander onto the abandoned property of a Polish magnate in Galicia and poke about the silenced, sooty rooms. All of Peter's childhood comes flooding back to him, for it was in such a place that he had grown up: a Polish son-and-heir in the spacious library, leafing through French poetry bound in red chamois and embossed in gold.

On the grounds of the estate, the sweet little straw-thatched cottages of the peasant-labourers, heavy-headed sunflowers and sun-bloated hollyhock up against the white plastered walls, cheeky little girls in bare feet driving the arrogant geese down to the pond. Peter breathes great lungfuls of nostalgia. "My country," he says and looks around with deep pleasure.

But what of Ivan, the illiterate from Carpathia? Ivan, who was born in the straw-thatched cottage and sent to the fields while Peter read Baudelaire and licked lollipops. If all this is "Peter's" country, then where is Ivan's?

When the Soviets occupied eastern Poland, now western Ukraine, in 1939, they required each villager to fill in a form indicating name, age and "nationality." The villagers wrote in "*tuteshni*": from here. Ivan the peasant is a citizen of hereabouts. Is "here" a country?

The Pole belongs to modernity – to the nation-state, to time present. The Ukrainian peasant belongs to "here," to everlasting time. Peter's lost Galician village, Tomasz's lost territories, were a restorative place, a plunge into time-out-of-mind. Is this why the loss has proved so traumatic? With the disappearance of Galicia into a modern Ukrainian state, the Pole has nowhere to escape to from his own unbearable history. He's trapped there. The Galician has more important things to do now than to lure the Pole back to his innocence.

I stand by Father Jerzy's grave, deeply moved, yet miserable. I am thinking too of the Ukrainian dead, the names of the numberless written on water and wind, the memorials never erected, or erected and cast down, the mourners unassembled, the stories dribbling away in privacy and whispers. Here am I, descendant of the Galician anonymous, at St. Stanislaw Kostka with nowhere to lay my wreath except over the bones of a Polish priest. It is as good a place as I will find.

UKRAINE

1939-1945: *incorporation of lands of western Ukraine (formerly in Poland, Czechoslovakia and Rumania) into Ukrainian* s.s.r. **1946-50:** *economic reconstruction under Five Year Plan; liquidation of Greek Catholic Church and Ukrainian Insurgent Army in western Ukraine; ideological campaign against "bourgeois nationalism"* **1953:** *death of Stalin* **1956:** *First Secretary of the Communist Party of the Soviet Union (*cpsu*), Nikita Khrushchev, denounces crimes of Stalin at Party Congress* **1956-64:** *thaw in cultural life and in the workplace, partial re-Ukrainization of intellectual life, discontinuation of terror, emergence of rebellious voices – the "sixties people" – at universities and in literary circles* **1965:** *trials of dissidents in western Ukraine* **1972:** *massive "pogrom" of intellectuals protesting Russification* **1975:** *formation of Ukrainian Helsinki Monitoring Group of human rights activists* **1975-85:** *imprisonment and sometimes death of dissidents in labour camps* **1986:** *Mikhail Gorbachev, First Secretary of the* cpsu, *institutes* glasnost *or "openness" policy* **1986:** *explosion of nuclear reactor in Chernobyl* **1989:** *founding congress of democratic opposition group Rukh* **1990:** *pro-democracy student hunger strikes and miners' demonstrations* **1991:** *failed* putsch *in Moscow; declaration of Ukrainian independence; illegalization of Communist Party; demolition of Lenin monuments; election of ex-Communist Leonid Kravchuk to presidency* **1992:** *introduction of "coupon" currency and price rises; indecisiveness regarding economic reforms; student hunger strikers call for parliamentary elections* **1993:** *parliamentary deadlock; introduction of limited privatization of state properties; alarming inflation; unresolved disputes with Russia concerning disposition of Black Sea fleet and ultimate status of Crimea; continuing construction of an independent state*

I

HOW DO YOU GO BACK TO WHERE YOU'VE NEVER BEEN?

CHERNIVTSI, 1984: I have been sitting in the hotel, waiting for my relatives. I am almost hoping they won't show up. Perhaps they aren't coming? Have had an accident? Changed their minds?

The hotel's forecourt is filling with clusters of families, Ukrainians and North Americans, visiting. They're all standing in various uneasy postures. In spite of the fact that for years this hotel has been the only "official" place that families may have their reunions, the villages being closed to foreigners, hotel management has provided few benches to sit on, no outdoor café, no privacy. So everyone is standing in bunches, chatting and weeping.

The westerners wear pastel-coloured, summery togs and designer sunglasses, and their children, who do not speak Ukrainian, hang back from the group signalling exaggerated boredom. The Ukrainians do most of the talking, and weeping, and huddle close together, all generations with shopping bags at their feet. From their villages they have brought flowers, bags of walnuts and dried mushrooms, and factory-embroidered blouses, tablecloths and table runners in crinkly cellophane wrapping – all of which will be handed over to the visitors and, on the last night in Ukraine, "forgotten" in the hotel room. The old women wear heavy floral kerchiefs tied in big knots under the chin, and they stand on thick-stockinged legs with their hands clasped behind their backs. The young women are bare-headed; their arms are crossed over their chests, holding closed the flimsy sweaters pulled over their dresses. The men, young and old, are in suits. They smoke and shuffle their feet.

How are we going to communicate? My relatives and I have nothing in common – least of all language – except that my grandmother and their grandfather were sister and brother. Baba got away. End of shared history. That was two generations ago. Even my own mother hasn't made the trip.

Family groups in the lobby, showing photographs. Ukrainian spoken with broad Canadian accents. Hotel staff watching with unconcealed petulance. I step out the front doors. Pavlina, yelling out my name, falls upon my neck. For a few months twenty years ago we exchanged letters. Ten years my junior, she is my second cousin. We wrote in Russian. The correspondence dribbled out, but news would still come from the family. Now Pavlina introduces me to her mother, sister, husband, brother and sister-in-law, all of whom have been standing back but now rush at me, pressing carnations into my hands and kissing me noisily on the cheek. I am overcome by their excitement, their tears, their fingers running in rough caresses over my arms and shoulders. They are familiar from their photographs, but I am thinking, Who are these people? We assemble for photographs on the hotel lawn and everyone is suddenly serious. When I look at these pictures back in Canada, I see that my relatives look well and relaxed, the women in cotton dresses and nylon stockings, the men in suits and white shirts. Only Katrusia, the matriarch, gives the scene away: she wears an embroidered blouse and a thick kerchief and looks wizened and worn out, my image of all Ukrainian women from the village since we received the very first photograph after the war. I have many relatives. These are the Ukrainian ones.

KIEV, 1984: It is about twenty minutes into the concert that the crone, stooped and dishevelled, makes her appearance at the concert hall's side entrance. She has shuffled into the open doorway, thick, dun-coloured stockings wrinkled loosely around her legs and her feet lost in old, too-large shoes. She wears a thin black coat and carries a cloth bag, and the way she is pitched forward with her arms clasped behind her back as though to ease a pain at the base of her slanting spine reminds me violently of my grandmother. (Just so Baba would stand, patient and meditative, at a bus stop in east-end Edmonton.)

The crone peers in to have a look, framed from behind by a cascade of flowering branches on a chestnut tree, staring with inexpressive concentration at the soprano – a fleshy woman wrapped in red flounces, her frizzy coiffure pinned down by a rhinestone diadem – singing Schubert. And then she turns away, in no great hurry but with deliberation, and leaves us, as though to say, with her broken back, that she knows her place.

She could have been my grandmother, had Baba not escaped the Sturm und Drang of revolution and the terrible violence done in her name. That hot wind rushed over the countryside and into the cities, leaving the old women much as it had found them: ankle-deep in the mud of the beet fields, stooped over the everlasting weeds. Seventy years into the revolution, they are still there.

Within hours of arrival in Ukraine, I am in a rage that will grow only richer and more textured as I travel around on the well-beaten Ukrainian-Canadian tourist circuit: Kiev (the capital city), Odessa (the Black Sea), Chernivtsi (closest open city to relatives' closed villages) and Lviv (major city of western Ukraine, region of principal emigration to Canada). I cannot say I have come unprepared: an upbringing in an East European ethnic community during the Cold War has impressed upon me the catastrophe that Soviet Communism has been for the Ukrainian nation. In my adolescence, I succumbed to the romance of the victorious proletariat that included Ukraine in the great sweep of revolution, but that exciting scenario has long since buckled under the weight of the sordid postwar reality of life in the Soviet bloc. Its features – economic wreckage, social inertia, aesthetic vulgarity and administrative cruelty – are notorious, and they have kept me for years from considering a visit to Ukraine, my grandparents' homeland.

Nevertheless, the rage overwhelms me as this reality unfolds in myriad manifestations. Downtown Kiev – bombed to smithereens – has been rebuilt in grossest Stalinist bravura. Only the flaring greenery of the chestnut trees on the main avenues, their white blossoming cones releasing an exquisite perfume on the late evening air of June, softens the brutalist perspective. The crowds shuffle about in ill-fitting jeans, cheap sweaters and appalling footwear, clunky and painful, to judge from the lurching gait of the women carrying shopping bags in the ever-hopeful expectation of coming upon something rare and wonderful in the shops. (New cucumbers? Baby clothes? Ukrainian poetry?) That some shoppers parade proudly with plastic bags displaying the company logos of Safeway and Eaton's and others flaunt the price tags still dangling from their western-made sunglasses and jewellery does nothing to dispel the visual insipidity.

I am not surprised to see the food queues, but I am stricken by the livid exhaustion on the women's faces and their stolid patience as they stand like mendicants in the line-ups at the bins of turnips and onions and the trays of fatback in the so-called meat shops. The land is broad and generous; why are people lining up for bad food? I am shocked by the beggars – palsied crones wrapped in bits of old coat – at church doors, the amputees and cripples on crutches, the legless man pushing himself along on a little trolley like a skateboard, his hands scraping the sputum-spattered pavement as he careers through the crowd. Even the most jaundiced western view of Soviet Communism concedes that the Party spread a wide social welfare net; why are people begging?

I rage against the obligatory first-class prices for second- and third-class service and facilities. In one hotel, no water for thirty-six hours. No toilet paper. No street maps. Exchange bureaus in the hotels that refuse to change currency from the fraternal socialist countries. Lifts out of operation. Slatternly service in the hotel restaurants: "Could we have soup?" "No soup." "But they're eating some over there!" Shrug ... And so on. The inconvenience to oneself is bad enough. But the certain knowledge that, if coveted western tourists are being treated with such insouciance, then Soviet citizens must be the objects of real contempt, drives me mad. Soviets take lunch in (very cheap) cafeterias, helping themselves to shreds of salad, bits of herring, watery bowls of dumplings, under the grim supervision of serving women dressed in white smocks like hygiene staff. They eat with gnarled tin cutlery while seated at wobbly furniture, chewing and swallowing quickly, faces close to their plates, as if they have only recently begun to eat their fill.

Come evening, we are deeply discouraged by the effort to find a bar, a café, somewhere pleasant to while away a couple of hours. By seven o'clock the few such establishments have filled up and even the usually efficacious "Please, we have guests from Canada!" cannot get us past the obdurate, bull-chested doorman at the Komsomol Youth Club (reputed to have the best ice cream in Ukraine). The alternative, then, to a brassy, smoky, boozy evening in the Intourist hotel restaurant, high-stepping it with Soviets in the fast lane, is to join the crowds milling about in the streets, sitting on park benches, street curbs, staircases, guardrails, in the passageways of the pedestrian underground. *This* is Kiev at leisure.

I do not complain in the company of Ukrainians. I am, after all, travelling, a feat in itself. A local schoolteacher, wishing to travel on a group excursion to Bulgaria, had first to secure authorization from three levels of authority at her place of work and to pass an interrogation. ("How many extra hours of work did you volunteer last month? Why did you drop out of Komsomol?") She lost her place on the waiting list to a colleague who had not dropped out of Komsomol.

Peace! Labour! Friendship! The flattened banality of the messages, the ceaseless inspirationalism of the gesturing Lenins, the exaggerated Aryan features of the New Soviet Man (like a Silver Surfer of the socialist cosmos) do not so much enrage as stupefy me; when "Fulfil the Ideas of the Great Lenin!" flashes on the electronic scoreboard at the soccer game, spectators take no notice of this "white noise," just as we in the West have stopped reading billboards in our arenas. But every trip to the newspaper kiosk and bookshop dispirits me utterly: the palpable insincerity of the language and the monotony of the predictable catch phrases represent to me a death by boredom. Imagine the reader for whom they are inescapable! In a nation of some fifty million, Ukrainian-language literature is available in editions of fifteen thousand or less. They sell out within hours and are never reprinted.

It seems that every public facility is pedagogical: the churches converted to showcases of local manufactured goods or to Museums of Atheism, visitors transfixed by the icons, the chasubles, the crucifixes – artifacts of a lost civilization – and the overwrought painting on the diorama depicting the torture of a victim of the Inquisition, hooded friars gloating at the torments of the sunken-chested heretic whose feet are being slowly roasted over a brazier of burning coals. A group of teenagers stands in silent meditation before the painting: what is the hidden message? Just so had people suffered in the cells of the prisons of the KGB?

Much is made of the opera houses, the symphony halls, the theatres named for famous (progressive) writers, as though whole generations of Soviet Ukrainians, having trooped through en masse for doses of Art, have at last left the village and entered European culture. Yet a friend tells me that, after seventy such pedagogical years, the system still can't fill a hall in the provinces for a concert by a touring opera company. On the other hand, I want to know, what does stuffing conductors into tuxedos and sopranos into ballgowns in order to mount Italian melodramas have to do with the achievements of socialism? The last time socialism experimented with art forms, dared to be modern, was in the years immediately following the Bolshevik Revolution of 1917. The artists and theoreticians of that experiment in Ukraine are now called the Executed Generation: they died in firing squads or in labour gangs, and their works have disappeared. Those artists whose reputations have survived are perforce linked with so-called internationalist traditions. This is especially striking in the museums dedicated to writers; catalogues invoke the Russian shades of Maxim Gorky and Nikolai Chernyshevsky, as if to demonstrate that the Ukrainian writer in question, far from being motivated by "narrow" national feelings, was an admirer of the Russian culture and promoted fraternization with it. The museums are admirable; the sycophantic notes make me grind my teeth.

One late evening, standing at a suburban tram stop, my companion and I are approached by two young men who have heard us speaking in a foreign language. Are we Ukrainians from abroad? What have our parents told us about Ukraine – that it is a "lost cause," its national identity and fate swallowed up in the Muscovite maw? Well, they are here to tell us it isn't true. The message is: Ukraine will yet be reborn. I am glad to hear they think so.

Among some western travellers to Ukraine it is a matter of principle not to sink into paranoia: by fearfully avoiding contacts with the local population you serve the system's purposes. Yet we are aware at all times that the smooth operations of Intourist and the Ukraine Friendship Society – the cab at the train station, the tickets for the opera, the interview at the Writers' Union – facilitate their surveillance of us. Our guides are also our "minders." We know that the woman at the desk on each floor of the hotel is there to keep track of the guests' comings and goings, the doorman is placed to prevent local citizens from entering, the cabbies waiting helpfully out front are informers for the KGB. We know when we are being followed as they always send the same type out after us – men in their thirties wearing stiff, belted black-leather jackets – and we know that there are "bugs" in the lamp fixtures in the hotel room. We do not use the hotel telephone and then fret that we are being observed using the public phone in the street. (What are we trying to hide?)

Local citizens move away from us when we sit down at their table in a crowded café. An art restorer from Latvia blurts out that, while the U.S.S.R. is "sick," "Latvian nationalism is alive and well," then flees, abandoning his torte on our table. Conversations take place in parks, eyes flitting in a ceaseless sweep of the vicinity.

To visit Jaroslav in Lviv we travel under cover of night: he lost his teaching job in the repressions of 1972 and is supporting himself by writing articles for publication in Ukrainian journals abroad. He would suffer the repercussions of our visit. I am so rattled by this pervading sense of being watched that I wait until I am in Poland to write up the notes of the entire Ukrainian visit. It is a measure of the stifling, breathless atmosphere of Ukraine that Poland, a mere year after the lifting of martial law, seems unexceptional.

In retrospect, though, I was to wonder at the inflexibility of my rage. Why was I not nearly so offended by the Stalinist features of rebuilt Warsaw, say, or the sullen brow-beatenness of the citizens of Prague, or the dilatory ways of business in Belgrade? I was to forgive and overlook much in those other capitals, but in Ukraine, in 1984, I overlook and forgive nothing. What is this double standard of evaluation and emotion?

Quite simply, for a Ukrainian Canadian Ukraine is not a country like other countries. Everything about it is "loaded," freighted with meaning. Kiev is not just a capital city; it is the mother lode of Rus, the mediaeval kingdom on the territory of future Ukraine. The Dnipro River is more than a major artery; it is the fecundating waters of Cossack settlements and steppelands ("free" Ukraine), and poets have addressed it for generations, in apostrophes of yearning and sorrow, epitomized by the poetic "Last Will and Testament" of Taras Shevchenko, the national Romantic poet who is buried on its bank. A baroque church is a reminder that the Ukrainian church has been driven underground or co-opted by the official Russian Orthodox Church: who then is to keep the faith? Folk songs at weddings in Soviet restaurants are subversive manifestations of the indomitable spirit of the narod, the people. The verdant, rolling countryside of my grandparents' home villages is a veritable boneyard of the victims of peasant wars, occupations, famines; this is why we kneel and kiss it. And so on.

Because Ukraine has for so many hundreds of years been subsumed within empires and other nations, the modest features of the modern community's cityscapes, topography, ritual and speech are forced to bear the entire weight of Ukrainian identity and purpose that normally would be borne by the apparatus of an independent state. For the visiting Ukrainian Canadian, then, the environment as a whole functions to remind her that Ukraine is not merely *interesting*: it is a disclosure of the meaning of Ukrainian history, whether in its eastern half, dominated by Kiev, city of Orthodox princes and Cossack chieftains and Russian hegemony, or in its western half, dominated by Lviv, Greek-Catholic and Polonized, home once of an awakening nationalist intelligentsia and the anti-Soviet "bandits" of the Second World War.

There was never a time that I did not know Ukraine was a special place, raised above the other nations by dint of its tragic history and its disappearance as a state. This often made me squirm (what had this to do with me?) and I understood it only sketchily, but this much was clear. Surrounded by neighbours who had always preyed on it – the open steppes defenceless against marauders from all directions – ground down by serfdom, poverty and the collective farm, threatened by overlords, landowners, czars and policemen who decreed that the people would not lift up their heads, abandoned by the fainthearted and the too-early deaths of poets, Ukraine had nevertheless managed to remember itself. It had survived the depredations of history to return again and again from the margins of oblivion and call itself Ukraina.

The suffocating realization in 1984 is that this identity is in deep peril. Ukraine is disappearing again, its citizens separated from each other and speaking in foreign tongues, its dissidents wasting away in the gulag and traduced by the political class. On the lands of Ukraine, I cannot walk lightly.

LAST WILL AND TESTAMENT

KIEV, 1984: Taras Shevchenko, nineteenth-century poet of humble origins and tragic life, has become a patron saint. Besides the monuments and namesake street and theatre and eponymous state prizes, Kiev has named an entire university after him. It is painted red. Perhaps it has always been painted red (it was founded in 1834) but I think of it as symbolic. For this most "national" of poets – chronicler of village life, peasant revolt, the Cossacks and national oppression, and exemplar of a literary Ukrainian language – has been appropriated by the Soviet state.

The visit to his grave at Kaniv, outside of Kiev on the Dnipro shore, is virtually obligatory. Intourist will arrange it quite happily. Unlike the clandestine visit to more subversive sites (graves of poets dead under mysterious circumstances), the excursion to Kaniv is positively touristic. One can take a boat down the river or motor through the bucolic countryside. The objective is the grave site. Once a simple wooden cross implanted near a burial mound, it is now a statue atop an impressive granite plinth reached by a flight of steps cut into the mound. There are always visitors and an accumulating pile of bouquets of flowers laid directly on the slab covering his remains. Inscribed on this slab are words from his most famous poem, "Testament": "And in that great family, in that free and new family, do not forget to remember me, with a kind and quiet word." This is the clue to the appropriation: in his radical and passionate advocacy of a Ukraine freed from social injustice and tyrants, he can quite easily be "de-nationalized" and incorporated into the pantheon of international freedom fighters. (He even wrote a poem about Jan Hus, the martyred freethinker of mediaeval Bohemia.)

This takes some getting used to: Taras Shevchenko as People's Poet. I buy a souvenir book. It talks of the great Bard and the " 'great new family, the family of the free' in which all the peoples of our multinational country have found their happy life." It's all lies, of course, both the sentiment and the pretension that Shevchenko would agree. Being a Ukrainian Canadian, I'm a few steps ahead. I know, from having heard about it all my life, that Taras Shevchenko was a Ukrainian patriot who hated Russian tyranny. "Murderers! Murderers! Cannibals!"

We agree, then, my Intourist minder and I: Shevchenko was a revolutionary.

He was born in 1814 to Ukrainian serfs Hryhorii and Kateryna Shevchenko in the central Ukrainian village of Moryntsi and was attached, with them, to the property of the Russian magnate Vasilii Engelhardt. In this district alone, Engelhardt owned a whole town, twelve villages and 8500 "souls" who were landless and compelled to labour without pay. Being a wheelwright, Hryhorii could keep his family from death's door. More than that he could not provide.

In 1831, Taras was apprenticed to a mural painter and discovered the pleasures of his own craftsmanship. Along with the servants and the baggage, he was transferred one summer to St. Petersburg in the household of his owner. He would wander through the Summer Gardens and sketch at the end of a work day. And here he was noticed by his countryman, the painter Soshenko, who introduced him to his friends at the Academy of Fine Arts.

It was decided Taras should study at the academy but since, as a serf, he could not, he first had to be freed. Engelhardt named his price: 2500 rubles. A portrait by the celebrated academician Karl Briullov was raffled, and on April 22, 1838, at the age of twenty-four, Taras Shevchenko was handed the papers that delivered him from bondage and into his life as an artist and poet. Two years later, he published *Kobzar* (*Bard*), the collection of poems that made him a household word, both in the salons of the progressive Russian critics and in the reading rooms of Ukrainian villages. When Ukrainians moved to Canada, they took along their family copy.

It is said of some antique and fabled civilization that it blinded nightingales to make them sing more sweetly. Just so the kobzars, *men blinded by the untended wounds of warfare, wandered the roads of the Ukrainian countryside, begging for alms in the villages where they sang, to the accompaniment of the lute-like* kobza, *hymns, ancient ballads of Cossack exploits, lyrics of love and yearning, and ribald improvisations: the people's collective memory on the tip of their tongue.*

His story goes on and is full of incident, but it is in the opening narrative of his childhood – the curse that lay within the heart of the squat, white-washed cottages nestled among the fruit trees, the despair resonating behind the bleating sheep and the buzzing bees in the clover – that the peculiar meaning of his life resides: the most-loved hero of the Ukrainian people was a self-taught poet who grew up the property of another man. "I dread remembering / the small cottage at the end of the village." It is not warrior heroes who give comfort to the Ukrainian soul but the notion of the simple man, the soil of his village still on his boots, who dies broken on the wheel of his own rhymed, avenging love.

In 1847, nine years into his freedom, Shevchenko was arrested in Kiev for his membership in a secret society known as the Brotherhood of Saints Cyril and Methodius, the "first Ukrainian ideological organization in modern times," according to the historian Orest Subtelny. For the crime of having attended, for fourteen months, clandestine meetings where philosophy and politics were discussed and serfdom denounced, he was found guilty. Because he wrote unflattering and caustic descriptions of the czars Peter and Catherine, he was given a particularly harsh sentence: ten years in a labour battalion in Central Asia.

This next part is notorious: how the autocrat Nicholas I personally scrawled an addendum to the sentence papers: "Under the strictest supervision, forbidden to write and sketch." After his release, Taras went to Russia. Broken, he sickened and died four years later, on March 10, 1861, exactly a week after Czar Alexander II signed the emancipation manifesto releasing the serfs from serfdom. The "old man" was forty-seven years old.

The czars feared Taras as a "democrat," the Soviets revered him as a "People's Poet" and Ukrainian youth read him for evidence of his subversive "patriotism."

"And why," asked the KGB captain of political prisoner Danylo Shumuk in KGB prison in Lutsk in 1958, "why did you underline the title of this poem, 'The Desecrated Grave,' in Shevchenko's *Kobzar* and underline every word of [certain] passages?"

Dnipro, my brother river, is drying up, me they forsake; and my beloved Cossack graves the Muscovite desecrates.

One hundred years after Taras's coffin came to Kiev on May 22, 1861, students and young people began the annual ritual of meeting at his monument near the university in Kiev to recite his poems and sing national songs. It was important – it was the whole point – to be there at his feet: "See how we remember where and from whom we come? See how we grow?" Bearing such witness led to jail. Nineteen sixty-seven saw the last official ceremonies for twenty-one years.

Taras is a young man. He doesn't have whiskers yet. He holds a candle up in front of the mirror and paints his self-portrait. I find it in a book of his paintings in my parents' library. He has the round moonlike face of the Ukrainian peasant and brownish circles around his deepset eyes that I associate with the torments of the poetic soul. I know he's the Poet, although I have never read his poems.

As I stroll through the small park surrounding the Shevchenko grave, little loudspeakers hanging up in the trees suddenly sputter into life and the stentorian cadences of an orchestra and choir blast full tilt from the greenery. Startled and annoyed, it takes me a few moments to realize that the entertainment is that universal hymn of Ukrainian communities around the world – "Testament" set to music – which, even when I was a little girl, broke my heart with its mournful melancholy. I only knew the first couple of lines to the verse but I *knew* the poem was about some great loneliness at the borders of the void, about an unforgiving soul dying exhausted. For the first time in my life, I wish I had learned to read Taras in his native tongue.

> When I die, then bury me
> in a grave on the wide, wide steppe,

in my beloved Ukraine
so that I can see, so that I can hear
the boundless fields and the Dnipro,
and the slopes,
and how the river roars.

This is the least I can do, this remembrance from the diaspora. And to be thankful that he lived while the Dnipro still did sweep down to the Black Sea over the rock beds of river rapids, before the dams went up and the river fell idle, and while the trackless fields still fed his people, before the commissars came and took the wheat away.

The poet's hands are empty. He is sketching in the sand with his finger, tracing the lines that rhyme before the steppe wind blows in and the dust of the prison camp covers his alphabet.

SPEAK WHITE!

KIEV, 1984: I stand on a street corner near a group of schoolchildren and listen to them speaking with each other in Russian. A battered delivery truck canters through the intersection, bearing the utilitarian inscription "KHLEB." Russian for bread. In Ukraine, legendary bread basket for eastern Europe, mythologized and memorialized as the Earth Mother cradling a sheaf of wheat in her round, stout arms, as the three-layered and crusty, coiled *kalach*, they eat bread in Russian.

A Kievan, addressed in Ukrainian, will answer in Russian. Backstage after their concert of Ukrainian folk songs, members of the Bukovynska Ensemble speak to each other in Russian. A cultural program by members of a music and drama theatre includes arias from the folk operetta "Natalka Poltavka" and, as if to give it ideological balance, a long monologue from Gogol's *Taras Bulba* evoking the "mighty Russian czar." I have been told that in eastern Ukraine Ukrainian-language schools in the villages are being closed down.

The Ukrainian language, as if by some scientific, philological law, is petering out. Russian, on the other hand, belongs to the ages.

The archdeacon of Aleppo, Paul, travelling in Ukraine in 1652, recorded his observation that almost every man and woman he encountered could read. In 1804, though, an imperial decree forbade all instruction in Ukrainian. By 1867, a census revealed that Ukrainians were the most illiterate people in the European Russian empire.

On May 30, 1876, Czar Alexander II prohibited the publication in Ukrainian of any original works or translations, the staging of plays in the Ukrainian language and the printing of Ukrainian lyrics to musical compositions. By the time of the Bolshevik Revolution in 1917, not a single Ukrainian language school was in existence and the peasants of Poltava thought so poorly of their own language that they considered it a sacrilege to have the Bible read in it.

Earlier, in Austrian-ruled Galicia, Jacob Holovatsky, philologist at the University of Lviv, had described his Galician counterparts in the Austro-Hungarian empire as "a dispirited and fractured nation ... a people without rights, without education, without schools." Anguished by this dismal social and moral topography, Galician deputies to the Austrian parliament had agitated in 1848 for the opening of public schools in the villages so that "persons of the lower estate can leave the darkness for the light."

From 1963 to 1968, I studied Russian language and literature as my major subject at the university. As I had earlier come to love the language of John Keats and then Arthur Rimbaud, I began to love the language of Alexander Pushkin. I learned whole poems by heart. *Ia vas liubil, liubov eshcho byt mozhet, V dushe moei ugasla ne sovsem.* I rolled the words around in my mouth like fruity lozenges, sucking out their hard sibilants, their throaty linguals, as though wooing the poet myself with my flickering tongue. "I loved you, and love, perhaps, still flares in my soul."

The Russian language had been presented to me, studying at Canadian and American universities in the sixties, as a world language: millions of people in an important country – "Russia" – spoke it. To those of us studying in literature faculties it signified the language of a world literature: major, canonical, essential. Every literate person in the world knew the country's writers. As my thesis topic I chose, unsurprisingly, Dostoevsky.

Screened from us, however, was the official Soviet state attitude to the Russian language. Because of the undeniable historical fact that the Bolshevik revolutionaries had spoken Russian to each other, the Russian language was deemed more "democratic" than other languages. It was not enough that this conclusion be merely "rational"; it had to be seen as irresistible. The non-Russian citizen was exhorted to learn Russian out of "love" and "obligation" to the Soviet motherland and by this means to gain access to the works of the titans, the patriarchs, the guardians of the revolution that had liberated them all, from the Black Sea to the Bering Straits.

Anais B., writing in L'Alternative *in April 1984: "The linguistic situation in the U.S.S.R. is deemed to be the model of what the Communist society, realized on earth, will be: a fusion, a total symbiosis of beings in a society where people, like angels, will be in perfect communication, that is, interchangeable, transparent to each other, the same.... The curse of Babel will be cancelled."*

A Ukrainian journalist went to visit a small town on the eastern bank of the lower Dnipro, Hola Prystian. Having had a disagreeable interview with the town authorities about the lack of Ukrainian-language signs in the town's public places, he went walking moodily about the streets and came across a brand-new house decorated with Scythian motifs.

Intrigued, he looked more closely at all the houses in the street and saw that each bore a masterfully carved *konyk* (a carving of a little horse at the peak of the roof's gable), a symbol which had, for a millennium, signified the past military feats of mediaeval Rus. One house even bore, at the peak of the roof, a coat of arms such as could be found on the coins minted in the time of Iaroslav the Wise. The journalist learned that a certain carpenter, Vasyl Ivanovych Veselovsky, had crafted them all.

Journalist: "So, you make these *konyky*?"

Vasyl: "What konyky?"

Journalist (switching to Russian): "Well, the *koniok*."

Vasyl: "What koniok?"

(The journalist points to the roof of a house.)

Vasyl: "Oh, that. You mean the *vershylo*."

Vershylo is an ancient Kievan word. It cannot be found in the eleven-volume (Soviet) *Dictionary of the Ukrainian Language*. But Vasyl Ivanovych knows it.

A cold hard rain has been driving down all day from the steely sky and I come back to the hotel room wet, cold and disconsolate. The whole day has been spent in a vain effort to contact a friend of a friend by telephone from public kiosks: broken connections, wrong numbers. I am scared to use the telephone in my room, telephone directories are classified literature and a taxi driver would take note of the address I gave him. I curse this society that won't allow me to meet the friend of a friend.

I turn to the television set, a bulky console on a table by the window where thin white curtains barely screen from view the sheets of rainwater falling into the mucky, rubbishy courtyard. The set is turned on to the so-called Ukrainian channel (the other two broadcast from Moscow). A children's program. A cartoon, of cuddly bears and fuzzy-wuzzy ducks and tiny, squeaky kiddies. In Russian.

And suddenly I can't bear it, the Russian language vibrating in my skull in sonorous clarity, choleric, harsh and disciplinary. I turn off the television with a savage yank at the cord and turn on the radio. A concert program. A Ukrainian baritone singing, with exquisite diction, a song by Glinka set to a poem by Pushkin. *"Ia vas liubil, liubov eshcho byt mozhet ..."* Am I now to hate Pushkin too?

CHERVONA RUTA

Once upon a time in Arcadia a youth and a maid fell in love and so extravagant was their joy that all the fields and forests burst into bloom as if to rejoice with them. Unfortunately, the girl's beauty reawakened long-forgotten desire in the breast of an elderly forest god. Day and night he wooed her with flattering words but she was unmoved and remained faithful to her lover. Enraged by this insult to his dignity as a male god and consumed by jealousy, he tracked the lovers, fell upon them and killed them both.

Miserable wretch! Even though he was a thousand years old, he didn't understand the simplest truth: love is firmer than rock, hotter than fire and stronger than death. The immortal love of the young couple was transformed into two plants: the rue with the yellow blossoms and pungent evergreen leaves, and the silvery ash. Like inseparable siblings, they always grow close to each other, the ash a little taller as though to protect the rue from jealous old men. To show her gratitude and her gladness, every ten years the rue bears a red blossom for the delectation of her companion. Happy the young girl who finds the blossom at the moment of its miraculous red flowering! She and her beloved will be happy forever, never knowing the bitterness of parting nor the wound of betrayal.

In 1966, when the young musician from Chernivtsi, Volodymyr Ivasiuk, was seventeen years old, he came upon the legend of the red rue (*chervona ruta*) in a collection of Ukrainian folklore assembled in 1906 by the celebrated ethnographer Volodymyr Hnatiuk. It was in several ways a fateful find. The legend became Ivasiuk's obsession. "That flower gave him no peace," his father wrote later in an article about his son's life. For three years, Volodia went tramping through Carpathian villages, recording variations of the story until, finally, one moonlit night (so his friends would relate), strolling distractedly outdoors, he caught the strains of a village girl's song:

> Red red rue
> Why have you blossomed?
> Young maiden,
> Why do you weep?

It was the Hutzul version: the girl who plucks the red flower under a full moon wields powerful magic.

> She gathered up the petals,
> The red red rue,
> For to bewitch me,
> A poor orphan boy.

Back home, in collaboration with his own instrumental group Bukovyna, Volodia penned a song inspired by his find and called it "Red Rue" to underscore the point.

> Perhaps somewhere in the woods
> You searched for the enchanted bush.
> You found the flame-coloured flower
> And then you enchanted me.

Recorded, it became phenomenally successful, a hit throughout the

Soviet Union, an astonishing accomplishment for a pop song in the Ukrainian language and for a young musician who had been paying his dues, along with his band, at the regional youth centre, at Komsomol gatherings and at a concert on the occasion of the Twenty-fifth Anniversary of the Reunification of Northern Bukovyna.

His genius and passion unleashed, Ivasiuk composed song after song – popular music rooted in folklore and folk melodies – that entered the musical lexicon of his generation. In 1973, he paid his debt to the man who had inspired him by visiting the grave of Volodymyr Hnatiuk in Lviv's Lychakivsky cemetery. He laid flowers there and had his photo taken. It is an "eloquent photodocument from his archives," his father wrote, for only six years later Volodia would be buried there himself. Fifteen thousand people would attend his funeral.

I heard about his death even before I had heard his music, fragmented accounts circulating in Edmonton of a portentous summons from the authorities, a black automobile pulling up to his house, a drive to the woods. It was Easter Monday, 1979, and he was never seen alive again. It took two weeks to find him, hanging bruised and lacerated from a tree within the boundaries of a closed military zone. The KGB investigated and determined it was a suicide. But no one in Edmonton believed that. We had heard another version of Volodia's death from a clandestine journal edited in Edmonton and Toronto. In Ukraine I heard this version again. People spoke of his eyes having been gouged out – or was it his tongue? – of his broken fingers and of a sharpened stake from a cranberry bush driven between his ribs. The implication was obvious: how was it possible that Volodymyr Ivasiuk, thirty years old and at the height of his powers, would take his own life? This was clearly a murder at the hands of the KGB, who could not tolerate his ideological heresy: at a time of the official "merging" of the nations of the U.S.S.R. into a single, Soviet identity, Ivasiuk had become famous and loved *in Ukrainian*.

LVIV, 1984: Typical of European cemeteries, Lychakivsky is a very pleasant place for a stroll, away from the fumes and clattering traffic of the city centre, under the old and heavy-limbed trees, along pathways marked by mouldering tombstones of now obscure notables and the occasional monument, heaped with bouquets and strung with banners, to Communist celebrities. There is no reason not to be making this touristic stroll and yet I feel furtive, for we've come to see Ivasiuk's grave. There is no tombstone, just a plate nailed to a tree (as if an official monument would be too hypocritical, even for the KGB), but his mound is a veritable garden of grasses and a grotto for the jars of fresh blossoms and the flickering beeswax candles. Someone has been here, to light the candles, but this afternoon we are the only visitors.

In a Lviv bookstore I buy his collected lyrics in a handsome edition and then worry about hiding it when we cross the Ukraine/Poland border. And then remember this will not be necessary. Ivasiuk was a *suicide*; the authorities have never deviated from this explanation of his death, and his official reputation remains intact. His records are for sale and his lyrics belong to the light of day. Still, it is the oddest thing: if *I* am aware of the rumours concerning how Ivasiuk really died, then surely the Soviet authorities know he is regarded as a martyred son of the Bukovynian soil? Even his associates hint at it. "The most dangerous human loss," I read in a tribute to Ivasiuk, "is the loss of grief for the vanished ones," suggesting delicately that, denied the true story of Ivasiuk's death, his public also has been denied the expression of their real sorrow. In Ukraine as in Edmonton, it is as if the lovers of the Ukrainian soul need this young man to have been murdered as the correlative of their bereavement. He needs to have been snatched from them, not delivered to silence by his own careless hand.

KIEV, 1984: One evening a group of us, four Ukrainian-Canadian tourists, find a table at a restaurant where we can dance. The place is very crowded and noisy and no one is taking much notice of us, which is why we are all startled when a young man comes right up to us and asks George if he can dance with his wife. There is some good-natured teasing about "women's rights" in the West – "Don't ask me, ask *her*!" – before Helen and the young man go sailing off in a waltz. After one dance he's back at our table, introducing himself, "I'm an electrician. I have my own flat!" He orders a bottle of vodka. "I was raised in Kiev. But I know things." He dances, he flits about, he's back at the table. He drops his voice. "I know about the famine." He's more comfortable speaking Russian than Ukrainian. In Russian he tells us that "thugs" run his society, "terrorizing" people, but he doesn't "give a shit" about them. We don't want to encourage him – he could be a provocateur – but we are all ears. He wants to know about Ukrainian-Canadian organizations and we tell him, sotto voce. He hails friends, bums cigarettes. Before he leaves us, he leans forward into our circle and whispers at my ear: "I know who killed Ivasiuk."

BLANK SPOTS

LVIV, 1984: The headquarters of the KGB in Lviv and the KGB "isolator" – the special cells for political detainees – are located at Number One Peace Street. We don't see the isolator. We hear about it from our unofficial guide for the day, a small, immensely energetic poet who speaks so fast we are forced to walk tilted in the direction of his mouth if we're to catch what he's saying in the racket of the traffic.

As a child he remembers his neighbours' and parents' satisfaction at the arrival of Soviet troops and a Soviet administration in Lviv in September 1939. They referred to this arrival as "historical justice," the reunification, after so many hundreds of years, of the western and eastern Ukrainian lands. Thanks to the fraternal troops of the Red Army, the Ukrainians of Galicia, so long immured within Poland, were incorporated together with their kin in the Ukrainian Soviet Socialist Republic. They would learn much later that this acquisition of eastern Galicia was part of the deal Stalin had struck with Hitler in the dismemberment of Poland.

Within days, the terror began: arrests and disappearances of local political activists, Communists included. The poet's father, a teacher, burned all his documents and photographs so the NKVD (People's Commission of Internal Affairs) would never be able to reconstruct his biography. Their belongings packed in suitcases, the family waited every night to be arrested. The boy bought a schoolboy's compass so that he and his family would be able to escape from Siberia by road.

In June 1941, the Germans crossed the border from occupied Poland and marched on Lviv. The Ukrainians welcomed them as liberators.

It took the Germans several days to get there. The Soviets retreated in a panic, the first day, leaving their prisoners behind. Then they came back, three days later, to murder them. Fifteen thousand detainees in the cells. The question is: why, when the Soviets had retreated and the Germans had not yet arrived, did no one in the city storm the prison and free those fifteen thousand wretches?

The warden and guards had left, forgetting the ring of keys in their panic; it lay there, tantalizingly, on the warden's desk, out of reach of the prisoners. But a civilian needed only walk through the unguarded gate and past the abandoned sentry posts, snatch up the ring of keys and open the cells. The prisoners waited. Nothing happened. They began to shout, then bang on the bars of their cells. Nothing. It was as though they were the only humans alive in the whole city. They were hungry, their thirst was terrible, their wounds, untended since torture, festered. The first sign of life they detected from the spooked city was the NKVD on their way back into the prison. They knew them from their boots.

Was everyone too frightened those three days to come out of hiding and find out what was going on? Someone who worked there later described "wading" in blood sluicing over the dungeon floors.

When the statue of Lenin in Lviv is taken down and dismantled in September 1990, it will be discovered that its base is made of shattered gravestones from Ukrainian, Jewish and Polish cemeteries. It would have been erected sometime after 1945, when the Red Army returned to western Ukraine, pushing the Germans out and re-establishing Red authority.

And now here are the names again, the dead contributing their vandalized inscriptions to the long roll call of the forgotten, spilling out on the pavement as Lenin is tilted sideways, as though to shake the names out of his pockets. The dead of the isolator on Peace Street were buried in a pit in the courtyard. They had no gravestones. There were no names.

PORTRAIT OF A DROP-OUT

ODESSA, 1984: Seriozha seems too good to be true: a soft leather bomber jacket, long legs in tight blue jeans, a face like Steve McQueen's and English spoken with a lilt picked up from the BBC World Service. He is waiting for us with his friend outside the opera house. We have absolutely no idea if either of them can be trusted, but we agree to go together to our hotel restaurant and have a chat. What the hell. It is his treat. He pays for all the champagne. He is "loaded" with rubles, he says, having just got paid handsomely by the family of an old man he had driven all the way to Ivano-Frankivsk oblast to an old age home. The facilities in western Ukraine are said to be superior. And for the women who are employed in them, he says, it is a blessing to work with bedpans and not on the collective farm, weeding beets. I make a note of his sensitivity.

He is an English-language teacher in a technical institute. He had once been very idealistic about his profession. If a student's work was worth only two out of five, then that was the grade he gave. This soon enough brought him to the attention of the Director. "What are all these twos?" "The work was unsatisfactory." "Well, you can't have taught them very well." The argument went back and forth inconclusively until it dawned on him that the Director *needed* threes and fours to fill his quota; his own standards as a teacher were irrelevant. Worse, they were obstructionist. He returned to his classroom, erased all the twos and made them threes. He had begun the swift slide into professional disillusionment. The students are no better. They memorize everything. Never speak for themselves. He is fed up with them. All year long the lift in the institute has not been working, but when he suggested they all do something about it – stage a sit-in in the lobby, for instance – they were scandalized.

He has a strong sense of belonging to a generation all its own. He had been in the army in 1968, in East Germany, sleeping fully dressed with his boots on because at any moment the Americans, invited in by the Czech counterrevolutionaries and hippies, were going to invade Czechoslovakia. The atmosphere was so tense even he believed the official version. They were on full alert – called up in the middle of the night, piled onto trucks and raced across the countryside, only to be returned to barracks. One morning he noticed fresh bullet holes in the barracks gates, as though someone, on driving past in the middle of the night, had sprayed them with machine-gun fire. But there was never an official explanation, and he wondered if he had had a hallucination.

He drinks without getting drunk. His smile is grudging. He has no compunction about saying the most damnable things in English. Perhaps he has been storing them up? "It's too bad the Soviet Union didn't lose the war," he begins. I hold my breath, waiting for the punch line. "Then the American capitalists would have moved in like they did in West Germany to reconstruct us and build us democratic institutions." He looks fierce and stubborn. I hold my tongue. "Good for Solidarity!" he cries, raising a toast. "They go on strike. They don't work. More power to them."

The next night he invites us all to visit his friend, the squatter. We take the tram and he refuses to pay his fare, arguing that one of the resolutions of the Twenty-Fourth Party Congress had promised free public transport by the 1970s; it is already 1984.

Together with a changing number of friends, the squatter is domiciled in the rooms of what had been the summer house of a Polish aristocrat. After the 1917 revolution, the house had been subdivided into communal flats for five families. The five gas ranges, encrusted with the grease and cinders of a thousand family meals, are still there in the kitchen.

There are almost no furnishings in the rooms, but the toilet works and the power has never been cut. At first our host seems rather gloomy about our presence, but when some friends of his drop by he brightens up. They are two fat blonde sisters, an Uzbek born in Odessa and an off-duty policeman. I briefly imagine a raid, a Black Maria, cold nights incommunicado on a treeless island in the Black Sea. Several bottles of red wine improve the atmosphere considerably. The cassette player is brought in. We dance. Outside the windows a cool thick fog is gathering in swirls from the sea; inside, Polish ghosts slide between us in the embrace of a mazurka. Seriozha is smiling.

On the third and last night in Odessa he invites us to his house. It is a two-room flat he shares with his mother in a very run-down building near the town centre; the toilet, he explains, is that malodorous biffy in the backyard. His mother is asleep. We tip-toe to his room where, in short order, we are served big mugs of tea, radishes, a hunk of bologna and slices of withered torte. He speaks of his mother in respectful tones bordering on the prayerful. She had come to Odessa as a girl to escape the famine ravaging her native province, had never been educated, still worked in her old age at menial labour. Her first husband had been drafted to fight the Finns in 1939 and then deserted the Red Army when Ukraine was overrun by the Germans and returned home to Odessa. He would die as one of the shock troops, barely armed, who were driven ahead of the Red Army to clear minefields behind the retreating Germans in 1944. Her second husband, my friend's father, was a Navy man who deserted his family.

The room holds a large bed, a small table, a short-wave radio and a shelf of books, including some in English. They are what is left of his education. He was never supposed to have been educated. He quit school when he was fifteen and went to work as a fitter's apprentice in a small factory. It was dreary work. He was well on his way to a life as a "hooligan" when he was called up for military service. It saved him from the factory. His language skills were spotted and, upon discharge, he was given the chance to finish high school and train as a teacher of English. The changes in his mentality were merely cosmetic: he had already "snapped" in the army. He refers to political education classes for the new recruits and the poster he stared at in stupefaction day after day, that "empty-eyed, square-jawed hero" with the submachine gun slung across his chest, the defender of the Motherland together with the menacing tanks, rockets, war planes and battleships swarming behind his back, the scene emblazoned with just four words: Party, U.S.S.R., Army, Peace – "in order of precedence." It was this argument, that peace was made through war, that unhinged him.

I look around at the things on his walls: a crucifix, a photograph of John Lennon, a calendar. He leaps up. He has two treasures to show, he says. When, I wonder, has he decided he can trust us? He lifts up the calendar. Taped to the wall behind it hangs the doleful mug of Alexander Solzhenitsyn. He walks to his bed, reaches under the mattress and pulls out a novel by Stephen King. I understand it isn't the novel that is the treasure; it is the means by which it has come to him. Under a mattress in a squalid flat I guess that my friend is hiding a few days of love that had once come his way.

FAMILY REUNION

CHERNIVTSI, 1984: My relatives refuse to come into the hotel restaurant, so we cross the street – Pavlina, Marusia, Katrusia, Maria, Dmytro, Petro and I – and enter a park where we find a picnic table and benches. We sit down. We stare. Dmytro asks the first question: "So, we hear you're a writer. Tell us about yourself." I am tongue-tied. I can feel the electricity discharging uselessly across synapses in my brain in that place where I once spoke Russian and babyish Ukrainian. I manage a kind of pidgin or proto-Slavic speech, and they all bob their heads in vigorous encouragement while I stumble around in search of a vocabulary for book writing, research, travel, impressions of Kiev... We drink beer. I am exhausted. They talk.

I get the drift of it: they are healthy, the children are doing well in school, Marusia's husband, Vasyl, hasn't come to see me because he is in Siberia working on a construction site, Katrusia's garden is spectacular this year. It is the sort of news they have communicated in their sporadic letters to my mother and aunt in Edmonton over the years, vaguely reassuring, bereft of detail.

It is agreed that I will come visit them all, in Katrusia's home, in my baba's natal village, on Sunday. Since this is illegal – the oblast in which the village is located is closed to foreigners – Pavlina and Dmytro will pick me up several blocks away from the hotel in a borrowed car. I will think of some excuse that will give the slip to my "minders" of Intourist, the official tourist agency responsible for my movements. The skulduggery, though amateurish, is unavoidable. It is within even Pavlina's living memory that contacts with westerners have had lethal consequences.

Sunday. As we drive through the countryside, I am impressed by how lush it looks, with stands of big, soft trees and rolling, swollen contours of farmland, the fields laid out in large splotches and not in the grid of the Canadian prairie. Ukrainian Canadians like to believe that the vast spaciousness of the prairie and parkland felt like home to the Galician pioneers, but I am thinking how dismal Alberta must have looked – bush and slough and stands of scrawny aspen – compared to this effulgent vista.

Dzhuriv, birthplace of my mother's mother, is tidy and colourful. I walk around it and take pictures. An abandoned blue cottage, overwhelmed by its ancient thatched roof and sinking somnolently into a yard gone wild with grasses and yellow daisies. Click. The field behind Katrusia's house – the celebrated, fecund private plot of Soviet agriculture – scrupulously clean of weeds and bordered by fruit trees. Click. A neighbour, stout, baggy-bosomed and kerchiefed, knee-deep in red and yellow tulips. Click. The church where Baba used to go, still in good shape, white-walled and tin-roofed with a single, squat, hexagonal dome. Click. The very pathway along which she used to drive the sheep out of the village and into the upland meadow. Click. The family and neighbours in front of Katrusia's house, the little girls with those oddly affecting enormous white bows on top of their heads; at the edge of the group, an aged, stooped crone who seems to have wandered into the picture on her way to the bus stop. Click.

In spite of the blatant illegality of my visit, once we are in the village my relatives make no effort to conceal me. If anything, they have roused the neighbourhood, and a small group of villagers follows me on my round of picture-taking, pointing out worthy sites – the cultural centre, the school, the single asphalted street through the village centre. They are very proud of these innovations, as though to prove to me that they live in the modern world. Yet it is obvious that one good rainfall must turn the roads into boggy mud holes. There is no hot running water in the houses nor indoor plumbing. Katrusia's outhouse has been lined fastidiously with long sheets of brown packing paper and four leaves of Kleenex hang off a nail, contraband hunted down in honour of my visit.

Katrusia and I stand in front of her freshly painted white door. She is holding aloft a shiny braided bread and a saltcellar poised on a long, embroidered cloth falling from her hands: the traditional gifts of greeting. I am unprepared for a ritual I have seen enacted only on stage, at Ukrainian-Canadian concerts. But here, in Dzhuriv, in Baba's village, this offering to the guest of bread and salt, ancient and habitual benedictions from the earth, is being repeated in real life, by real Ukrainians, and handed over to *me*, granddaughter of the beloved young woman who left and never came back. I take the bread and hold it a little gingerly and look into the camera with a rather weepy look, as though the significance of the moment were just then sinking in: "Paraska Kosovan left and never came back. In her place, you have come. Welcome. Welcome back."

We sweep indoors for the meal. It will go on for hours, with many toasts and a staggering amount of food – lettuce and tomato salads, head cheese, sausage and ham, boiled eggs, perogies and crepes and homemade bread – and much to drink, as though they hadn't heard they were supposed to be on the verge of starvation. Between courses the women scurry out to the kitchen to prepare the next one and I hippity-hop around the table in a little dance with Petro and Dmytro to the sound of Ukrainian country music off a cassette. The feast concludes with the sated company polishing off the peppery vodka and singing folk songs. I hum along, because I know the tunes.

Before setting off for Chernivtsi, I am taken to a monument at the top of the main street. The relatives stand around me, arms crossed over their chests, stern, even a little proud. I look. There's a list of names, including my baba's brother's name: Iurii P. Kosovan. And sixteen other boys – M. S. Nikoliuk, P. F. Nikoliuk, V. V. Fedoruk, I. M. Ravliuk, M. V. Ravliuk, and so on – engraved under large gold lettering: "These

Perished at the Hands of Ukrainian Bourgeois Nationalists." Next to this plaque is a statue of a Soviet soldier, stalwart, broad-shouldered, Aryan, one arm cradling a rifle, the other protectively resting on the shoulder of a little girl who holds a wreath of victory. On the plinth under them: "To Our Countrymen Who Perished on the Fronts of the Great Patriotic War and at the Hands of the Ukrainian Bourgeois Nationalists, with Gratitude from the Workers of the Village of Dzhuriv." Someone has left a basket of lilacs at the base.

I take a couple of pictures but ask no questions. I am not supposed to have any. I'm supposed to know about this, and I do, in a garbled sort of way. I've heard snatches of it since girlhood, how Baba's brother was killed by shadowy figures who were waging war in the villages. I thought it was tragic; I didn't know that Iurko Kosovan was a Soviet hero. I would like to argue the point with my relatives, but this is not the place or time. Besides, the history is a mishmash in my mind and I haven't got the language.

I leave Dzhuriv as I arrived: ignorant of the foretime of this land and speechless. When I get back to Canada, my muteness will seem to me an affliction I no longer wish to bear.

BEGIN WITH A BOOK AND A MATHEMATICIAN

"Christa T. realized that we all had to share in the mistakes we'd made, otherwise we'd have no share in the truths." – Christa Wolf, *The Quest for Christa T.*

I am in the basement rec room, reading a book from my parents' library. It is thick and heavy, like a bible, printed in the typeface of a church bulletin and with a number of foggy black-and-white photographs. Although it is in English, there is something queer about it. It is called The Black Deeds of the Kremlin: A White Book.

In Edmonton, in 1984, I am trying to remember that reading. The photographs were grainy and imprecise, but I was horrified and fascinated all at once. I remember skeletal figures in the throes of an unimaginable anguish – death by starvation – and withered flesh retreating from around the black eye sockets of the dying. Or am I superimposing the images of all the starving wretches I've seen since 1960?

I remember stories of peasants scrabbling through piles of horse manure, looking for undigested seeds and grasses, and of the Red Army soldiers guarding grain piles at railway stations, and of scarecrow-survivors reduced to eating their boots and, later, their children. I remember pictures of wagons filled with frozen corpses like cords of wood. And the portrait of a madwoman who had pickled her own dead children, stuffing chunks of their flesh into large glass jars that she lined up on a shelf like a proud, thrifty housewife.

It is revolting. I slam the book shut. I don't believe a word.

I have already read Anne Frank's diary. I have seen my first photographs of the Holocaust, have ardently watched war movies, and I believe. But for seven million Ukrainians dead of starvation, I have no belief.

Victims in 1930 of an economic "strategy" to squeeze as much grain out of the peasantry as possible – the instruments were Stalin's collective farms and the outright expropriation of all land, grain reserves and livestock – Ukrainian peasants were obliged to turn over all their produce to the state and give up their household stores. Then they began to starve. But I shut the book on them. I had no pity for the dead (who were they?). This would remain true for the next twenty years.

I don't remember anybody talking about the famine, although I suppose my parents must have done. Our relatives lived in western Ukraine, at the time of the famine still part of Poland, and the catastrophe had not struck them. Certainly it was never brought up in school or in the newspapers. It was a non-event. It existed only in that hysterical book in the basement. (Try to remember.) I hated the language of the title: the unredeemed darkness ("Black") of the demonized enemy ("Kremlin") and the innocence ("White") of the victim.

If someone *had* talked about the famine, it would have been the shrill, anti-Communist immigrants who had arrived from the displaced persons' camps of Europe into our Canadian communities in the 1950s, unhinged, as I saw it, by their dispossession, their loss. In the church basement, in the community hall, at picnics and commemorations, I watched the faces and heard the voices of these patriots, and I cringed at their venomous rhetoric, their histrionic gestures. I shared nothing of their fanaticism, their trauma or even their hatred of the Russians, the Soviets, the Communists, the Reds. The Enemy. The Other Ones. (This is hard, this remembering. This isn't just about Ukrainians dying of hunger. This is about me, trying to get rid of them.)

Nineteen sixty. The Cold War. Us and Them. Choose. Right here, right now. Choose these dying Ukrainians. "They" have done this: the wolves in the Kremlin have visited upon your kin a terrible violence. "They," bent on world conquest, have done this in the name of the future and have delivered into its maw the shrivelled bodies of Ukrainian peasants who dared to refuse it. So choose. What are Cuban sugar cane cutters and South African schoolchildren to you? Choose your own. Choose these Ukrainians.

I could not. Behold the second generation born in Canada. Lost to the language, lost to the stories, lost even to the territory known as the diaspora. (We *had* a home; it was right here under our feet.) Lost to the sense of tragedy. It was not just that we could not hate the enemy: we could not feel the terror and pity of his victims. In that chamber of the heart where Ukrainians love their people's struggle to live was a great carelessness. The consequences were predictable. Truth-telling was left precisely in the mouths of those who didn't mind being labelled Cold War hysterics: the North American ultra-right, the ethnic fanatics in the church basement and, eventually, students in Eastern and Central Europe, with whom we of the 1960s imagined ourselves in deepest and reciprocal solidarity.

But then, following a public meeting held in Edmonton in 1977, there was a private party for Leonid Pliushch, the Ukrainian Marxist mathematician who had recently been released, after an international campaign on his behalf, from psychiatric prison in Dnipropetrovsk.

Thirteen years earlier, he had been a young cybernetician at the Academy of Sciences of the U.S.S.R., by all accounts a career man. But in 1964 he wrote a series of letters to the Central Committee of the Communist Party in which he disinterestedly pointed out certain discrepancies between Leninist texts and contemporary Soviet reality. In response, he was visited by agents of the KGB and warned to keep quiet. But in 1968 he wrote a letter to *Komsomolska Pravda* protesting the trials of dissidents and was fired from his job. In 1969, now working as a book stitcher, he joined the Moscow-based Initiative Group [for the defence of human rights] and once again lost his job. Finally, in 1972, he was arrested, in a great wave of arrests across Russia and Ukraine, for "anti-Soviet agitation and propaganda," and imprisoned. In 1973, diagnosed as suffering from "sluggish schizophrenia," he was detained in the Dnipropetrovsk Special Mental Hospital. Treated with neuroleptics and insulin, he suffered from prolonged anxiety, confusion, restlessness, convulsions, coma and memory loss. After a visit, his wife reported that his body had swollen up "to incredible proportions" and that he no longer spoke at all. In 1976 he was released and, along with his family, expelled from the Soviet Union. In 1977 he made a speaking tour across Canada.

His story excited me. Tales of Hungarian and Polish resistance to Soviet power were well known and the formation of a dissident group, Charter 77, had recently been announced in Prague, but, except for Ukrainian-Canadian and Ukrainian-American students who had been protesting for some years the imprisonment in the gulag of numbers of Ukrainian intellectuals, little seemed to be known about resistance in Ukraine. Now here was a real Ukrainian dissident in our midst.

Shy, I hung back and watched the skinny, sallow, bum-legged, chain-smoking dissident from Over There drawn into the heart of the party like a long-lost relative. He was surrounded by students in embroidered shirts and "Free Valentyn Moroz" buttons and pins bearing the black flag of anarchism, singing songs of the Ukrainian partisans from the Second World War. He was singing along with them, beating out the rhythm on his knee.

Pliushch was a man who had suffered much, but he was no martyr: it isn't funerals and icons the Ukrainian people require, he seemed to be saying, but survivors, the men and women returned from the gulag, who carry on doggedly the unspectacular resistance of witness: "Here is where I've been, this is what happened to me, this is what I did, and here is what I'm going to do next." He drank a prodigious amount and was drunk. The young people were taking care of him. He was precious, a hero snatched from the jaws of madness.

The next day I interviewed him. I had heard and read gulag stories. They were usually Russian. Here was one survivor who told it in Ukrainian, and I was unexpectedly moved. At the end, I asked him: "How is it that, although we come from opposite ends of the world and we do not speak each other's language and I cannot begin to imagine your experience, still I feel close to you?" And he replied: "Because, in the end, we come from the same village."

So there finally it was: the Ukrainians and I: kin. This time I did not deny it.

"They sang, their mouths full of earth." – Wislawa Szymborska, "Starvation Camp near Jaslo"

NAFPLION, 1984: On the fiftieth anniversary of the 1933 famine, the Ukrainian-Canadian community produced a large number of materials relating to it. I have brought them with me to a hotel room in Greece. With the scent of almond blossoms on the moist air outside the unshuttered window, I read again about the famine in Ukraine. I make myself read.

"The Soviet state was viewed in the countryside as an occupying regime."

Ivan Tukhonovych Zahorulko, born 1917, Dibrivka village: "The people in our village were all swollen up. And yet people arrived from God knows where, from other starving villages, to barter for bread. They brought cloth with them – who needed it? At the market they practically offered gold for bread. They died anyway."

A peasant woman who had worked on a collective farm had been accused of hoarding food. The GPU (State Political Police) searched her hut and demolished it. They found fourteen potatoes. She was tried for sabotage and admitted that she had taken home one or two potatoes each night and hidden them. The local papers later carried headlines: "A Fiendish Attempt to Wreck the Soviet Has Been Thwarted."

In 1930, a decree authorizing the recruitment of 25,000 proletarian volunteers to assist in the implementation of collectivization sent out a wave of Communist activists to the villages to agitate against "rich" peasants. They were known as the Twenty-Five Thousanders. Three years later, in the midst of the famine, thousands more organized into special political departments were dispatched to the villages to supervise the requisition of the crop and to guard against the pilfering and hoarding of grain. In the villages they made their rounds, looking for caches, carrying long iron spikes that they stabbed into the earth as though it were a sack of loot.

Those peasants not dead on their feet struck back and burned down the newly erected buildings on the collective farms, rioted en masse with pitchforks, axes and shotguns or shot at brigade workers who wandered into view of an open window. They slaughtered their own cattle and, having no means of selling the beef, gorged themselves on it. "For the first time in their sordid history," a future People's Commissar of Agriculture is reported to have said, the peasants "have eaten their fill of meat."

In 1932–33, the Soviet Union exported 1.7 million tons of grain to the West to pay for industrial equipment.

Mykola Hryhorovych Mukha, born 1913: "Father had horses, cattle – so he was afraid to join the *kolhosp*. When they took everything, even the cow, he lay down and died. I was already too feeble to dig him his grave.... I went once to Kharkiv. I stopped to ask for water in the ancient villages of Malii and Velykii Rublivki. All the houses stood unlocked, the floors strewn with scattered human bones."

The writer Mykola Khvylovy, travelling through the countryside in the disastrous season of the famine – he would shoot himself a few months later – lodged overnight with a farmer who had managed to keep his family alive by hanging onto his cow. "He slept in the stable with his most precious possession, barricaded and armed to the teeth."

In January 1933, Soviet newspapers reported that members of the Ukrainian Communist Party apparatus who had distributed bread to the starving farmers had been arrested for going over to the class enemy.

From *The Black Deeds of the Kremlin: A White Book*: "Having cut off their children's heads, Myron Yemets and his wife, Maria, salted them away for meat."

Boris Pasternak: "Such inhuman, unimaginable misery, such a terrible disaster, that it began to seem almost abstract, it would not fit within the bounds of consciousness.... For an entire year [after a visit to the Ukrainian countryside in 1933] I could not write."

I make myself look at the photographs. The decomposing body of a young peasant is laid out on the steppe, his pelvis already mouldering and mingling with the black loam of the prairie. In a snowy cemetery, bodies – some naked, some in bits of clothing, all stiffened in the dance of rigor mortis – have been left in a pile, as though there had been no neighbour with the strength left to dig a pit. Near Kharkiv, in a peasant's hut with dirt floor and thatched roof, a girl sits holding her infant brother in her lap; she sits serene, a bit aloof, or perhaps benumbed, like a Madonna; the child, shrivelled and bandy-legged, looks like a fetus. A photo with caption: "Boy standing beside his dying father and weeping bitterly. The father had been shot for approaching too closely forbidden territory while the two were picking up grains of wheat spilled on the ground. Now the boy must wander alone, almost certainly to die of starvation."

And I read, in an autobiographical essay by an émigré poet, that his mother, a teacher in a village school in the Mykolaiv region in 1933, was required to teach singing to the children swollen and stupefied by hunger. Singing! It was in the curriculum.

What had driven me to slam the *White Book* shut so many years before? What was it about these chronicles of the most elemental suffering – hunger – that had provoked my disbelief? Behind these simple stories I had imagined the machinations of "hysterics," "fanatics," "nationalists," as though to plead the cause of the hungry were *unseemly*.

Well, they were right and I was wrong – not about everything, but about this. Wolves *did* patrol the cellars of the Kremlin, the dictatorship of the proletariat *did* roll over the modest lives of those whose very souls it had invaded the villages to save.

When I finally reread *The Black Deeds of the Kremlin*, thirty years after I first came across it, the book has the heft I remember and the same murky photographs, although not nearly so many as I thought there were. The pages do not look at all like those from a church bulletin, although there is a textbookish air to the typeface. I had not remembered the name of the publishers, but here they are on the title page: Ukrainian Association of Victims of Russian Communist Terror. This no longer sets my teeth on edge. I find it admirably straightforward and unsentimental. That is who they were – victims – and terrorists were responsible. I read their stories now with an open heart, and I believe them.

Sitting in my Greek hotel room, with the scent of almonds on the humid air, I read of the little boy, swaying unsteadily on his rickety hands and knees, who had crawled into the village cemetery to find something to eat.

When his rescuers find him, he is feebly grinding blades of luxuriant grass between his rotting teeth. I choose him.

THE POWER OF SPEECH

EDMONTON, 1984: I decide to learn to speak Ukrainian. I begin where I left off thirty years earlier: the Saturday School.

I had always perceived the Ukrainian language as some great obligation. It was never just a means of expression; it was a carrier, a veritable caravan of cultural and psychic and political import, and to cease speaking it, individually as well as collectively, was held to be a national catastrophe, as though one had stood idly by while a whole wagon train of goods – flour and tea and frying pans – had gone tumbling over a cliff while on its way to a beleaguered colony of countrymen. I cannot speak Ukrainian. I have been found wanting before the ancestors, and I have much to make up for.

My reader has fallen apart utterly, although the pages remain clear and clean. I leaf through it: the illustrations are acutely familiar to me – the frog, or *zhaba*, the fairies floating on dewdrops like miniature parachutists, Marusia gathering flowers from the garden, the teacher, in a splendid green coat and matching green hat, greeting Marusia and Roman. Even the lessons resonate like fragments of poems once memorized whole and now remembered only for their refrains: *Dzvony dzvoniat, bam-bam-bam. Hen vysoko u dzvinytsi, tam-tam-tam. Dzvony dzvoniat, dzvony klychut, nas-nas-nas. Chy do shkoly, chy do tserkvy, chas-chas-chas.* The bells are ringing, ding-dang-dong. From afar in the bell tower, there-there-there. The bells are ringing, the bells are calling us-us-us. To school or to church, it's time-time-time.

There is nothing remotely "ethnic" in these lessons, save for a story about lighting candles on Christmas Eve. Marusia and Roman live in Middle Canada, in a suburban bungalow where Mother wears an apron and serves supper and Father appears twice – to eat and to dandle the baby – and summer is spent at the lake, building sandcastles, and children go to sleep with teddy bears. This is upwardly mobile, lower middle-class hyphenated Canada seduced not by its own "difference" but by its adaptability.

And yet the little book, published in Saskatoon in 1947, is redolent of that quintessential "ethnic" pastime – the mother, her children gathered around her, reading in the mother tongue a text that if not almost banal (the bungalow, the teddy bear) was nevertheless other than everyday life. For this is how I learned to read *Marusia*, curled up against my mother's shoulder, my sister at her other shoulder, while the book lay open before us and we read out loud, along with her, chanting the text like a trio of cantors in church. The point was: this was outside school.

The anecdotes, about fairies and frogs and going to school and telling the time, were told in that same Ukrainian language reserved for extraordinary occasions and places – church, concerts, speeches, the national anthem, prayers and those mysterious but clamorous arguments that broke out between my father and grandfather, voices rising, hands slapping authoritatively at their respective newspapers.

How I loved to write out the letters, all the curlicues and whorls and slanted strokes of the Cyrillic alphabet, *drawing* them, for long before the letters arranged themselves into discrete, meaningful words, the written Ukrainian language was a design, such as one could trace in a carpet or on an embroidered cushion. Pleasing. Like the swirl of my name written in Ukrainian in the front of the reader in my mother's hand.

I had seen the letters all my life – in my father's newspapers, on the envelopes that came all the way from Dzhuriv in the U.S.S.R., crabbed and cuneiform on the icons in church. And had heard the language from birth (Baba holding me gingerly, her first grandchild, as she stood in front of her root cellar) and had even, so I was told, spoken it baby-ishly. It was synchronous with my sensory life. What perverse process alienated it from my mouth?

Together with some twenty teen-agers, I enroll in the senior class at Saturday School. The teen-agers radiate a self-confidence in their youthfulness and their ethnicity that was quite absent from my genera-tion at their age. I remind myself that these kids are the *great*-grandchil-dren of Galician immigrants; their "ethnic baggage" carries purely Canadian content and the last immigrant in their families died quite some time ago. I sit at the front of the class, take notes, listen attentively, raise my hand to answer questions and do all my homework. I am a model student.

It is a humbling experience – this forcible return to baby talk, to sim-ple, declarative sentences and the present tense for all actions – but I bend my head to it and persevere. Finally, the day comes when I open my brand-new copy of Taras Shevchenko's *Kobzar*, his collected poems. It is my very own copy, just purchased at the Ukrainian Book Store, a Soviet edition with extensive notes.

I begin with "The Bewitched Woman" and read every word, consult-ing the dictionary and underlining words to remember, poem after poem. When I am a third of the way through the book and reading one of the most famous poems of them all, "The Haidamaky," I suddenly realize I am not just reading Shevchenko: I am *inside* the language, understanding it directly, the profoundly familiar sounds carrying a story, a voice, a personality where before there had been only babble. For just a few moments I am in the company of literates who have known all along the beauty carried by the Ukrainian language and the splendid architecture of its poetry. Soon enough I am stumbling and tongue-tied and overwhelmed by the learning still to be done. But I know that I have for a very short time been inside the words, without translation.

To learn this language is also to keep a kind of faith with my grandmother, the gentle, pink-cheeked, round-headed old woman who could speak no English but who never, not once, reproached me for my speechlessness before her. Now it is I who reproach myself for having taken up this learning too late. Baba was the last person in a long line of generations who spoke only Ukrainian; I broke the chain, speaking it not at all. Now I pick it up, wanting to hammer back my link, so that Baba might live again in my broken, stammering syllables.

In 1988 I travel again to Ukraine, this time endowed with the power of speech. As before, I hear the Russian language everywhere. It is pervasive, like a gas – in the airport bus, the Customs Hall, the hotel restaurant, on the rock videos, in the boutiques. But this time I do not stand by rainy windows and weep. I revel in the sounds I am making, even though I often retreat to my hotel room, my tongue swollen with exhaustion, my brain depleted of all vocabulary. The Russian I once knew is filed in some deep archive of my brain; the Ukrainian I am speaking has risen up and inscribed itself on my tongue as though I once knew how to speak it and had only now to remember. And so I go to the provinces, to the village, meet my relatives, open my mouth and speak.

II

FILLING IN THE BLANKS

KIEV, 1988: Huge, triumphalist signs still announce that we have just arrived in the "City of Heroes" where we are encouraged to give a cheer for "Peace and the Friendship of Peoples." But two years of perestroika in Kiev have otherwise altered it so profoundly that I am initially quite disoriented. I grope for the props from the "good old, bad old" days of my last trip, four years earlier, in an effort to get my bearings. For instance, I am relieved to see that, although the Customs officer is not the least bit interested in my bags, she is still obsessively concerned about the amount of foreign currency I'm bringing in with me, requiring me to count out in front of her, down to the last zloty, all the loose change from my recent trips to the fraternal socialist republics, although its combined total – she knows this as well as I – is worth almost precisely nothing.

Cousin Pavlina is at the airport to greet me, having taken the overnight train from Lviv, as are representatives of the Ukraine Friendship Society. We drive to the hotel in a taxi and the lackadaisical chat is about Chernobyl and the weekly announcement of the radiation level in foods and in the atmosphere – people accept the official statement that the readings have returned to pre-accident levels – and how Kiev is crawling with priests and nuns from all over the world, gathered to celebrate the millennium of Christianity in Rus.

Without so much as a glance over to the dragons at the reception counter in the hotel, Pavlina accompanies me to my room. While waiting for the bottle of champagne to cool off a bit in the toilet bowl, we flop on the beds and watch TV, Pavlina providing a running commentary. *I* am the one to caution prudence, signalling the "bugs" in the telephone and behind the wallpaper; Pavlina tells me not to be so crazy.

And so we watch an exposé of the deplorable food prepared in the school cafeteria for schoolchildren (when they're fed at all), an interview with members of a fashion house, man-on-the-street opinions of the upcoming Gorbachev/Reagan summit, a news item concerning the amount of money to be made in the private markets selling T-shirts bearing western logos (Mickey Mouse, Garfield the Cat), and the speech of a poet at the Academy of Music, evoking our continuity with the shades of our ancestors every time we open our mouths in folk song. To all of this, Pavlina responds with snorts, sarcastic whistles and indignant harrumphs as though to make up for the years of well-bred silence in which she had pretended to agree with everything.

I invite her to the hard-currency bar of the hotel. There are three other people there, not including the barman who is draped moodily over the taps of the bar sink.

She begins. "Let me tell you about Stalin." Slurps of Heineken. "The thirties," she continues – she who was born in 1954. Great violence in the villages during collectivization, villagers driven out naked into the snows, political commissars torn limb from limb as they made their way down the muddy streets carrying the long steel rods with which they'd prod and poke and pierce the walls and garden plots in search of hidden caches of grain. Fear and terror. She mentions the purges of the intellectuals and the dissident Communists, at this point collapsing all the generations of the tormented into one great slag heap of the gulag. She mentions Trotsky. Where is this conversation going?

Back to the war, the purges of the army officers and Stalin's great crime against his people: their helpless vulnerability to the Nazi blitzkrieg from the west. She recites her knowledge to me as one who has come to it for the first time – fiery, evangelistic, half out of breath – and aches to pass on the news. I say gently: "I know this, Pavlina, but how do *you* know it?"

"I watch TV."

The film she saw was the story of two Communists in the Siberian camps, one of whom survives and returns home after thirty years. He had promised his dying comrade that he would visit the comrade's widow and now-grown son to let them know what had happened to him. They know nothing except that their beloved was arrested and taken away with an official explanation – given once and never retracted – that he was a "wrecker" and "saboteur." Under this rubric he had vanished into the void. "And was my father guilty?" the son pleads to know. "Was he? Was he?"

And now the survivor, the wretched helpmeet, is finally given grace to say it: No. And my second cousin weeps and weeps.

"I read it in the newspapers! I read it in *our* newspapers." Pavlina straightens up and beams at me not a little cockily.

I understand the declaration: See, I'm not so stupid. I have my own ways of knowing now. I'm no intellectual. I had no under-the-counter foreign newspapers to read, no foreign guests, no invitations abroad. Those people knew all along what was what and still they kept their mouths shut. But with every newspaper and magazine I open these days, I get smarter. I can find out things on my own. Now I read about them in the newspapers – and I don't mean those hoity-toity papers from the capital cities, the literary gazettes and the sermons of the democrats – I mean *our* papers, the inky provincial rags. Even a sooty smudge of cheap printer's ink can fill in a blank.

Out in the streets I notice that some effort is now being made to decorate store windows, that some enterprising café manager has hauled a few tables and chairs out onto the sidewalk under a canopy, and that the citizens, walking about in decidedly more stylish shoes, are all licking ice cream. At the cinema you can see "One Flew Over the Cuckoo's Nest."

Small businesses such as restaurants, operated as co-operatives, have been allowed to organize, and I join two friends at a basement bistro for dinner. The brick walls have been scrubbed down, candles placed on the tables and a piano shoved into a corner for dinnertime music. I am charmed. In spite of the fact that our host promises to find us some beer or champagne, none ever materializes (we are in the midst of President Gorbachev's anti-alcoholism campaign), but the food is delivered in a nonstop series of well-presented dishes – bowls of fresh vegetables, platters of rare cold roast beef and smoked chicken decorated with carrot curls, fresh strawberries and cream – until we yell, Stop! and ask for the bill. It is the equivalent of one-fifth of an average monthly wage. I think I am witnessing the beginnings of the two-tiered economy.

Outside on the main shopping streets, the rest of Kiev is still lining up in queues – their second job – for food, for shoes, for a haircut, for a newspaper. First you line up at the counter, then at the cashier, then at the counter again. It takes hours to get a lettuce, a slab of fat, a tired fish displayed in a wooden box on the sidewalk.

And after dark the rest of Kiev congregates in the dreariest spot in the city – the cavernous underground passages that link the major intersections in the downtown core. Under low concrete ceilings, in a yellowish light, huddles of young people smoke feverishly and pace the littered concrete floor, flipping their cigarette butts into the little pools of water left over from the rain, or, sitting cross-legged against the walls, play guitars and sing Russian pop songs while young lovers neck at the edge of the crowd.

LETTER FROM ODESSA

I had prepared conscientiously for this trip, reading the papers and attending lectures of visiting Ukrainians, and so I was aware of the dramatic changes since 1984. And then, after a long silence, had come a letter from Seriozha.

March 26, 1988

Dear Myrna,

I'm very glad to have heard from you again. I was beginning to believe of late that we'd lost contact for good. About three or four years ago I found a note in my mail box from the postwoman saying that I should come to the post office and get a registered letter. That was the only time I signed to acknowledge receipt of mail. Apparently, ever since someone's been signing for me.

Back in 1985 I found a lucrative new job and have been doing well ever since. I didn't write to you about it at the time because I didn't want my *other* readers to know. Now I don't care. I completely renovated my old place and turned it into a decent flatlet with flush toilet and hot water heating. Unfortunately, my mother hardly had any time to enjoy improved living standards – she died only a month after the work was finished. I bought a car but the only rides she had were to hospitals and clinics.

There was a brief period when cars were freely on sale, naturally those the least in demand. Of these I purchased the best – a five-door hatchback, "Moskvich," for 7600 rubles [the equivalent of thirty-one months' average salary].

Now, as to perestroika or perebudivlia and an insider's point of view! When you write of impressive changes in this country, I understand you mean marked changes in attitudes. As to innovations in the physical sense, there aren't many to see yet. The old socio-economic structure is still in place and until it's dismantled progress is going to be slow indeed. Society is divided over the issue of constitutional changes – whether the entrenched bureaucrats and die-hard Stalinists and Brezhnevites will succeed in crippling the proposed changes by vague formulas and foggy wording, leaving loopholes to render them ineffective, or will the democratic stream prevail and achieve a directly elected parliament and president, and local self-rule. The most complex problem is how to take away power from party functionaries and committees. They've got lots of it and practically no responsibility. They can bully and push people and officials around, and then when something goes wrong just step aside and let others take the rap.

What's more important is that the era of the slumbering mind, which according to Goya breeds monsters, seems to be over. The nation's stirring to life.

I've been on a trip through the Crimea and on to Georgia. The flat sandy soil of the area immediately beyond the Dnipro River must be particularly good for pine trees for they grow and prosper there in great abundance. But even more abundant are watermelon fields. They are said to be the best melons in Ukraine. I don't know why they grow so many of them as a good deal of the crop remains unharvested. It's simply pushed by bulldozers into heaps and fed to cattle.

The motorway ran along the North Crimean Canal and brought me to the Krymskii Val, a system of fortifications built in the Middle Ages and rebuilt several times since to keep out invaders. Villages in Crimea look particularly unattractive for the barrack-like ugliness of the new housing. Almost every village has a row of tiny identical cottages for migrants. I think the idea is that these new inhabitants are going to be able to claim that there's no way the Crimean Tatars can come back to their land as it's all been resettled!

On the way to Tbilisi, I turned off the main road and headed south via Bakuriani towards the pass. To keep me company I picked up a local fellow of uncertain age. Locals usually have such growth on their faces that it's very hard to tell their age. He was sitting next to me, chatting cheerfully, bragging mostly, until we passed another character, who looked to me like a twin brother of my passenger – the same dark, unshaven face of uncertain age and also dressed in black. He was tending a flock of sheep. A dark cloud came over my passenger's face, he jumped in his seat and fiercely declared: "He's a Tatar. They should all be killed!"

I've also motored around western Ukraine. Unlike in Odessa or Kiev or eastern Ukraine, you can hear the Ukrainian language everywhere and the most promising sign is that children use it in play. The changes in Lviv over the last two years really impress me. The blue-and-yellow flag [established as a symbol of Ukrainian independence in Lviv in 1918] flies proudly right in the heart of the city. Billboards are set up all around the centre posted with newspaper cuttings, type-written articles and hand-written poems in defence of the Ukrainian cultural and linguistic identity and for the restoration of independent Ukrainian churches.

It's very different in Odessa. There's a small Society of Enthusiasts of the Ukrainian Language but even this has split into radicals and moderates who function separately. Their impact on public life has been minimal. True, the bulk of Odessa's population speaks Russian now but its roots are in the surrounding countryside where the Ukrainian language still lives. Given the right circumstances, it could make a comeback. The fact that *you*, thousands of miles away from the Old Country, are learning the language, is helpful to the cause, I am sure.

Only recently it has been made public what a lot of people knew all along, that for the better part of a century the Soviet nations were forced to live in a world of twisted ideas, inverted morals, all-out brutality and suppression. Duplicity and dishonesty were a way of life. The country is only beginning to try to rid itself of this horrible legacy. As a headline in *Moscow News* had it, "Life Is Getting More Complex and Troubled, but Fairer."

Hear from you soon?

Love,

Seriozha

WITH ONE MOUTH AND ONE HEART

KIEV, 1988: We are entering the foyer of the renovated opera house.

"Please note," says my escort from the Friendship Society, Olha

Vasylivna, "that the seats have all been recovered with their original pattern and reproduced by the firm in Vienna that first executed them" – as though this marvel may somehow remind us that Kiev was once equidistant between Moscow and Vienna, culturally speaking.

There are a great many patriarchs seated on the stage, in the purple and white and black robes fashioned after the court dress of Byzantium, and they bring greetings in Greek from Jerusalem and Cyprus and Athens, in Rumanian from Bucharest, in Macedonian from Skopje, in Serbian from Belgrade. Then their host, Metropolitan Filaret, Exarch of Ukraine, father of the Russian Orthodox Church (the only official church in Ukraine), makes a long sermon in which he instructs us, without once availing himself of the Ukrainian language, in the meaning of the Christianizing of Rus. Civilization arrived among the "brother nations" of Russia, Ukraine and Byelorussia with the Bible, the sacraments, art and literature and conscience. How happy he is tonight, he tells us, his smooth, pink face glowing cherubically above his long, white beard.

This gathering is one in a series of public events organized to celebrate the millenium of Christianity in Ukraine – a conversion that brought the people of Rus into the community of European cultures – but a dampish melancholy settles on me as I realize how much of this long, long story is not being told here. It is narrated outside, in the still illegal, furtive services of the Greek Catholic faithful in their apartments or in clandestine Easter Masses in the woods, in the long-buried bells and church treasures hidden by Orthodox peasants from the rapacious representatives of official atheism, in prayers whispered into the cupped hands you bring up to your face as you stand before the icon in your grandmother's house.

We assemble again for a concert the next evening in this czarist confection of an opera house, creamy and gilded and velvety, its stage curtained with a splendid red and gold tapestry, the hammer and sickle woven among its threads like a coat of arms.

I tell myself that I do not mind, for even thirty generations later, here we all are, here we *still* are, each mindful of our place in the genealogy of Rus.

It is said that the Apostle Andrew once passed by the hills of the future city of Kiev on his way north from the Greek colonies on the Black Sea.

He stood on the shore of the Dnipro River, his disciples gathered around him. "See ye these hills? So shall the favour of God shine upon them that on this spot a great city shall arise, and God shall erect many churches therein."

The scaffolding at the church of St. Sophia is down in time for the millennium and I am whooshed in ahead of the daunting queue of Soviet visitors gathered massively and patiently at the main doors. This is not a practising church; this is a museum, an art gallery, whose treasures are frescoes and mosaics. Visitors, having forgotten how to make the genuflections of the believer, come to admire the handwork of men. Still, a certain piety hangs in the air: we feel the faded presence of the ancient ones, and we read their passion flung on the walls in pigment and tesserae. Here are the angel Gabriel, the theologian Gregory, Saint Nadia, the holy warrior saint Michael, John the Baptist and all the rest of the pantheon of Christian notables, wonderfully expressive with personality. No two faces are alike; there are round and smooth ones, lined and gaunt ones, bony and fleshy, startled, pensive, serene, bewildered, stricken, perky – a portrait gallery of the artist's familiars, on whom they were modelled: the baker, the fur trader, the monk, the boatman, the fishwife, the artist's aunt, the artist's nephew, the artist's confessor. This was the beginning of the Christian era in Kiev; how was he to know he wasn't supposed to paint like this? I imagine his pleasure in the crowds that came to Mass, their heads craned back as they looked up and down the tall pillars of the cathedral, looking for a face they recognized, their smiles when they saw themselves.

How was he to know that church painting is "about" the repeated, coded gesture and not this display of exuberance in particularity, in the vain, ephemeral diversity of human society? Nor could he know that in only two hundred years the hordes would arrive from the East to ransack the sacristy and scrape the walls with the edges of their swords and scimitars as though to erase the offending features of their contemptible victims.

In 987 A.D., Volodymyr, Prince of Kiev, summoned his vassals and the city elders to a counsel. He was disturbed, he told them, by the frequent representations made to him by the ambassadors of foreign religions – the Muslim Bulgars of the Upper Volga, the German Christians of central Europe, the Greek Christians of Byzantium – all pressing conversion upon him. They were arguing that it was unseemly that a prince of his stature, lord of Rus who had made even the gates of Constantinople shake, was still worshipping barbarian idols.

Not far from where Volodymyr and the elders were meeting, the tall, carved wooden effigies of the gods of Rus leaned over the banks of the Dnipro in an assembly of their own. They were the most powerful agents of the natural world: Hors, the sun god; Volos, god of cattle; Striboh, wind god; Dazhboh, god of abundance and fertility; and, mightiest of them all, Perun, god of thunder, with his head of silver and his moustache of gold. For generations, Kiev had worshipped and honoured them. But now, aware of the role it had to play in the international scheme of things, the great city was casting about for more brilliant patrons.

The vassals and elders advised Volodymyr to dispatch ten wise men to visit the lands of the neighbours of Rus so that they might see with their own eyes how others worshipped. They were to return to Kiev with a recommendation. So it was done.

"When we journeyed among the Bulgarians," they reported, "we beheld how they worship in their temple, called a mosque, while they stand ungirt. The Bulgarian bows, sits down, looks hither and thither like one possessed, and there is no happiness among them, but instead only sorrow and a dreadful stench. Their religion is not good. Then we went among the Germans, and saw them performing many ceremonies in their temples, but we beheld no glory there. Then we went on to Greece [Constantinople], and the Greeks led us to the edifices where they worship their God, and we knew not whether we were in heaven or on earth."

Marriage forced Volodymyr's hand. As his bride he had chosen Anna, sister of the emperors of Byzantium, Basil and Constantine, but they would not give her up until Volodymyr had promised to be baptised into the Christian faith. Anna herself walked out of the gates of Constantinople accompanied by a retinue of priests and her own loud and eloquent lamentation that she was being married off to an idol worshipper and slave trader. Volodymyr was duly baptised and married. Then, with the ardour of the newly converted, he directed that all the idols of the old faith should be overthrown.

The stout ancestral totem poles were pulled crashing to the ground, set upon with axes and put to the flames, and almighty Perun himself, tied to a horse's tail, was dragged about the city and down to the river, beaten by citizens wielding sticks as though to punish the Fiend for having chosen Perun's attractive form (the silver head, the golden moustaches) to walk temptingly among them. And so Perun was pushed into the water and disappeared over a waterfall. The following day, summoned to the river, the inhabitants of Kiev celebrated a mass baptism, standing breast-deep in the water in their white shirts, and sang Hallelujah! And where the gods had once stood, on the deconsecrated ground of Perun, Volodymyr built a church.

Volodymyr begat Iaroslav, called the Wise, whether for his love of books and the monumental achievement of his library, or for St. Sophia, the cathedral that he caused to be built in 1037, I am not certain, having heard both explanations. The chronicles incline to the former; indeed, the scribe is almost ecstatic with admiration of this feudal paragon of learning – the prince who read day and night; who assembled about him scholars to translate the lives of the saints and the liturgical texts of Byzantium from Greek to Slavic; who wrote books himself and who deposited all this learning into a library within St. Sophia, as though to make an offering. When Iaroslav's daughter married King Philip I of France, she was the only literate member of the court.

The scribe reminds us that "books are like rivers that water the whole earth; they are the springs of wisdom." In reading them, we converse with God and the holy men. Now the books are gone, but the church still stands.

In 1240, the Mongols, under the leadership of Batu, grandson of Genghis Khan, arrived at the Golden Gates of Kiev and sacked the city, then moved on to Poland and central Europe. Kiev never recovered, and the civilization of Rus shrank to a shrivelled remnant of ancestral memory up and down the Dnipro River.

It was the modus operandi of the Mongols to burn settlements to the ground, to enslave the able-bodied and slaughter the rest. Plano Carpini, papal envoy to the Mongols, mentions in 1246 the "countless skulls and bones of dead men lying about on the ground." I imagine him an elegant figure on horseback, headed east from the river, his animal skittish as they make their way through the ossuary of the steppelands. The Mongol invasion is followed by famines, locusts, forest fires and twenty eruptions of the plague between 1338 and 1448.

At the beginning of the eleventh century, there had been four hundred churches in Kiev. Now one single glory remained, the *nerushyma stina* of St. Sophia: the "indestructible wall" of the east-facing apse, cupping in its dome the monumental mosaic figure of the Virgin Orans, the *Oranta*, she-who-prays, her arms upraised in the primordial gesture of reverential greeting to the (sun) God, her face a mask of serenity, her gaze directed to eternity, her body draped in twenty-one shades of blue, a little Ukrainian embroidered cloth tucked into her belt. The church collapsed around her, but her perpetual upstandingness, upright over the charnel house of Kiev, over the stinking smoke of its ruins, over the nettle and thistle growing up between the fallen slabs of libraries and bathhouses, was her gift to the generations to come.

In 1934, St. Sophia housed the Spartacus Brewery. To one writer who walked in there, the "sour smell of hops and malt" brought to "the ancient walls" the smell of the "boundless steppes." In 1943, in wartime Moscow, the exiled Ukrainian filmmaker, Oleksandr Dovzhenko, despondent in the grey, cold city, made a list in his notebook of the monuments of architecture that, in his own lifetime, had been destroyed in Kiev. He listed twenty-three, including monasteries, academies, churches and even whole streets. He named no perpetrators, no guilty parties; only the "twentieth century" stands accused: "It has ridden roughshod over the remains of the nineteenth, seventeenth, and eleventh centuries, leaving debris, a crippled land, and disgusting stone boxes." On the site of the demolished belfry of the Piatnytska church in Chernihiv, ancient city upstream from Kiev, former seat of princes and bishops, the city council decided in 1963 to erect a public lavatory.

The climactic event of the millenium celebration is Mass in St. Volodymyr's Cathedral to commemorate the baptism of Rus. Thousands of would-be celebrants swarm in a heated, aggressive crush around the doors, where men like bouncers in a nightclub heave them away. One old woman pleads with a priest – "I've come all the way from Ivano-Frankivsk!" – and wrings her thick, knobby red hands. I think of giving my pass away. She, after all, is the believer.

Inside, a spectacle has overtaken the highly ornamented nineteenth-century nave – cameras, floodlights, sound booms, ponderous lighted chandeliers, choirs, bells and a score of patriarchs in glittering ceremonial headgear and gorgeous brocaded robes lined up along the iconostas. I am standing crushed upright against a pillar, holding fast to my resistance with private recitations of the sins of this ceremony's Russianness, its pomposity, its hypocritical obeisances to the memory of the first saints of Rus. But eventually the full-throated rumble of the familiar responses, the yearning melancholy of the hymns and the collective, devotional intonation of the creed break me down.

How do they remember? A thousand years of violated memory – Mongols and Tatars, slavery and serfdom, Poles and czars and Bolsheviks, war, terror, famine, occupations, gulag, silence and fear – and yet they remember how to do this: how to be the faithful of the Orthodox Church and of the saints, how to sound the words of the blessed poet John of Chrysostom, how to take communion. Village women bearing sickly children in their stout, chafed arms make their way to the priest holding the chalice. Middle-aged women off the collective farm, squat bodies presented in their best cotton dresses, cross their arms over their breasts and receive the bread and wine from the golden spoon. They turn away with expressions of beatitude, as though they have seen the face of Sophia.

In Lviv, in the fall of 1989, to the huzzas of thousands, the statue of Lenin in front of the opera house will be taken down, lowered by ropes in a slow descent onto the platform of a flatbed truck. Several young men will jump onto the truck. As it lumbers along, they will beat the prostrate man of marble with two-by-fours. It is an echo of the rage of Kievans a thousand years earlier who had pursued the disgraced idol, Perun, through the city streets, beating at his gimcrack body with sticks.

THE HISTORY LESSON

KIEV, 1988: Viktor was going to be an engineer until the day in 1967 when, three weeks before the final exams in his diploma studies, he spent the afternoon on the banks of the Dnipro below Kiev. He lounged in the sunshine, chewed on grasses and sang to himself all the songs he knew that had set to music the words of Taras Shevchenko, the poet, so many years in exile, for whom this river had a special meaning. Viktor suddenly and irreversibly realized that, by calling, he was not an engineer; he was a rememberer.

He's a small man with a fine head of hair and moustache and a crisp polyester shirt pulled tight around his narrow chest. He does not seem to be a bum, but on the other hand neither does he have a place to live. Or, rather, he seems to live all over Ukraine, popping into Kiev every few weeks and kipping out in friends' flats and then disappearing again, who knows where. "But in my heart," he tells me, "I am a Kievan." Every visit to his hometown yields him new treasures: "I keep rediscovering this beautiful city." I tell him I am not so impressed, and he is a little offended. Now we are on an evening stroll, so that I might see what he sees.

On our way to the riverbank we walk through a park, examining the monuments. Here is a statue of the nineteenth-century poet Lesia Ukrainka by the celebrated, if persecuted, modern sculptor Ivan Honchar. This is the first I've heard of him. The sculpture looks unremarkable enough, until Viktor tells the story of how, when it was finished back in 1925, Honchar and his friends went out under cover of night to erect it on its spot in the park and stood in a circle around it, arms linked, to repulse the efforts of the police to topple it to the ground in the morning. The story sounds apocryphal to me – were things so bad in '25? – but I accept the spirit of it.

Here's the bust of an actress, famous at the turn of the century, another whose name means nothing to me. Viktor is disgusted. "You call yourself a Ukrainian?" We stand at her monument so he can deliver a lecture on the development of post-Romantic theatre in Ukraine and the actress's contribution to it. Because the Ukrainian language has been suppressed periodically in theatre and in publishing, "Ukrainian literary aspirations flowed into songs," and Ukraine developed an intensely musical theatre and an "incredibly rich" repertoire of song. It wasn't until the revolution and the arrival of the avant-garde dramaturge Les Kurbas that Ukrainian theatre entered the modern age. I brighten up. I've heard of Kurbas! Viktor looks sceptical. But did I know he was arrested in 1934 and vanished? This doesn't surprise me in the least, of course, but I look astonished and say nothing.

On the cool descent to the river, under the heavy, broad-leafed canopy of trees, we come upon what looks a kind of ramshackle gazebo. Viktor says this is an early nineteenth-century church rotunda that marks the spot where the ninth-century Kievan prince Askold was murdered by the craven prince of Novgorod, Oleh. I idly observe that Askold's name "sounds Scandinavian" to me. But I have got it all wrong. It seems that the old way of seeing things – the origin of Kievan

Rus in the Scandinavian princes who sailed out of their Baltic fortresses down the riverways of the Slavic lands to establish a principality on the Dnipro – is hopelessly misbegotten. It's true, this is just the way I heard it in Russian history classes. It didn't occur to me then to be suspicious of theories that grounded the origin of Kiev in *non*-Ukrainian folk. Viktor, determined on my reeducation, informs me that "the most recent research" seems to be pointing at the emergence of Rus from the merging of Slavic and *Celtic* cultures. This produced a higher, synthesized culture, namely Ukrainian. "U - kraina. At the edge. The frontier. Ukrainians emerged where the tribe ended and the state arose." He seems so pleased by this possibility that I do not bother to ask what his sources are.

Viktor and I continue down the slope, slapping at mosquitoes while he moves to questions of etymology. He doesn't exactly hector, but there is an insistent emphasis to his words and intonation that brooks no argument. I have no stake in it one way or the other, so I let him go on, trying to pay attention at the same time to this beautiful riverbank just below the lip of the city where the peace is complete and we are sheltered from views of the disastrous postwar suburbs built right across from us on the other bank. Viktor's right: Kiev can be pleasing.

"A friend of mine has spent years and years on a dictionary of the etymology of Ukrainian geographical names," he is saying. And he has proved – certainly to Viktor's satisfaction – that the roots of these names lie not just in Indo-European but in that protolanguage from which the very oldest Indo-European language, Sanskrit, was derived. "Get it? Ukrainian is the oldest European language. It's there *before* the Indo-European. All other European languages emerge from it!" This theory hasn't been easy for his friend to prove; in fact, he's done nothing of the sort, because so little material evidence concerning the development of the Ukrainian language exists. And the reason for this, says Viktor, is that it has always been in the interest of the enemies of Ukraine to "ban, suppress and burn" the evidence for the "uniqueness and antiquity" of Ukrainian culture.

"Did you know that archaeologists working in Kiev early in the century did in fact come upon the eleventh-century library of Iaroslav the Wise?" We have come to a stop again so that he can have my full attention. The Kievan's library is as legendary as the lost libraries of Alexandria and the incinerated codices of the Yucatan. "They reburied it right away, realizing that Russian scholars would not be able to absorb this shock to their ego. While a Ukrainian prince was commissioning manuscripts and translations from the Greek, Muscovites were still running around in bear skins!"

"Think of our alphabet," Victor continues. "You're going to tell me it comes from the Greek via the missionaries Cyril and Methodius. But the Greeks got it from the Phoenicians. And where did the Phoenicians get it? From the Trypillians. And who were the Trypillians? They were here in 3000 B.C. and they made the most beautiful ceramics and jewellery and they made magic... Okay, so they weren't Ukrainians, but they lived *here*, on our Ukrainian lands."

That seems to be the decisive point. Victor may be bluffing for all I know, making it up as he goes along, with the deep assurance of the true maniac. He speaks with passion and broad gestures. But the point is that, after seventy years of official historical expurgation and erasure, he narrates nevertheless the history he was never supposed to be able to imagine.

I am astounded. Seventy years of lying and forgetting, yet Victor remembers all the same. It doesn't matter if he embroiders and embellishes, making up for uncloseable gaps and wounded pride. What matters is the process he is in: constructing a necessary, if improbable, history. When I get back to my room I write it all down.

RED, RED RUE

LVIV, 1988: "Look here, it was all his mother's fault." I am back at Volodymyr Ivasiuk's grave, this time openly and in the company of an aged member of the local branch of the Writers' Union of Ukraine whose job it is, this late in his fading career, to take foreign visitors on little excursions. He had suggested the cemetery, I the grave. "You don't know this story?" We are looking at the mound of grasses and flowers, unchanged in all respects since 1984, and still without headstone and noncommittal as to the manner of the deceased's passing. It's a rather long story. Several other visitors come and go, having laid down their bouquets and stood in brief meditation, strolling away without a flicker of furtiveness. I stand rooted to the spot. This is my penance for having doubted.

"The dear lady, visiting her son at Eastertime, discovered him 'shacked up' with a mistress – forgive my bluntness, madame – and hit the roof. She knew he suffered from alcoholism and schizophrenia, yet she hounded him all the same for a couple of days – driving him to drink and the brink of madness – about his sinfulness, which was breaking her maternal heart, and at Easter, *hospode*! Then she went back home to Chernivtsi in a huff. Two days later he disappeared... Of course he hanged himself, he was *unbalanced*. Wouldn't you be? Look, I *know* his family."

I report all this to friends at dinner that night. They hem and haw. Well, they hadn't heard that story, but it's true that there seemed little reason for Ivasiuk to have been persecuted by the security forces – he wasn't political, strictly speaking. Yet there *had* been malicious gossip that he had been murdered for refusing to hand over his hard currency royalties to the State Cultural Fund for retired and indigent artists. But can one really believe such a tale? On the other hand, there are those who claim that at the time of his disappearance he was working on an opera about the Cossacks. Someone they know saw him being bundled into the black Chaika outside the Conservatory of Music. Personally, they thought he had been made an example of: he had refused the one offer you do not turn down – the invitation to move to Moscow and make an all-Union career. He had wanted, he said, to live in Ukraine and write Ukrainian songs.

"What about the plucked-out eyes? The cut-out tongue?" I ask. This is the first they've heard about the tongue; as for the eyes, they had probably been plucked out by birds. Remember, the body had been hanging for two weeks when it was found. Yes, and about that fact: it *is* odd that a suicide should choose a forbidden zone and manage to suspend himself two metres up in the air. As for the spear from the *kalyna*, the cranberry bush, they had never heard that variation. And it occurs to me, for the first time, that the image comes from the wound in the side of Jesus at the Crucifixion.

"Tell me volodymyr how did you really ascend the kalyna tree..." – Andrew Suknaski, "What Is Remembered."

CHERNIVTSI, 1988: The Historical Museum of Kitsman, a Bukovynian town not far from Chernivtsi, is hosting a small exhibit dedicated to the memory of Ivasiuk. It is a modest display, but all the more poignant for that. His school notebooks, his composer's drafts on sheet music, the first albums, a violin, a portable record player, the suit, shirt and tie he'd worn on stage. The curator has added traditional embroidered cloths – one bears Volodia's face in cross-stitch – as though to reclaim him for the village, away from the blandishments of international stardom. Because of that peculiarity of Soviet photographic processes by which all lines and shadows and facial curves disappear in a flat, dingy light, in his official portrait he looks terribly young. This is, of course, the way the sons of the soil should die: young, violently and borne away in great innocence, never knowing what hit them.

There is talk of a song festival in his name, and indeed the First Republican Festival of Modern Ukrainian Song and Pop Music will be organized within a year, offering the Volodymyr Ivasiuk Grand Prize and dedicated to the "memory of this outstanding Ukrainian composer who died under obscure circumstances." In 1990, with funds raised by a cultural foundation, community subscriptions and a donation from Ivasiuk's parents, a truly hideous monument will finally be erected on his grave in the Lychakivsky cemetery: the composer as a Byronic youth, posed romantically at a baby grand piano in an open-necked shirt, his left hand lying upturned as though waiting for the centurion to drive in a nail and impale it to the piano lid.

Ivasiuk has been beatified and his putative killers reborn as the Security Services of independent Ukraine. There is no need to investigate further.

> I see you in dreams
> in leafy green groves,
> along forgotten pathways
> you come toward me.

There are those who claim that there is no such plant as the red rue. And others who say it grows only in Ukraine. This is a political question. "It is *our* flower," the patriot will say, "and there is nothing so beautiful in the woods." In the same way, fans of Ivasiuk, when it became possible to express their feelings of loss, described his song "Red Rue" as a "spring whirlwind," a "swift flight of a bird," "honest" in its exploitation of the traditional Ukrainian song. "It was not borrowed," one artist is quoted as saying. "It is as though the people themselves had written it." And for the director of Chernivtsi television, Ivasiuk is important not just for "sincerity of heart and soul" but for the seamlessness of his art with the heritage of the folk song, "wondrous songs, not blown in from other people's fields."

Ivasiuk was a graduate of medical school and operated confidently in the Soviet spheres of media and entertainment; he lived in the big city and drank too much. But this is unessential information, and not nurturing. The truly important thing he did, from which the rest of his life, including his success, flowed, was to go looking for a song in a village. The cities are a hodgepodge, he might have said; the village is ours.

As for Ivasiuk himself, he used to say that the reason "Red Rue" could be sung everywhere in Ukrainian, accessible even to those who didn't know the language, was that it was the "spiritual achievement of youth, independent of nationality."

I will think of this a month later, in Sopot, Poland, as I sit with my friends around the table in candlelight, reluctant to get up and break the circle. Someone suggests singing. Judit and I sing some verses of Negro spirituals, and she and Gabor sing a romantic Hungarian ballad, crooning cheek to cheek. I offer the Russian chorus to the Internationale, but Anatol covers his ears and howls for me to stop. Then there is silence. The Poles, oddly, don't know any songs. Anatol, who is from Kazakhstan and knows something about music – about wine and dance and horses – begins to hum a tune under his breath, his lips moving to the words. The melody gets stronger and with its deepening bittersweetness his face softens and he smiles dreamily. He is singing "Red Rue." *For your beauty is pure water, the swift water of mountain snows.* Into our festivities he has conjured up the ghost of the boy-faced musician from Bukovyna who wrote this song, became famous and well-loved, and then died, by hanging.

THE CIRCLE SHALL BE UNBROKEN

KIEV, 1988: I've caught her standing in her paisley housecoat in a corner of her "studio," and I've taken the picture at such an angle as to show the length of the wall behind her on which hang her "gallery" of ceramic panels. She wears a radiant smile as well as the mustardy-orange robe.

Halyna Sevruk lives in one of those endlessly reproduced apartment blocks in suburban Kiev whose age is impossible to discern: you simply cannot assume, from its dilapidated façade, filthy entry and dark and corroded stairway, that it is old. But the sunlight streams into her two-room flat through thin white curtains as though bleaching the home of the soil and stain leaking in from the outside world.

I walk through the largish main room. Blind and senile, her ancient mother leans into a pile of large white pillows as though she had been toppled there and shouts gibberish at the flickering black-and-white television screen. I pass into the apartment's other room: books, shelving holding toiletries and mementos, photographs of friends in the heady days before the treks to the labour camps, the narrow bed wrapped chastely in white sheets pulled with savage tightness across the mattress.

A scrunched-up space by the window, the table's surface burdened by pots of brushes and pencils and tubes of paint, has been her "studio" for the last fifteen years.

She is a ceramicist. The panels on the long white wall of the room are a portrait gallery of the notables of Kievan Rus: Prince Kyi, Queen Olha, Prince Iaroslav the Wise and the learned Anna Iaroslavna, queen of France, their emblematic faces crowded in with mediaeval heraldic blazons and the symbols of their renown – the churches they built, the manuscripts they wrote, the totemic animals (gryphons and lions and horses) they elevated to state mythology – all set in glazes of vivid reds and blues.

These are her themes, and her magnum opus, a wall-sized series of ceramic panels, presents on one seamless plane the history of Rus. Here are the merchants and boatmen of the great river Dnipro, the armies marching against the nomads of the eastern steppes, the church builders and scribes and icon painters, the cities and their sovereigns. The roots of the short and branchy Tree of Life coil deep in the river in whose stream Dazhboh, pagan god of fertility, falls, drowning, and with whose death the epic of Rus begins.

In 1968, for signing the Appeal of the 139 protesting the arrests of writers and artists, she had been expelled from the Union of Artists of Ukraine. She lost exhibition rights, royalties, welfare benefits, access to materials and her studio. At night she would creep to the studios and kilns of friendly associates who were willing to risk the consequences of their clandestine charity. In 1989, Sevruk will show her work of the 1960s and 1970s, the work created in that narrow space of her apartment between the bleaching sunlight and the shouts of the crone in front of the television set. Among these works is a portrait of her dead friend, the artist Alla Horska.

Poet Vasyl Stus at the grave of Alla Horska, December 1970: "When a black chill shrouds our sun, seek the berry's scarlet shadow ... for we are few, a tiny handful, fit for hopes and prayers."

The grave had been dug at the edge of town, and a funeral band, hired by the Artists' Union, had already taken up position, frigid and fidgety, by the pile of excavated earth, waiting for the mourners. A hundred arrived. An official from the Artists' Union delivered the eulogy, and every now and then the band would strike up a doleful tune and then subside, stamping their feet and blowing on their frozen fingers. The official from the Union praised Alla Horska's exemplary life – her commitment to Communist ideals, her gratitude for the education she had received from Party organs. More funereal oompah-pah. End of ceremony.

Then began the *real* funeral. Her friends – some of whom had already been to trial, prison camp and back, some of whom would be going in the next great wave of arrests in a year or two – drew closer together at the lip of the grave and summed up the life of the woman who had been snatched so violently from them.

Alla Horska, artist, forty-one years old, had been murdered.

Her body had been found in the cellar of her father-in-law's house in a town outside Kiev. And when her father-in-law had also been found, sprawled decapitated on the railway tracks at the edge of town, the local militia advanced the theory that he had killed Alla and then himself, by hurling himself headfirst under a train. No relative or close friend had been allowed to examine her body nor had the coffin been opened. Rumours flew about that she had been, on the one hand, a participant in a sordid sexual drama and, on the other, the victim of a plot by "nationalists" to silence her because she "knew too much" and was already singing to the KGB. In a photo in an underground journal, she is wearing a dark sweater with a white Peter Pan collar; she has short blonde hair and a grave, close-mouthed expression. Full lips. Broad chin. Nobody's fool. Her friend, the dissident mathematician Leonid

Pliushch, loved her for never losing her "sarcastic calm." Another friend, writing from Camp Number Eleven in Mordovia, said her works had given him "reassurance."

In commemoration of the 150th anniversary of the birth of Taras Shevchenko in 1964, Horska and three fellow artists, including Halyna Sevruk and Liudmila Semykina, had been commissioned to design and execute a stained glass window that would be placed in a wall of Taras Shevchenko Kiev State University. Preliminary sketches were approved by the rector of the university and the municipal council of art.

Liudmila Semykina: "We had to work day and night and even slept on the scaffolding. We put our very souls into it. We wanted to show the grandeur, the indestructibility, the revolutionary rebelliousness that was Shevchenko, his filial ties with mother Ukraine whom he defended." But when, on March 8, 1964, V. A. Boichenko, secretary of the Kiev Regional Committee of the Communist Party of Ukraine in charge of agitation and propaganda, inspected the first completed panel, he hated it. The artists – and a growing number of curious citizens who were gathering to see what all the fuss was about – insisted that a commission of artists from the Artists' Union be convened to evaluate the work so far. Boichenko agreed. But when the commission gathered on March 18 at the artists' workshop, they discovered the window had been smashed to bits.

A photo of the window was said to have made its way eventually to Poland, where it lay unexamined in the archives of the Ukrainian Social and Cultural Society of Poland. Anecdotal accounts and descriptions by eyewitnesses in Ukraine reported that the window depicted a wrathful Shevchenko, one arm protectively embracing a young woman (Violated Motherland) and the other raised as he triumphantly wielded a book. Further, the window included a fragment of Shevchenko's verse: "I shall glorify these small, mute slaves and put the Word on guard beside them." Because of the placement of the panels, Shevchenko seemed to be standing behind bars. On April 13, under the chairmanship of Meritorious Art Worker V. Shatalin, the executive of the Kiev branch of the Artists' Union met in a closed session with Union members to discuss the vandalized stained glass window. Official: "Had you concentrated on the vertical, you could have avoided all this.... Instead, you followed the road of contemporary abstract generalization." Meritorious Art Worker V. Chernikov: "Comrades! Turn your attention to the [sketches of the] stained glass window. There is no picture there, only Shevchenko behind a grating. What exactly is this supposed to be? I have finished." The meeting decreed that Alla Horska and Liudmila Semykina be expelled from the Union rolls.

Horska's friend Nadia Svitlychna: "There were all kinds of reproaches. Yet no one had seen the window, although they exhibited ... the broken bits, which they displayed in a special room in the basement. But you could imagine how it must have looked.... For myself I'm convinced that the KGB was involved in her murder.... Having killed her, they then zealously and painstakingly wiped out everything associated with her name."

Horska's last work, in collaboration with her husband, was the painting of a restaurant in Cherkasy oblast. The painting was done in a village for a collective farm. She took her fee in food, filling up her car and distributing it among her friends. She was dead a month later.

BLANK SPOTS

KIEV, 1964: On May 24, 1964, V. Pohruzhalsky, an employee of the State Library of the Ukrainian Academy of Sciences in Kiev working in the Marxism-Leninism section, stayed behind in the library after the other employees had left for the day. Carrying phosphorus, magnesium and other inflammable materials, he went up to the seventh floor and set thirty separate fires to the Ukrainian collections – documents relating to folklore, literature and history. He was, as would emerge at his trial, a "Russophile." The fires spread swiftly through the dry, wooden shelving of the stacks and burned for three days, the fire hydrants having unaccountably failed to operate when the firemen arrived on the scene.

Rumours immediately spread through the city that the fire was the work of Ukrainian bourgeois nationalist arsonists, which was illogical. In any case, by the time of Pohruzhalsky's trial the following August, he took responsibility for the action, claiming "patriotic motives." The court found him of "unbalanced character," motivated by personal grievance against his boss, the chief librarian, and sentenced him to five years' imprisonment and five years' servitude in labour camp. At his trial, Pohruzhalsky had been questioned in some detail about his private life and his relations with his three former wives but was never questioned about how he got hold of phosphorus and magnesium. Pohruzhalsky never served his sentence.

In Kiev, in 1988, they will tell you that, for the three days the library was burning, volunteer firefighters were turned away. They will ask whether the library burned through an act of sabotage or through sheer incompetence and bungling – the shabby buildings that acted as firetraps, the lack of instruction in fire prevention measures among the staff, the slovenly, indifferent firefighters. Does it really matter, they ask, what the reason was? The library burned all the same.

LVIV, 1952: For months, an "expert commission," headed by the diplomaed artist V. Liubchuk, sat in judgement of the collection at the museum. In the end, the commission sentenced to be burned, shredded or otherwise destroyed 315 works of art by 61 artists. The works of all diaspora artists – those who found themselves outside the borders of Soviet Ukraine in 1920 – were singled out, as were the works of western Ukrainian artists deemed "bourgeois nationalists," even when it was a question of a landscape or family portrait. (In 1988 I will read in the catalogue of the Museum of Ukrainian Art in Lviv that "A characteristic feature of the artistic process of the 1920s and 1930s was the orientation of western Ukrainian artists to social themes and their lively interest in the culture and art of Soviet Ukraine.")

To get them out of the way while the dirty work was being done, the museum's director and librarian were sent to a spa. On their return and upon discovery of the spoliation, the director is said to have gone into a sudden decline. He died shortly after. In deep despair, the librarian had only one thing to say to artists of his day: "Do it! Paint! Who knows when Liubchuk will return and start burning again?" It has been suggested that a Wall of Shame be erected at the museum, hung with photographs of Liubchuk and his co-commissioners and with a complete list of all the works they destroyed or mutilated.

From the list on the Wall of Shame, someday: a bronze by Oleksandr Arkhipenko, thirty-one paintings by Petro Kholodny, Sr., "Annunciation" by F. Pekutka, "Self-Portrait" by Mykola Fediuk, "Hutzul Group" by Mykhailo Moroz, "Dead Cossack" by Antin Manastirsky ...

My guide, Olha, tells me that all of the early sculptures of the avant-gardist Arkhipenko have been destroyed, but she has heard there are some sketches somewhere. I tell her that when I first heard of Arkhipenko, as a student, he was a Russian Cubist.

"That's my point," she says.

LVIV, 1988: They are born, they paint a while, they are cut down. In the 1920s and 1930s they were dragged off to secret trials in the middle of the night, shot in walled-up courtyards or transported north of the taiga where they were last seen disappearing into a whirlwind. In the 1950s and 1960s they were sentenced in closed trials and shipped off to labour camps, once, twice, three times, until they were toothless and rickety and repentant. In the 1970s, during the Great Brezhnevite Stagnation, their creative juices were leached out by stupefying duties in the institutes or in deadening loneliness in exile. The miracle is that there are still those who know where and who they come from.

One day in the early 1970s, the painter Panas Zalyvakha looked out his window in Ivano-Frankivsk at a winter scene that pleased his eye: a flock of raucous, bustling, coal-black ravens settling down on the frosty branches of naked trees, outlined with great clarity against the frozen landscape. He painted it. Shortly after, on an official visit to his studio, a "commission" of fellow artists evaluated his work as "professionally undeveloped" and the winter landscape as "blackening," "calumnious" and "anti-Soviet." Why winter? Why black? Why frost?

Zalyvakha had just been released from the camps to which he had been sentenced for five years' severe hard labour in 1966. He had worked as a loader and stoker. He wrote from prison: "The epidemic of flu is over and I remained alive and well, God be praised. I continue through manual work to 'atone for my sins.'... Painting is forbidden.... I watch the sky and the stars."

Zalyvakha's *Self-Portrait with Oxen*, 1970: The planes of his face echo the long, flat bones of the bovines; his eyes, like theirs, are rimmed with black and gaze out at us with patient vehemence. He has painted himself strapped into the yoke.

Years of obscurity and loneliness after the funerals of his generation, and then suddenly, in 1988, Zalyvakha is rediscovered by the young and returned to the public with an exhibition at Lviv's Museum of Ethnography, an old man holding a bunch of red carnations, tears streaming down his cheeks as three hundred well-wishers press their admiration on him and his forty-three paintings.

KIEV, 1988: Sponsored by the glasnost-era Ukrainian Cultural Fund, Feodosii Humeniuk's first ever one-man show in Kiev opens at the Kiev Lavra Museum of Decorative and Applied Arts. He had studied and painted, in the 1970s, in Leningrad and Dnipropetrovsk but was denied permission to exhibit in Ukraine and, in 1982, was denounced for his "excessive indulgence" in national "romanticism," meaning the iconic and colourist canvases of folk legends and historical tableaus for which he had become admired and loved. As recently as 1984, the Ukrainian press had called him a "morally degraded person enticed by foreign parcels and invitations" for having sold works abroad.

"Ukrainians must be born twice," Humeniuk once said, "the second time spiritually, as I was."

A public meeting has been called at the museum to discuss Humeniuk's work. The artist is in attendance, wearing an embroidered shirt under a suit jacket. He speaks briefly, mumbling into his handsome moustache in a self-effacing manner. Then many people stand up to speak, including a young art enthusiast from Lviv, her blonde braids twined in a crown on the back of her head, and an old man with thick, white whiskers. The speakers talk loudly, clearly, sometimes at great length, but no one interrupts or betrays signs of impatience, even at the repeated expression of the same sentiments, for such a public forum, so recently permissible, is precious, and time must not be squandered in bad manners and bickering.

They are articulating a communal testimonial of thanks to Humeniuk: for his rootedness in them, in his narod. For his courage in bringing to his canvases artistic and spiritual practices so violently truncated. His sincerity, his honesty, his manliness (*muzhnist*), his clear-sightedness, his conscience. And they want to let this artist know that they have made the same journey – to sources, to roots, to the people, the narod. ("Look! We're still here and we call ourselves Ukrainians to this day!") Not a single member from the Party-based Artists' Union has been to see the show.

A Humeniuk painting, *Carol Singing*. A Cossack in boots and voluminous pants, with a sword. Rooster on his arm. Woman bearing bell and wine jug. Cow. Pig. Angel, stepped out of icon. A star. A halo. Blocks of colour slanting across the scene. The edge of a figure becomes the throat of a beast. Folklore deconstructed as circles and arcs, cylinders and surfaces. Humans and animals, angels and music, colour, line and meaning exist on the same plane. There is no perspective. All worlds inhabit the same space.

What is Humeniuk doing here, with this lexicon of folk memory, tapping the despised and the left behind? The New Order is about the city, the machine, the newspeak; the Soviet person does not dream, s/he *plans*. If you do not want to live there, if you do not want to speak that language, where do you go? First, to your own studio, shutting the door on academies, unions, exhibits, critics, commissions, tours, catalogues, etc. Then you go *back*, back to that place the revolution and war heaved you out from: the village.

The here and now is constantly being interrupted, interfered with, ruptured and erased. The point is not to argue with the "collective," the "social," but to rejoin it. There is no art in the solitary gesture, the private quest; that way lies only idiosyncrasy. Art is born in the ethnos, the place everybody comes from: the village, its tales, its adventurers. This will be yours. You will claim the detritus of a revolutionary upheaval: village cottage, village church, gull, sheaf of wheat, the angel. These remain uncorrupted. The forward vision, the plan, begets only sterility, only the perpetually unrealized. The dream backward yields connection.

I sit in the museum gallery riveted by this savage nostalgia and my own speechless ambivalence. Humeniuk's paintings enclose us in this room in a kind of rapture of remembrance of the "eternal village," the place that remained, no matter what, *ours*. Here, in this zone of mud and land hunger, people spoke Ukrainian and kept the Ukrainian ways while the cities were won by the colonizers and the colonized elite. It is no wonder that, at the times of our collective reawakening and restoration of our memory (as now, in 1988, in Kiev), we remember where we came from. But I chafe with impatience. Behind this fantastic village of Humeniuk's desire lies the *real* one, the one I've heard about all my life, the one that my grandparents fled and, in fleeing, saved me from.

The farmers collapsed, struggled to their feet, then fell again on the earth which ran uselessly through their fingers. Or they went seeking land beyond the seas while others in despair squandered it in drink or walked among the landlords and their lackeys clutching their blue work books. And out there on the landlord's field, an old woman gathers bits of gnarled wood and hides corncobs inside her shirt. Poor Dmytro patches women's boots. And the hut is such hell that even the birds will not come to sit here.

I want *this* village to end. I want Ukrainians not to have to live in it. Or, having escaped it, not to keep wanting to merge with it in nostalgia for a lost self. I want Ukrainians to assume a modern identity, a *psychology*. "You are our heart and our brains," the villagers cry out to the doctor, the writer, the teacher. "Show us the world, lead us out to it!" I want to know: when do Ukrainians finally live in their own time?

STEPPE BALLAD

"Ukrainians: The Ukrain... is inhabited by the refuse of several nations, who came from the neighbourhood of the Black Sea, among whom are Poles, Russians, Hungarians, Turks and Tartars, who, however, pretend to be Christians. They are usually Cossacks, are noted for their cruelties, and there is no sort of crime they are not ready to commit." – Jacobus Barclay, 1774

ODESSA, 1988: For years and years, long after their defeat, aged Cossacks who had not been exiled or imprisoned could be seen tramping the dirt trails of the steppes. They were sellers of salt, the *chumaky*, and they plied their trade from the salt marshes of the south. We wait for a sunny day, and when it comes Seriozha takes me to the outskirts of Odessa. There, from a sandy hillock on the shore of the Kuialnitsky Estuary, we can see, under the clear taut skin of the pools in the salt pans, the pattern of the wooden stakes driven into the pans a hundred years ago by the saltmakers at the origin of the Salt Route. Trundling over the steppe, leading teams of oxen yoked onto wooden-wheeled carts, the old Cossacks, as white and flaking as their cargo, bore the blocks of salt from the Black Sea to Kiev. Cossacks of the brotherhood of the *sich*: travelling salesmen. Cossack, or Kozak: from the Turkic, *gazag*, freebooter.

The focal point of Illia Repin's picture *The Zaporozhians* is the Cossack with the quill pen who is drafting a letter in reply to the Ottoman sultan. The content of this letter – presumably dictated by the company of Cossacks assembled around the scribe – is hilarious, for one man holds his belly in laughter, others smirk, jeer and grin, stroking their moustaches and puffing on their pipes in deep pleasure. One Cossack sprawls expansively on a wooden barrel while another, bearing the wounds of war (a bloodied bandage around his head) gazes down at the letter writer with fixed satisfaction. Cossack accoutrements – swords and scabbards, water flasks, lutes, muskets – clutter the space while in the background can be made out the tent poles and tents and milling throng of the sich in Zaporozhia. The Zaporozhians have received a communication from the Turks, demanding tribute. This is the Cossacks' reply: they laugh.

I am ten, and I have seen the "funny picture" everywhere for as long as I can remember: fat-bellied, bald-pated men in animal skins enjoying a good joke. I know these funny men are Cossacks and that they are some- how related to us Ukrainian Canadians. But I can't place them, either in my grandmother's village or on a northern Alberta homestead. They live in some never-never land, east of the sunrise, without children, without women (who cooks? how do they wash their clothes?) in an exotic summer camp that is both dangerous (all those swords) and entertaining (the belly laughs). They wear costumes – peaked caps, bearskin capes and pantaloons – and gesture theatrically: the sich is a stage and I sit in the dark, looking on.

The Cossacks had come in the mid-sixteenth century to the lands once held as Rus by the princes of Kiev and Chernihiv, lands that had lain empty after the fall of the cities to the Mongols. They were runaway serfs, defrocked priests, army deserters, townsmen on the lam, adven- turers. To hear tell of it, theirs was an idyllic existence, a Boy's Own story: tightly knit groups of free men, self-governing, making forays into the steppe to hunt and fish, to graze cattle, capture wild horses, even raise bees for honey ... and to gather at night around the campfire to sing the *dumy* (ballads) of their peculiar fate. Any Christian male, no matter his social origin, was free to join them. As a brother of the sich, he had co-equal rights with all the others and had a vote in the election of the hetman. He could leave when he wanted to. Women and children were not welcome. The sich was not a village; it was a war camp.

They lived on the edge: the edge of cultivated Ukraine, *u krai*, facing out towards the "wild fields," just beyond the reach of landlords, tax collectors and recruiting officers; the edge of Christian communion and Slavic speech, glaring ferociously eastward at the dust devils on the steppe horizon raised by the Tatar horsemen returning to Crimea on their ponies after a raid.

"They Trade in Slaves in Turkey," a painting done by Ivan Iznakevych in 1926–27, shows a mosque, a minaret, the awnings of a bazaar. Ukrainian men bound in ropes, prostrate on the bare ground. A pile of loot: swords, caskets, carpets. On the carpets, Ukrainian women, semi-naked and

dishevelled, huddle in an imploring heap as their Moorish master menaces them with a whip and a trio of ogling fat men in turbans look on.

The Tatars, volatile Turkic nomads under the overlordship of the ottoman in Istanbul, twenty-five thousand strong, advanced in an immense semicircle across Ukraine, burning, looting and ravishing. According to the chronicles, in 1575 alone they plundered along the Dnister for two months, taking fifty-five thousand prisoners, including Cossacks, and driving them in herds to the slave markets in Smyrna and Crete, where the captives were loaded onto caravans with spices and carpets and silk for Istanbul. The Tatars had been making their raids every year since the early 1300s and would continue until 1769, when they were absorbed into the Russian Empire.

In 1553, under imperial orders from Moscow, a fortress was built on Khortytsia Island in the bend of the Dnipro River (across from the modern city of Zaporozhia) as part of a line of defence against the Crimean Tatars. The sich became the headquarters of the Dnipro Cossacks, who proceeded to stage their own "unbelievably daring raids in all directions," in the words of the Russian historian Nicholas Riasnovsky. They became a legend because they created the Zaporozhian Host, terror of Tatars, Turks and Poles. As fortress and brotherhood, the sich stood like a bulwark of strength in the sea of the Ukrainian oppressed.

The Hetman, gorgeous in red tunic and sash, red boots and pantaloons, crowned with fur and eagle feathers, sits astride a dainty white horse, holding aloft in his right hand the mace of office. He points up and for-ward, as though in the direction of Warsaw, to lead the way for the Cossack army assembling behind him. It is 1648, and they are on the warpath. Across the horizon trudges a shadowy horde of peasants on foot, armed with stakes and scythes, a wall of flames backlighting them as they cut their bloody, vengeful swaths across Ukraine. They have joined the Cossacks under the leadership of "Batko" (Papa) Bohdan Khmelnitsky, the Hetman in red, in what will be one of the most violent and protracted peasant uprisings of early modern Europe.

I have seen the famous painting of Khmelnitsky hundreds of times in Ukrainian-Canadian halls and offices. The portly Hetman, surrounded by a jubilant crowd, has achieved the impossible – he has thrown out the Poles and restored Kiev, the heart of Old Rus, to Orthodoxy and Ukrainian heroes. The price the Ukrainians have paid for this liberation is war.

Khmelnitsky was hailed a "second Moses": the deliverer of the Ukrainian people from an alien king, alien landowners and an alien church. If there was any moment in Ukrainian history when the possibility of a Ukrainian *state*, autonomous and institutionalized, could have been realized as well as dreamed of, this was it.

Instead, Cossacks and Poles continued to fight inconclusively. The Ukrainians' old enemies, the mercenary Tatars, with whom Khmelnitsky had adroitly contracted an alliance, withdrew their support, and many landlords, slipping through loopholes in treaties with the Cossacks, reclaimed their estates and re-enserfed their peasants. By 1654, Khmelnitsky was forced to choose a "protector" for his vulnerable people and the fledgling state that was caught between more powerful governments. He could choose the sultan in Istanbul or the czar in Moscow. He chose Moscow, signed the Pereiaslav Agreement in 1654 and died in 1657. He ended as he had begun, outmanoeuvred by potentates, and his failure marked the beginning of a period in Ukrainian history known as the Ruin: civil and fratricidal wars, foreign and mercenary intervention, hunger and epidemic and ravening death. Ten years after his initial triumph, at the bloodletting of the battle near Poltava in 1658, rival Cossack armies were slaughtering *each other*.

In 1775, incensed by the last great Cossack and peasant uprising in Ukraine, Catherine the Second, known to Russians as "the Great," razed the legendary fortress at Zaporozhia, distributed the Cossack lands among German, Mennonite and Serbian colonists and exiled the leaders to Siberia. For the Cossacks' last commander, Petro Kalnyshevsky, whom she had once decorated with gold and diamonds in thanks for his campaigns against the Turks, she reserved a special fate: twenty-five years in solitary confinement in a windowless, man-sized cell in a prison on the Solovetsky Islands in the White Sea. It was the first trek of the Ukrainians to the gulag.

The Cossack – bold and fearless and independent – is a kind of ur-Ukrainian. The Cossack, laughing derisively at the pretensions of a Turkish sultan, is the symbolic reminder of what we once were, before we became engulfed by our modern history, laid low by our enemies, dispirited by our own helplessness.

I want to come to the Cossack romance as to a restorative, to accept in these heroic horsemen the symbols of the possibility of a people's independent communal existence. They occupied the wide-open wild lands so recently despoiled by the Mongols: they evaded serfdom, scorned overlords and measured a man's worth in battle. They were fugitives, squatters, brigands, mercenaries and artisans who staked out autonomous territory and held it, in that space known to faraway Polish and Lithuanian serfs as the "divinely protected zone of freedom."

The rude reality, though, is that the admirable "brigandage" of the freebooters was too often garden-variety plundering, pillage and rape by bandits who robbed the poor, never gave away their loot and kidnapped women for the slave markets or as sexual slaves for the sich itself.

The celebrated, if rudimentary, democracy of the Cossack fort looks to be the familiar fraternity of men bonded together by secret oaths and ceremonies, symbols, taboos and fetishes, with privileges of self-rule that were never extended beyond the "blood brothers" themselves. The Cossacks lived in a military, not civilian, institution. Their loyalty was to each other, and their alliances with other groups were mainly opportunistic. To all accounts, they were not above selling out the peasant rabble for the promise of a land grant or an army commission or the chance to own some peasants themselves. And they were at the head of the furious peasants when the wars against the Polish landlords swept up the Jews who worked for them.

In the great uprisings of the Cossacks and the renegade serfs between 1648 and 1656, tens of thousands of Jews were killed. The purgatorial flames of the burning countryside – that "necessary" conflagration of social war – fed on the terrible fuel of Jewish houses, Jewish merchandise and Jewish bodies. The peasants rose up, armed themselves, joined with the Cossacks and marauded. They assaulted their oppressors, put their properties to the torch and danced on their graves.

What is a massacre like? The sepia-coloured illustration in the history book I found as a child in my parents' library showed its aftermath: the Gothic ruin of the Catholic church, the black cloud of carrion crows and the jackals feeding on the bodies of the dead, among whom, in the light of the fading day and the democratizing anonymity of death, it is impossible to distinguish Pole from Jew, priest from leaseholder. All the worse for the living: the priest skinned alive and the seminary students buried deep in wells, their heaving lungs sucking in the muck. As for the Jews, they met their nemesis in the woods in a vain flight from the

Cossack youths in pursuit, terrible angels of justice, knives poised above the yawling throats.

From a Cossack duma: "*When God sent a child to a Cossack or a peasant, / The father could not go to the priest for a blessing, / But had to go to a Jewish leaseholder / And give him six small coins.*" Jews, barred from the professions and from owning land, leased revenue-producing enterprise from Polish landlords, thus becoming the primary instruments of serfdom's oppression of the peasants. Wherever the serf turned – to have grain milled or timber cut, to sell at the local market or drive a cart down the highway, to drink in the tavern or baptise a child in the church – there was a Jewish leaseholder skimming off his own surplus along with the taxes to be delivered to the pan. The landlords sometimes granted Jews disciplinary authority as well, with the right to judge infractions on the estate and to impose punishment, up to and including death. For the Jews, survival lay in the patronage of the pan; for the Ukrainians, in stoking resentment against those they saw as their oppressors. It was not until serfdom itself was abolished – that "rotten, pathological society," as the historian John-Paul Himka describes it – that Ukrainians and Jews in the villages of the Polish kingdom could begin to disengage from their broken-winded, bloodied embrace.

I wonder how we Ukrainians are to find communal healing in these ambiguous images of peasants maddened by their own oppression, freebooters at their head? How can a community find self-respect in such hosannas to violence? There is so much death here – in the bootless serfs shaking pitchforks at field cannons, in the twisting bodies of the lynched and the torments of the flayed and burned, in the raped and disembowelled women and the babies tossed to the dogs, and so on, and so on, the blood running as though it were sap draining out of the tree of life and not, as patriarchal mythmakers would have it, the "fertilizer" of future generations of warriors, themselves of course to become the quick and the dead.

I was a grown-up before I learned that the Cossacks also built schools, had a style of church architecture named for them and, in at least one case, produced a philosopher who could speak six languages, including Greek.

I dance in the basement of the church. The whole dancing class is on stage for the grand finale. We know our parts. Girls in a line at the very back, mincing girlishly with little pointy steps and holding our hands coquettishly to the side of our heads, smiling, smiling, smiling. At centre stage: the boys doing a Cossack dance – the whirlwind of males, their frisky dashes across the boards, their drumming and stamping booted feet carrying them in cartwheels through the air and soaring, catapulted leaps over our heads as we all go "Ooh" and "Aah" until they come down to earth again with a smart bow and a kick. Sixteen-year-old farm and small-town and city boys who play hockey and snap their fingers to Elvis Presley reenact for us the dance of the wild men of the steppe who will redeem us all, if we will just keep the faith.

The liberation of Ukraine is the affair of men, and even these crew-cutted and pimply adolescents with names like Johnny and Orest and Fred, who sit in Saturday School dreaming of cruising down Highway 45 between Willingdon and Myrnam with an arm around a girl and a case of beer on the back seat – even they are the representatives of the Zaporozhian sich.

ZAPOROZHIA, 1988: We are clattering along the ruinous highway to Zaporozhia, a cheerless itinerary through a cold and despoiled countryside, once the honeyed steppelands of the sich. In the 1930s, Soviet authority, dreaming of cheap hydroelectric power, flooded the fertile settlements along the Dnipro to create putrid seas that lie like bilge water over the bones of villages. Back home in Edmonton, I had read in *News from Ukraine* a story about this area: "Waves of the man-made sea go on to submerge former Cossack lands and undermine the banks. The land of Khortytsia has lost hundreds of hectares of ancient Cossack land over the past years. The local authorities over the years distributed historical territory to build holiday homes, enterprises, whatever you like. Concentrations of industrial enterprises on this land, and the tons of toxic discharges, exceed several times admissible norms."

Riding the highway on the outskirts of town, I can see the "satanic mills" of the enterprises – steel and auto plants – right in the town centre, engulfed in yellowish vapours and discharging their emissions on the populace below. In the breakneck period of industrial expansion and the first Five Year Plan (1928–33), it had been considered a proletarian distinction to live in the embrace of the mill.

No one can give us directions to Khortytsia Island. They doff their caps, scratch their heads, point at various possibilities. Once we have found it ourselves, no one knows the way to the site of the sich. I am exasperated. What is the matter with these people? They are living on or near some of the most hallowed ground of Ukrainian history and they *don't know how to find it?* We stumble across a parking lot and a small, hand-printed sign, "Museum." I stand on the lot, looking around me in all directions: phalanxes of pylons, colossi bearing power cables, criss-cross the whole length of the island. The shrubbery is dusty, exhausted. Near the doors to the museum, two ancient and defaced crosses slump into the soil. Beyond the humps of the island the Dnipro hydroelectric works are flung across the river in triumphalist bravado. *This* is why there is a museum here. The rooms are full of Cossack memorabilia and bric-a-brac, but the pièce de résistance, the installation towards which the whole museum has been directed, is the wall-sized painting depicting the exhilarating and prodigious labour of thousands of shock workers building the dam.

THE OLD MAN

LVIV, 1988: From my window in the Intourist Hotel I have a fine view out to Lenin Street and the fin-de-siècle monument to the Polish poet Adam Mickiewicz. He stands halfway up the impressive column in a great deal of drapery, an arm extended as if to receive the lyre held out to him by a hovering angel. Some citizens of this city would like to tear the thing down. They want to put up a statue of Taras Shevchenko or, at the very least, to place Taras somewhere equally prominent. Unfortunately, the other pride of place, in the opera square, is already taken up by Lenin.

The citizens have been struggling for a hundred years for a monument to the Old Man. Now, in this age of reconstruction, their wish has been granted, in principle, but no site has been designated as yet. Perhaps foolishly, the civic authorities have decided to confer with the public about how to proceed. What should the monument look like? Where should it be?

All proposed sites have so far been rejected by public opinion as too unimportant, too cluttered or out of the way. If a Polish poet stands downtown, how can the Old Man be shunted off to a suburban round-about? As for the statue, none of the designs in competition has met with approval either. Too Leninesque (Lvivians are very proud that their city never had a Stalin statue) or too reminiscent of extant statuary, such as at Kaniv: the Old Man as bald-headed, brooding Conscience.

I have heard that, only a couple of days ago, fifteen thousand people were turned away by ranks of police from the stadium where they had gathered to discuss the question of the Shevchenko monument. A ban on "demonstrations" has been declared. It's been explained to me that these "Shevchenko meetings" have lately turned into mass forums on the state of everything – a great hue and cry about the paralysis of pere-stroika in Ukraine, the snub of cultural activists by the organizers of an upcoming Party conference, the deplorable state of the Ukrainian lan-guage, the failure of the civic authorities to remove the Russian-lan-guage signs on shops and streetcars and at intersections.

To gather in his name and raise hell: the Old Man would have been pleased.

He wears an astrakhan cap and long whiskers. He has bushy eyebrows, but he does not glower. He's stout. He's been dead more than a hundred years. He's a saint. He likes children; I'm convinced of this. Once a year, in March, the whole family gets dressed up in our good outfits to go to the church basement to honour him on the anniversary of his birth. I have never not known his name: Taras Shevchenko. I have always known he was a poet. The poet. Others don't count. For him I'm dressed up in a starched cotton dress and polished white shoes. There's his picture. It is ubiquitous. It is an icon. Alongside the family portraits, the group photographs of the members of the women's associations and the painting of Bohdan Khmelnitsky entering Kiev, he watches over us.

Children step forward on the stage and recite his poems in a dogged singsong. It is difficult to tell whether they understand what they are say-ing, but it doesn't matter. Everyone adores them. Everyone smiles and claps. I'm on the stage too, in the children's choir, thrilled by the lights, the paper streamers crisscrossing the ceiling, the rapt faces of my parents as I croon the words that will not die. My understanding is not required, only my bearing witness even at a tender age to this collective rite of recollection.

I remember the little boy in the embroidered shirt and pressed trousers who stood on a battered metal chair in the meeting room of the Ukrainians in Gdansk, Poland, in 1984. He stood up there so we could all see him. We had teacups and pieces of cake. It was the Old Man's birthday party. "*Iak umru, to pokhovaite mene ...,*" the boy began.

He twisted his hands and pulled at his sleeves, but we all smiled extrava-
gantly at him and nodded our heads in sympathetic rhythm as he completed the mantra. "*I mene v semi velykii...*" The Old Man hung there,
in his whiskers. This was for him.

Like a blind man Shevchenko saw, with a third eye, into the humiliated hearts of his countrymen and countrywomen. He was ours, the
peasants', the illiterates'. I think I understood this right from the beginning: my barely literate grandmother draped her picture of Taras hon-
orifically with an embroidered towel. It was not required that she be
able to read. In 1988, a picture of the Old Man hangs in a corner of the
main room in the home of a collective farm worker of Soviet Ukraine.
Icons are discouraged, so she says her daily prayers to Taras.

"That's Taras Shevchenko," my Saturday School teachers would say,
pointing at the icon. "He's our bard. He's our Robbie Burns." They
always added that: "He's our Robbie Burns." We already knew who
Burns was; his funny poems were in our books in "English" school and
the "English" made a large, noisy, public fuss about him on Robert
Burns Day. Only Ukrainians made a fuss about Taras Shevchenko.

*I am fifteen years old. In a big picture book I look at the reproduction of
one of Taras's paintings. It shows a naked-chested man sitting splayed on
the stone floor of a prison cell, his ankles in manacles, his muscled arms
pinned back by rope, his head turned away and up towards a tiny barred
window from which streams the little beam of light in whose pool the prisoner sits. In his mouth – this is what agitates, even excites me – a bar of
wood, clamping down his tongue. I am lured by the disturbing confusion of
sadism, pity and indignation it evokes in me. I know that Taras was a
political prisoner. He must have painted this picture from bitter experience, and I ache for the dumb ardour of that head turned to the light. But
the sunshine washes over his naked shoulders and across his straining
breast and belly: behold the Ukrainian Prometheus. It is not a political
prisoner I admire but a god on the rack.*

Later, when I visit Tulova, the home of my ancestors, I will stand in the
middle of the village common near the bushy tree under which a grave
mound for Taras has been erected. A picket fence, a grassy hummock
green as jungle, a white plaster pediment trimmed in blue paint and the
bust of Taras, exactly the same head and face and jacketed shoulders as on
the little plaster bust that supervises my study in Edmonton: the high-

domed, hairless forehead, the luxuriant whiskers, the eyebrows drawn together not in irascibility but in some far-sighted anguish, as though he were looking straight into this very day and finding it wanting.

I stand awhile, mulling. I want to say something to Taras but I feel tongue-tied by my own desire to do so. All my life it has been Taras Shevchenko who has had something to say to us, down through the generations. We lend an ear, murmur appreciatively, vow to recommit ourselves to this or that. The elders recite the well-known details of Taras's biography as an exemplary narrative we would do well to ponder as we take the measure of our own self-satisfied lives. The poems remind us of the dog-weary field serfs, the ravished maidens, the patriots at the dark end of obscure lives, the once-brave Cossacks lost under the erasing drift of steppe dust. Even I, squirming in the audience, got the drift of it.

Now I want to say something about how, when Taras imagined a free Ukraine, he never imagined someone like me: granddaughter of a Ukrainian peon upended from the "eternal" village and cast upon the North American plain to breed a second generation of anglophones practising professions in the cities. He never imagined that this was what the struggle was for: to leave this godforsaken place and not come back, sending instead a grandchild who recognized nothing but could make out the names of the family on the village gravestones. This, at last, was the free Ukrainian.

Peace, old man. I've been to the village. It lives, and it is ours.

SCRAPBOOK OF THE VILLAGE

"Women so gaunt and pale you want to cry… / the men morose, of stern, fanatic glance… / their ragged, dusty bundles round them piled – those are the emigrants." – Ivan Franko, "The Emigrants"

TULOVA, 1988: In the plushy back seat of the sleek black car provided by my hosts, the Writers' Union of Ukraine, and driven by an official chauffeur, I am rolling through Ivano-Frankivsk oblast, driving the route back into Tulova, Galicia, that my paternal grandparents rode on their way out to Canada in 1901.

The scenes scrolling past the window are pleasing – very green, gently contoured fields, small groups of old women and children tending the cows and goats that graze in clover-carpeted ditches, swaying horse-drawn wooden wagons that take up much of the pitted roadway. Because the collective farms are so huge, I have an impression of the unfenced expansiveness of northeastern Alberta, and I take a deep breath as if to draw it all in.

If I shut my eyes, I see the village of Ukrainian-Canadian imagination: cowbells, geese, fiery red poppies glutting the garden, an old man in an embroidered shirt and straw hat. I am brought back to Ukrainian earth, however, by a series of spine-cracking jolts as we pass over craters and veer smartly around piles of gravel left in the middle of the road, as though the road workers had suddenly been called away on a more urgent assignment.

We wheel leftward off the highway and up a dirt road to the village. I take in the green sward of the common, the tethered cow, the church just beyond it and the splotches of colour of the houses sheltered in the village greenery. We pull up at the first building and stop. The chauffeur says I must go in here first.

The building is a crumbling structure with brilliant blue wainscotting and an agitprop poster on the outside wall: "The Fulfilment of the Food Plan Is the Nation's Business." Above the open door, in red and white letters, a sign announces this as the headquarters of the Village Council Committee of the Village of Tulova. I walk in and find myself in a shadowy room set up with wire racks displaying yellowed newspapers and pamphlets and some dark, clothbound books. Behind a counter stands a young woman I take to be the librarian, if not the council in its entirety.

I have startled her, as if the last thing she expected was clientele. I introduce myself and tell her why I've come. Her face lights up. "Come," she says, "I will take you to the Kostashchuks."

We trot down a sun-dappled dirt road and turn into the yard of a rather handsome newish house (again that brilliant blue, in the plastered exterior walls). Just to the back of it is the original dwelling, a low-roofed hut with small windows and a large nail by the door holding up a pair of men's pants. There is no grass in the yard, only chickens pecking at the gravel and two thin trees. (Where are the blossoming pear trees, the sunflowers and fat red pumpkins on the stem?) The front door is open and the librarian waves me through. The three women seated inside, who don't seem at all surprised to see me, are introduced as the mother, wife and daughter of my kinsman Hryhorii. We kiss cheeks and stand speechlessly, smiling at each other.

I am given a tour of the house, three large and airy rooms papered with bright red rose garlands running up and down the walls and decorated with embroideries and Turkish-style carpets. Enormous cushions are piled five high on the divans: leaning against them, you'd send some tumbling down upon your head. I note a virtual gallery of essential Ukrainian scenes in frames throughout the rooms: Taras Shevchenko brooding on a rock in the middle of the steppes, a blind kobzar singing under a tree in a village, Batko Bohdan's triumphal entry into Kiev, an icon of the Mother of God. The women point out the photographs of family members taken many years ago, naming them all precisely and indicating the nature of their relationships to each other, but I recognize no one.

Preliminary hospitality having been exhausted, we all sit down at a table to await the arrival of the man of the house, Hryhorii Kostashchuk, on his way home now from the kolhosp fields. We sit and talk of genealogies and of how a branch of the family grows now in Canada, thanks to the enterprising spirit of the one Kostashchuk who got away. He married Anna Svarich from two houses down and left with all her relatives, including her irascible brother, Peter, pedagogue and adventurer, who had arranged the whole thing. I am the first Kostash to come back.

Hyrhorii arrives, we embrace – the traditional three wet kisses on the cheek – and he proposes a little walking tour of the village. He is a real *muzhyk*, a collective farm worker with a grizzled, knobby skull and steel teeth, who, because he is in his work clothes, will not go inside the church out of respect to the Mother of God. But he leads me to it and has the sexton throw on the switch and so I see it in all its renovated, repainted splendour, readied for the millennium: the wall paintings and icons, banners, chandelier, embroideries and plastic flowers, and a row of fat light bulbs casting a glow of pink around the mild face of the Mother of God Herself.

Next, the cemetery. Here lie the Kostashchuks, including the boy killed in 1944 on the western front. There is a whole row of these boys, their headstones shoved up along the fence, the village's truncated family lines. And the grave of Vasyl Kostashchuk, a village schoolteacher who wrote a book. I sit down on the grass to take the measure of this information. I am not the family's first pen pusher after all and I do not come, not entirely, miraculously from illiterates. Witness this Vasyl, this toiler in the village schoolhouse, beacon of light in the village reading room.

"How did Tulova get its name?" I ask Hryhorii as we walk towards the village green. "From *tulub*," he replies. Meaning "trunk of the body." "The Tatars chopped off our heads," he explains, with a descriptive gesture, "and left the bodies behind." As if this had happened the day before yesterday. I see the green littered with the decapitated, veins pumping out blood into the root systems of the linden trees, while the skulls of the villagers hang bleached on the tent poles of the Crimean Khanate. This happened in Galicia! In the bosom of European landlords!

At the village common we stop at a desecrated plaster monument effaced of its cross. It had been erected shortly after the abolition of serfdom in the Austro-Hungarian empire in 1848 and been knocked down by "*them*, from Moscow," says Hryhorii, winking meaningfully at me, "in the 1950s."

I think of the map my father showed me just before I left for Europe. Drawn from memory by my great-uncle Peter Svarich, it showed the layout of all the villages on the road from Sniatyn to Kolomyia, including Tulova. In a meticulous hand he had drawn the central plan of his village, how it was arranged around the common: the properties of Hryts Onyshchuk, Vasyl Poraiko and the blacksmith Budakovsky; the school with its two swings, the orchard, the willow fences, the conical haystacks, the triple-domed church and the reading room. In the centre of the common, he had drawn the four trees sheltering the monument dedicated to the abolition of serfdom. In his sketch, the monument still bears its cross.

The Kostashchuks of Tulova, in bare feet and with bared heads, with too many children and not enough land, would have received the news of their liberation from the pan himself, standing in a black mood within the arches of his porch. Did they sing his praises, offering thanks also to God?

Before I knew there had been Ukrainian saints and well before I had heard of Ukrainian scholars, I knew that Ukrainians had been serfs. *Kripak*: serf, from the verb *kripyty*, to fix, to fasten.

In a letter written in 1783, state official Mikolaj Pobog-Rutkowski pleaded with the higher authorities for permission to beat every tenth peasant in the village of Vyshatychi. "The local peasant is as stupid as he is stubborn," he wrote, "and the cudgel will instruct him more quickly than hunger or imprisonment."

Working hilly terrain on small plots, owing the pan five and six days of labour a week and delivering up to him half their produce, losing communal forests and pastures to their landlord's confiscation, the average Galician serf family in 1819 was reduced to fourteen acres from which to support themselves on one or two days' labour a week. In 1848, on the eve of emancipation, this had shrunk to 9.6 acres. Emancipation came not a year too soon: with a food intake (mainly cabbage and potatoes) one-half that of the western European farmer, a life expectancy of thirty to forty years and a death rate that exceeded the birth rate, the destitute Galician peasant was on the verge of extinction.

Even with emancipation, the landlords retained ownership of forests and pastures, charging the "independent" farmers a fee for firewood and pasturage. Of thirty-two thousand court cases that disputed this arrangement from 1848–81, the landlords won thirty thousand. Half of the village children died before their fifth birthdays. There was only one hospital for every 1200 inhabitants, one tavern for every 220. At the point of mass emigration to Canada in 1902, 80 per cent of the peasantry was classified "poor" and some 50,000 were dying each year of hunger. (Why, then, did the emigrants weep, huddled on the station platform? Did they not know they were about to save, if not themselves, then their children, and their children's children, and their children's children's children?)

Fedor and Anna Kostashchuk, along with Anna's family, left Tulova for Canada in March 1900. I imagine the days before their departure, their neighbours milling about the common, restless, shaking their limbs as if they don't know whether to dance or weep. Fedor moves among them with a large stone jug, pouring out the *horilka* into their wooden mugs. The women do not drink. They sing a sad song of farewell, joined by a pair of blind musicians who have been singing for their supper up and down the King's Highway. The young people, in crisp white shirts, hold each other by the waist and sway like branches in a slow, drifting *kolomyika*. A scythe against the tree stump. A goose in the reeds of the pond. Anna Kostashchuk walks backwards out of her house, stopping at its stoop, and genuflects deeply, three times, in propitiation to the gods of the hearth. Then, on hands and knees, she kisses the stoop and rises, brushing the dust off her apron. Fedor is already on his way to the church with his neighbours; there will be one last Mass and the funeral hymn: *Vichnaia Pamiat.* Eternal Memory. It is a kind of death. Anna and Fedor are leaving forever. They are dropping off the face of the earth.

The leisurely drive to the Kostash homestead always seems to take forever, east on Highway 16 and around the curve leading up to the Royal Park grain elevators and the gas station that marks the point where we leave the highway and turn onto a gravel and dirt road that will take us to the farm. We are instantly in the country, among poplar windbreaks, ditches filled with wild roses, orderly fields laid out with oats and barley, then a dip in the road and there we are, at the track that leads us into the yard.

I love this place. Games around the pigpens. Games in the lilac bushes and caragana hedges. The creak of well ropes, the splash of the pail hitting the water down near the centre of the earth. The barn, vast and cavernous, a cathedral of wood and chink-filtered sunlight, grain dust in the hazy atmosphere, smells of dung and horse piss, leather harness and straw.

Back at the house, in the lean-to kitchen, Anna Kostash (the "chuk" having been dropped by my grandfather) ladles out chicken soup into the flat soup bowls of her daughter-in-law's wedding china. She is tiny and dressed in black, her head in a woollen cap; she has always been the same age – very old – and peers out at us from behind cloudy glasses. I never understand a word she says, nor she me. I think she has been in the kitchen a hundred years.

It has never occurred to me that the farm has not always been here, or that someone had to come along from some other place to build it. And so, to be told that my grandparents had emigrated from Ukraine to Royal Park, that they had broken sod and harnessed themselves to the plough, that Uncle Harry had lived in a dugout and that my own father had walked the miles to school, kicking buffalo skulls out of his path, that after many hardships the family had prospered and produced all the aunts and uncles, cousins and second cousins, of the family reunions, is like the recitation of a well-loved tale: it is marvellous, but it all happened in some other, primordial time, having come to its satisfying conclusion well before my arrival.

The landlords are gone now from Tulova and the land, collectivized, is officially "the people's." Yet old women, swaddled in layers of ragged clothes, trudge through the small forests in wintertime, chopping feebly at spindly trees with little hatchets and dragging the virtually worthless timber away, hoping to sell it in the village. It is an intensely familiar little scene.

In 1988, in a typical Ukrainian oblast, two-thirds of the villages have no public baths, some 160 have no hard-surfaced roads and fewer than 1 per cent of the households are hooked up for gas central heating. Many state shops have no flour, milk, oil, fish products or even salt. Villagers heat their homes with wood, piling it in the corridor between the two main rooms of the house and burning it in a tiled stove. In the land of the latifundia, the peasant is still a pilferer from her own larder.

Earth, *a 1930 film by Oleksandr Dovzhenko. The first section of shots, as described in the script: beautiful views of the Ukrainian village; haycutters; the river; vegetables; fruits; wonderful field of rye, like the sea; flowers; a girl, like the sun, hot, vital, dreamy; flowers; scattered flowers; children; horses; colts; oxen; scattered flowers.*

The backdrop on the stage in the basement of St. John's Ukrainian Greek Orthodox Church, Edmonton, never changed. A local artist, a war refugee, had been commissioned to paint a village scene and there it hung, throughout my childhood, his charming and enchanted dreamscape that became mine too. It was a never-never land of blossoming cherry trees, thatched-roof cottages and maidens in embroidered blouses – a kind of Ukrainian *Heidi*, or *Anne of Green Gables*. A vanished place made all the sweeter for having disappeared into the black hole of famine and war.

Dovzhenko's script: pears; melons; vegetables; the old man is chewing, and the cow is chewing, her calf beside her; the child chews the melon; various kinds of food; a child is suckling; another child beams with happiness; bees on flowers; seeds.

There was nothing real about this village, nothing of small prairie towns: no broad, treeless avenues stacked with pickup trucks, no garbage dump, no rusted and pock-marked Orange Crush signs flapping against the ramshackle boards of an abandoned pool hall.

It wasn't until I was a grown-up that I understood finally the "meaning" of that bucolic scene on the backdrop of the stage. In spite of the allotments of history, Ukrainian villagers had continued to imagine a village of harmony and hope. *This* is what I was doing, second-generation Ukrainian-Canadian teen-ager whirling around in my costume in time to the dance music coming out of the portable phonograph placed just inside the wings, whirling like a whirligig in my flying ribbons and skirts in front of the pretty backdrop, flinging out my arms in greeting to that perpetual village couple, the maiden and the Cossack swain: I was dancing that other village back out of nostalgia into a place where we could *see* it and, on the boards of the stage in the hall of a prairie church, dream of Arcadia again.

I take my leave of my relatives at the door of their house in Tulova. Hryhorii, the sleeves of his green-checked work shirt rolled up to the elbow, presents me with a good-bye gift, a souvenir of my visit to the ancestral village. He explains that his son-in-law is a bit of an artist, a woodcarver, an engraver in wood, and this is his work: he hands me a large, oval-framed portrait of the ineluctable Taras. He is wearing an astrakhan cap and long whiskers.

I know what to do; I say the right thing.

FAMILY ALBUM

HORODENKA, 1988: The zone in which my cousin Pavlina and her family live is still closed to foreigners, but this time, thanks to the Writers' Union, I can write my own itinerary: "Let me go see my relations in Ivano-Frankivsk!" The chauffeur waits at my hotel in Chernivtsi to whisk me off. I have permission to stay overnight.

Pavlina, Dmytro and twelve-year-old Halia live in a comfortable one-bedroom flat dominated by a living room chock-a-block with enormous pieces of furniture – sofa bed, china cabinet, bookshelf, television set – oversized embroidered cushions and, in pride of place, a very large "boom box." There is a smallish kitchen and bathroom but no hot water after nine in the evening. Not bad for a truck driver at a jam factory and a bookkeeper at a sugar beet farm.

There is a tableful of food – fried fish and beef stew, new potatoes and strawberries, cherry-filled perogies and champagne – and all the usual toasts. Pavlina's mother, Katrusia, has been brought in from Dzhuriv for the occasion.

From all the food on my cousin's table, Katrusia eats precisely nothing.

It is a Friday night and she is fasting until she receives communion on Sunday. Fasting! This wispy, toothless, gnarl-fisted woman who already looked seventy in her fifties, who has probably never once in her life eaten her fill. She sits at the table in a kerchief, hands in her lap. Every few moments she interjects some story of her own, whether her grievance against her children that none of them has stayed on with her in the village, or her recollection of a particularly rich harvest of plums, or her sorrow – undiminished over the months – that she has had to get rid of her old cow, her pride and her joy, because it had stopped producing.

Katrusia had sent a photograph of this cow to my aunt in Edmonton. It is a fine photo in black and white of a very large spotted cow with a thick dewlap, high haunches and a certain cast to her head, as though she were tired of having to hold it up. Katrusia stands beside the animal looking out at the camera with a rather severe expression. Perhaps she already knows that the cow has got to go. On the back of the photograph she had written, in fractured Ukrainian: "This photo was taken in 1987. I stood in the backyard with the cow and I felt very bad that I didn't have a memento of her. She lived with us by the haystack. She was born in 1970 and was always very good to us."

We go for a postprandial stroll down the main street of town, Lenin Street, to see the sights. They are not many: the bulky, yellowish Russian-Orthodox church, the concrete post office, the cement and concrete government buildings, the Gastronom where, from dusty shelves, the state is in the meagre business of selling greyish packages of soap and salt, sludge of pickle, sludge of jam. At the bottom of the street, though, there is evidence that Horodenka, too, has felt the seductive breezes of privatization: a five-member co-operative has bought up the Komsomol youth centre and turned it into a café. They have tried to liven the place up with bright oak panelling and rustic furniture. Eventually they hope to serve pancakes as well as Turkish coffee, but it is hard to see how five young people could make a living selling pancakes in this sleepy, no-account town.

Pavlina is talking about her father, Baba's blind nephew, whose picture I remember from the letters sent to my mother – a youngish, stalwart man, deep-shadowed eyes opened on the darkness, his family stiff-backed around his chair. I don't remember any stories, only the epithet "*Bidnyi, bidnyi* Petro," poor, poor Petro. It was an incantation to elicit in us not only the sorrow we shared with Baba at her family's plight but also our own profound thankfulness that we were well. We were in Canada, and we were well.

Petro suffered from a degenerative eye disease that, had it been treated promptly in a modern hospital, might have been arrested. But after six operations in faraway Odessa, without proper nutrition or appropriate medications and under threat of war, he returned home to Dzhuriv in great pain and increasing darkness. For weeks he was in postsurgical agony. Desperate, his wife Katrusia trekked on foot across country to a gypsy camp and approached a female healer. "He may be helped with *zhinochi liky,*" the gypsy said – "women's medicine" – which Katrusia reasoned was mother's milk. And so she went to visit a sister-in-law who was nursing a newborn. Three times the sister-in-law came to Katrusia and Petro's home to express milk, three times it was applied to Petro's eyes and, thanks be to God, the pain subsided and never returned. But Petro was blind.

He would die at age forty-seven of lung cancer, victim of the wretched cigarettes he smoked in a rage against his condition. He felt crippled, unmanned. But taught himself to play the violin, the accordion and the zither in order to support his family by making music at village weddings. He would listen with insatiable auditory greed to the radio and to friends who would read newspapers and books to him. His knowledgeableness impressed the young Dmytro, a shy, gawky village boy who was courting Pavlina and who loved to listen to the blind man talk. "My father was a tall and strong man. He made fun of Dmytro. Called him puny," Pavlina says. Dmytro says, "I loved him like a father."

Dolia. Fate. One's lot. A family as a whole, as well as its individual members, has a fate. The blind man's father – my baba's brother and Pavlina's *dido* or grandfather – had likewise come to a bad end. This is one story I had heard as a child that, though sketchy, had satisfied me, somehow represented a whole story nevertheless. Baba's brother Iurii had been murdered by the Banderivtsi, the "bourgeois nationalist" guerrillas of wartime Galicia. Thus I imagined a Ukrainian farmer much like my own dido in Edmonton (wiry, grizzly, in heavy denim overalls) having dinner with his family when suddenly there is a knock on the door (heavy and insistent); wiping his mouth on the back of his hand, he goes to the door, opens it, is grabbed by the collar by men in black berets and masks and dragged out into the yard, where he is shot and left to bleed to death face down in the muddy, piss-stained straw. The assassins escape while the dead man's family clutch each other in terror over their soup bowls.

He is harmless, innocent, felled by bad luck: dolia. His assassins are wild-eyed and fanatical, burning in their guts and their hearts with hatred for the Russians. I fail to make any connection between the hatred and its victim; it never occurs to me that this needs to be explained. The important information is that he was Baba's brother and the story always made her cry, wiping her tears away with the apron bunched up in her rough red hands.

Now Pavlina gives me her version. In 1934, when western Ukraine was still a part of Poland, her grandfather had joined the underground Communist Party. He was a Communist for the most unimpeachable of reasons, struggling for justice in the Galician countryside where generations of peasants had been ground down by landlords of all descriptions. This, however, apparently failed to mollify the Banderivtsi, the anti-fascist, anti-Communist guerrillas who haunted the Carpathians until well into the 1950s.

At Christmastime, 1945, they came looking for Iurii Kosovan. Among them were a couple of cousins who knew he was home for the holiday. (Again I imagine the knock on the door, the spoons poised frozen over the soup bowl, the masked men.) He was seized and taken away and never seen again. For two weeks, his wife scoured the woods for his body but found no trace. Thirty years later, his daughter-in-law, Katrusia, Pavlina's mother, took his photograph to the local *vorozhka*, the fortune teller. The woman meditated upon it, then took out her astrological chart and read there that this man was living in a faraway place with a new wife and family but that he wanted very much to return to Dzhuriv. He would set out but would die on the journey. Pavlina is sceptical. She says that her dido was taken away for his documents, which could prove useful as false identity papers for a guerrilla trying to cross the Ukrainian frontier, and was probably shot somewhere on a forced trek out of the mountains.

Katrusia's dolia: a blind husband, three children, a father-in-law sucked into the void, a household stripped of its patriarchs along with its booty of food, clothing, linens and utensils by "bandits" who were blood relations. What could she do? It had to be borne.

And then, in 1954, the first of the *banderoli* arrived from the relatives in Canada: boxes of clothing, cloth, knitting, what have you, and a letter. Stalin had died the year before. Katrusia, says Pavlina, still keeps the kerchief from that first box.

At this point, Pavlina is crying, so I take up the story. How I remember from that time and after, for years, the hustle and bustle in my mother's kitchen as she and my aunt prepared the banderoli – big cardboard boxes stuffed with secondhand clothes and some bright new gifts such as the highly prized floral kerchiefs sold in the Polish and Ukrainian shops near the farmer's market – tied them up with many yards of twine and addressed them in bold, Cyrillic script, worrying all the while that they would be pilfered by some greedy Soviet customs agent.

I sensed their anxiety and the undercurrent of urgency that attended their work, but it all seemed quite exotic to me, if a little d.p.ish (as though we had relatives in refugee camps!), suggestive of shadowy figures with hats pulled down over their eyes in black-and-white movies about the war, of ragged soldiers and emptied, cobble-stoned streets, burned-out villages and civilians digging for rotting potatoes in the smoking fields.

Then came the letters in reply, and the family photographs, those black-and-white studio portraits that seemed to have been taken in another era: the heavy drapery, the bulky, ill-fitting clothing too short in the arms and legs, the artless haircuts, the unsmiling, almost stricken faces with eyes sunk in dark circles. The poor cousins. The Soviet relatives. The *Ukrainians*, over "there," trapped, frightened, hungry, from whom came letters saying they were fine.

I look over to Dmytro. It occurs to me that I know nothing about *his* family, and so I ask. "Poor," he says. "We were poor." Pause. He looks humiliated, then anguished. There were five kids, he was the youngest, the runt... The village was poor. His father was in the army during the war. End of story. Pause. Then he goes on a little about his father, how he spent a month in the bogs of Belorus, water up to his waist, fighting on the western front, but made it home in '45.

As for his grandfather, he was a savage who tried to get through life not by doing honest work but by making deals. And when he couldn't make a deal, by raising hell. He walked into a pub one day and demanded one hundred grams of vodka, free. The publican called him "scum." The old man left, returned with an axe and split the man's head open. The old man's daughter got him out of police custody by bribing everyone in sight. Pause. This is Dmytro's one and only story. His hand is over his mouth. His eyes look out at me as though I had him cornered.

I suddenly feel very young, although I'm ten years older than both Pavlina and Dmytro. Nothing has happened to me. I live on the first day of creation. People are good and there are pleasures to be had. But these two are already members of a generation of pain and suffering who join the gnarled and toothless and haunted ones at my table and hold their hands over their mouths so as not to howl at my banquet.

BREAD BASKET

Diary, June 1988: "The Ukrainian lands seen from the air in June are green, green and green again."

When Adam and Eve had eaten the forbidden fruit in Paradise, God appeared before them and, more in sorrow than in anger, expelled them from the Garden. "But I will not destroy you," He promised, and handed over a sack of treasures to help them survive on earth: honey, poppy seeds and kernels of wheat.

Kutia: a dish of cooked grains of wheat mixed with honey and poppy seeds. It is the food of the gods of harvest. On Christmas Eve, the master of the house throws a spoonful of kutia three times at the ceiling: once for the calves, once for the lambs and once for the bees. The word is ancient, from the Greek *koukkia*, grains. The custom of boiling grains of wheat with honey and dried fruits as an offering to the dead dates back to the Neolithic. The dish is called *kolyvo*. Among the Hutzuls of the Carpathians, a funeral procession is led by a priest on horseback, followed by a village elder bearing a large bowl of kolyvo.

It is more important than the coffin.

Oleksandr Dovzhenko, *The Enchanted Desna:* "If only I could die here under the raspberry bushes, I thought. Let them look for me, then, let them cry and grieve over me, recalling what a darling boy I had been. Let them carry me to the grave and there I'd come to life again ... and then we'd go to the cottage to eat some *kolyvo*."

The basic word is *zhaty*, to reap, to harvest.

The harvest depended upon the goodwill of the god of the sun,

Dazhboh, and of Perun, god of lightning and rain. They are praised and propitiated in elaborate rituals carried over into Christian times. The last clump of uncut grain at harvest time, for instance, is left uncut; its stalks are woven and braided together and into their heart the farmer presses a loaf of bread, some salt and water, kneeling in thanks while the women of the family offer a prayer. *God, let the earth provide for all, the poor and rich, widows and orphans.*

This braided wheat has many names, among them *Illi Boroda*, Elijah's Beard, for the saint of lightning and thunder. (For Perun, perhaps? The pagan god of thunder?) The last day of harvest is a holiday, *Obzhynky*. The last sheaf of the best grain is ceremonially reaped, tied and decorated with flowers and ribbons. This will become the *didukh* – the honorific wheat sheaf in the corner of the main room of the house under the family icons – for Christmas Eve. The master of the house addresses the didukh: "You have made us full, given us drink, fed us, warmed us and our animals, guarded our fields – give us even better in the new year."

Zakrutka: a knot tied in a handful of growing grain to prevent the evil eye from spoiling the bread that will be baked from this wheat. *Babka*: the Easter bread, the holiest bread of all. Babka: grandmother, or old woman. Babka: women's work, women's ceremony.

The wood for baking was gathered during Lent and the kindling from the branches of pussy willow blessed on Palm Sunday. The ashes were scattered over the garden when the first seedlings were planted. Into the dough of the babka go at least sixty egg yolks: intensification of the female. In the villages of the Lemko region, on Holy Thursday, the eggshells from the baking were strung out on bushes and tree branches along the road: Behold the blossoming trees!

In Kiev, at the colossal feet of the statue of Hryhory Skovoroda, the eighteenth-century psalmist, philosopher, satirist, translator of Cicero and Plutarch, the wanderer whose memory is sacred to the people, someone had left a small shiny crusty bun.

In the eighteenth century, the main export from the Black Sea coastal cities was grain. Between 1778 and 1787, the harvest in southern Ukraine increased by 500 per cent and Ukraine became the granary of Europe. By 1900, the average Dane was consuming 2166 pounds of bread a year, the average German, 1119, the average Hungarian, 1264, and the average Ukrainian, 867.

In the 1930s, Ukrainian peasants died of hunger in the middle of their fields. In retribution, grain requisitioners, who had been sent to the villages by the Party to confiscate the harvests, were seized by the vengeful starving. The people slit open the requisitioners' bellies and stuffed the cavity with their own purloined wheat. While five million or so died of starvation during collectivization of the countryside, the poet Pavlo Tychyna agonized over the question: What do the people of Ukraine need more – my sonnets, or bread? He chose bread. He degenerated into official poesy, and the people died of starvation anyway.

Prisoners on their way from Liubanka prison in Moscow to their execution by firing squad were transported in trucks marked "Bread."

In the corner of the old palace courtyard off Market Square in Lviv, there stands, rusted and neglected as though of no account, a machine that looks to be a kind of hand-pushed seeder. And so it is. With just this instrument, I am told, the Nazis fertilized the fields around Lviv with the bone meal delivered from the crematoria.

Khrushchevka: The flat, oblong loaf of corn and pea flour named for the Chairman of the Communist Party of the Soviet Union whose disastrous agricultural policies in the 1960s reintroduced hunger in Ukraine.

Pavlina: "People began queuing up early in the morning for this bread. As the eldest child, I was sent to stand in line for the whole family. I was so hungry! I trembled and shook, waiting for that 'brick.' The smells drove me crazy. I could taste, I could *chew* that smell. I died a hundred times, worrying the bread would run out before I got to the head of the queue. Finally, when I had reached the front and had the loaf in my hands, I couldn't help myself. On the way home, I tore at it, stuffing my mouth. When my grandfather saw the mangled loaf I handed over, he beat me black and blue. I had taken food from the mouths of my family. I had no right."

In the forced labour camps of the 1960s, the nutritional minimum of 2400 calories was never met because of the poor quality of the bread. Sixty per cent of the weight came from non-flour additives such as sawdust.

A Ukrainian will kiss the bread knife before she cuts the loaf, she will kiss the piece of bread that has fallen to the ground and beg its forgiveness for her lapse of reverence. "Remember," says a prisoner of the gulag to the newcomer, "a *zek* must never let a single crumb of bread fall to the ground." He is holding his slice of bread over his bowl as though to baptise it.

"My own dreams assumed a cannibalistic, erotic form," wrote Gustav

Herling of his experience in the gulag. "Love and hunger returned to their common biological root, releasing from the depth of my subconsciousness images of women made of fresh dough whom I would bite in fantastic orgies till they streamed with blood and milk, twining their arms which smelt like fresh loaves round my burning head."

In the 1990s, when it became safe to talk of these things, survivors would come to the public seminars bearing enormous loaves held tenderly on embroidered cloth like so many village pietàs.

In 1962, when Les Taniuk, Alla Horska and Vasyl Symonenko visited the Bykivnia Forest near Kiev together, the earth was springy under their feet, as though it were not bound with roots but with moss and the slowly decaying matter of a forest floor. They did not know then that they were ambling on the surface of a mass grave filled with the refuse of the prisons of the NKVD.

On the eve of the Nazi invasion of the city, some seven thousand prisoners of the Soviet secret police were shot and buried en masse in Bykivnia. As recently as 1988, an official commission of investigation "confirmed" that they had died at the hands of the invaders, and city authorities announced plans to build a railway station on the site. By 1989, though, the population of Kiev had "taken back" Bykivnia for themselves. As the pits were opened up and bodies exhumed, priests led prayers for the dead over their bones while their sons and daughters clutched photographs brought out from hiding places. And on the edge of the pits, laid devoutly in a plastic bag beside the heaps of flowers and the stands of sputtering candles, a loaf of bread.

Earth: a film. The old man is dying under the apple tree, chewing one last fruit so he may enter Paradise with apple on his breath.

His grandson, Vasyl, the local revolutionary, has been assassinated by his enemies in the village. Now he is being borne to his grave on the shoulders of his friends and comrades, his body hoisted to the caressing, blossoming trees. This nineteen-year-old "new Soviet man" had delivered the first tractor to the village, riding it like a charioteer over the fields, contemptuous of the field markers that demarcated one family's property from another's. He knew this would all soon be collective property and the will of the revolution would be fulfilled in wheat and steel.

Vasyl danced, under the moon, on the earth. The exultant tattoo of his feet drumming in the dust reminded him that, to fly off the earth, you must first be standing somewhere.

There is an earlier earth. It precedes the furrow and the dance. It is the earth to which Vasyl's assassin flees, circling crazily in the open fields, bellowing out his guilt to the blooming buckwheat and the swarm of bees: "It was me! *I* killed him!" When he flings himself down on this earth, it is as though to burrow in the dark alongside his victim's corpse. The place he seeks is the ancient ossuary of the underground, it is the fertilizing black loam, and it is the beginnings of bread.

NOTES

CZECHOSLOVAKIA

For a historical overview I found no single authoritative account but made use of relevant material in Leslie Tihany's *A History of Middle Europe* (Rutgers University Press, 1987) and Robin Okey's *Eastern Europe 1740–1985* (Hutchison University Library, 1986), as well as the robust lecture notes of Dr. John-Paul Himka of the Department of History, University of Alberta.

Marian Slingova, whose husband was executed in the Stalinist show trials of 1952, gives a deeply felt account of that sinister period in *Truth Will Prevail* (Merlin, 1968).

There is a broad range of material on the Prague Spring of 1967–68. Some highlights are Yorick Blumenfield's touristic wander-through, *Seesaw: Cultural Life in Eastern Europe* (Harcourt Brace Jovanovich, 1968), Josef Skvorecky's saucy memoirs of the arts scene of the 1960s, *All the Bright Young Men and Women* (Peter Martin Associates, 1971), and a critical retrospective on the era, *The Prague Spring: A Mixed Legacy*, ed. Jiri Pehe (Freedom House, 1988), which discusses the Spring's relationship to reform Communism, the behaviour of journalists, the Spring's effect on a textile factory, the politics of the student movement and much else. By far the most detailed journalistic account is Z. A. B. Zeman's *Prague Spring* (Penguin, 1969), a book that I found in a secondhand bookstore and have never come across again. I also consulted an unpublished thesis by Katherine O'Leary entitled "The Rise and Fall of Independent Political Groups in the Prague Spring" (Princeton University, 1986).

For their contextualizing of the 1967–68 period within a large European setting, I found helpful *Eastern Europe since Stalin*, ed. Jonathon Steele (Crane, Russak & Co., 1974), Jacques Rupnik's *The Other Europe* (Schocken, 1989) and David Caute's *The Year of the Barricades* (Harper & Row, 1988), a tour de force of reportage on that extraordinary year of international student militancy, 1968.

For its meticulousness, nothing surpasses *The Interrupted Revolution* (Princeton University Press, 1976), an account of the Spring and its violent aftermath by that doyen of scholarship on modern Czechoslovakia, the

Canadian Dr. H. Gordon Skilling. Three French journalists, Pierre Desgraupes, Pierre Dumayet and Alain Stanké, write with gusto and outrage of the invasion and occupation in *Prague: L'été des tanks* (Les Editions de l'homme, 1968). For the Petru Popescu quote about the "heavy" heart of Europe, see *Index on Censorship* (Autumn 1976).

The long, melancholy, inspirational history of the Czech and Slovak dissident movements and debates can be tracked in a number of directions. Imaginatively, there are the novels of Josef Skvorecky and Milan Kundera, the plays and essays of Vaclav Havel, the short stories and feuilletons of Ludvik Vaculik, Jiri Grusa and Ivan Klima. (Unfortunately, women's writing has not been so well-served by translators, and there is a dearth of books available.) Polemically, Kundera's themes and variations on the Sovietization of Czech culture appeared with some regularity in the British quarterly *Granta* (see particularly the interviews with him and his "A Kidnapped West or Culture Bows Out" in *Granta* 11). Jaroslav Seifert's remarks to the Writers' Congress were published in *Index on Censorship* 2/85.

The activists in the opposition were indefatigable archivists of their own activity. The Charta 77 Foundation in Sweden published their documents in two useful volumes – *A Besieged Culture: Czechoslovakia Ten Years after Helsinki* (Charta 77 Foundation, 1985) and Karel and Ivan Kyncl's *After the Spring Came Winter* (Askelin & Hagglund, 1985), which features Ivan's fascinating snapshots of the everyday lives of Charter 77 signatories. In London in the 1980s, Jan Kavan of Palach Press was publishing and disseminating *Bulletin*, a periodical compendium of news, manifestos, press releases and editorials that had come his way via the clandestine networks of his homeland. Zdena Tomin's quote is taken from an article in *Index on Censorship* 2/83.

YUGOSLAVIA

Concise and even-handed, Fred Singleton's *A Short History of the Yugoslav Peoples* (Cambridge University Press, 1985) is an admirable general introduction to the ancient and modern history of the South Slavs. For a sprawling, opinionated and impassioned historical sweep that refuses to go out of date, read Rebecca West's *Black Lamb and Grey Falcon* (Penguin, 1986), written just before the outbreak of the Second World War and packed with curiosities, telling anecdotes and observations as often skewed as acute.

Yugoslav writers have contributed idiosyncratic versions of their respective national histories, notably Ivo Andric's panoramic *The Bridge on the Drina* (University of Chicago Press, 1977) for Bosnia, Milovan Djilas's autobiographical *Land without Justice* (Harcourt Brace Jovanovich, 1958) for Montenegro, and Dobrica Cosic's martyrological epic of Serbia's coming-of-age in the First World War, *This Land, This Time* (Harcourt Brace Jovanovich, 1983). As someone who spend most of his adult life in the United States, Slovene-born Louis Adamic wrote from a decidedly "ethnic" and elegiac slant in *The Native's Return* (Harper & Brothers, 1934; reissued Greenwood, 1975) and *My Native Land* (Harper & Brothers, 1943).

Not long after the events of 1968, Robert S. Cohen and Praxis participant Mihailo Markovic published *The Rise and Fall of Socialist Humanism: A History of the Praxis Group* (Spokesman, 1975). Milan Nikolic, 1968 activist, published his critical assessment of student protest in "1968 Protest in Yugoslavia" in *New Politics* 2, no. 2 (Winter 1989), while David Caute, in *The Year of the Barricades, op. cit.*, grounded the events in an international context of student upheaval. The line "Oh, let all our losses be light" is from a kolo song based on Montenegro's national poem, "Mountain Wreath"; see *Introduction to Yugoslav Literature*, ed. Branko Mikasinovich, *et al.* (Twayne Publishers, 1973).

Chronicles of the Battle at Kosovo Polje have been translated by John Matthias and Vladeta Vuckovic in *The Battle of Kosovo* (Swallow Press, 1987), and Vasko Popa's poem "Earth Erect" is quoted in their introduction. The epithet "And there was a dancing girl called Macedonia" is from Procopius, *The Secret History* (Penguin, 1985). Ivan Lalic's poem "Word of the Warrior on the Battlements" is from his *The Works of Love* (Anvil Press, 1981). Ljubomir Simovic's "The Migration of Serbia" was published in *Relations* (Serbian Writers' Association, 1988). Maggie Helwig's "The Lost History of Byzantium" appeared in *Conspiracy of Silence* (1989).

That perennial dissident, Milovan Djilas, in writing the demystifying *Rise and Fall* (Harcourt Brace Jovanovich, 1985), set the stage for a literature of post-Tito reevaluation of the Yugoslav experiment. This includes a 1987 Helsinki Watch Report, *From Below: Independent Peace and Environmental Movements in Eastern Europe and in the u.s.s.r.*, and sociologist Sonja Liht's analytical essay, "The Yugoslav Experience: The Failure of Reform without Democracy," in *New Politics* 2, no. 3 (Summer 1989), which importantly does not lay the (impending) Yugoslav collapse at "tribalism's" door. Arishi Pipa on "Ethnic Phobia" is in *Across Frontiers* (Winter-Spring 1989). Misha Glenny, the canny journalist of bbc's World Service, writes more in sorrow than in anger in *The Rebirth of History: Eastern Europe in the Age of Democracy* (Penguin, 1990), of the "tragedy of revenge" that is ex-Yugoslavia in war. Glenny's most recent book is *The Fall of Yugoslavia: The Third Balkan War* (Penguin, 1992).

POLAND

Of all the Slavic countries with which my book is concerned, Poland has consistently attracted the most attention from non-Slavic historians and journalists. Poland's inarguable importance in European affairs, from its dynastic involvements in royal families to Solidarity's impact on a disintegrating Cold

War world order, is one explanation. Another is the undeniable romance of the country's long history of cultural and political resistance to national oppression. Sometimes this romantic identification reproduces the excesses of Poles' own self-regard, as in British historian Norman Davies's *Heart of Europe* (Oxford University Press, 1986), an eccentric retelling (he goes backwards from the 1980s to the beginnings of the Polish state in the tenth century) of his earlier two-volume *God's Playground: A History of Poland* (Oxford University Press, 1982). He systematically assumes a Polonocentric view of the prewar Polish state's relations with Poland's minorities, for instance. (It is Davies who referred to the concentration camp at Bereza Kartuska as a "minor aberration.")

But other foreigners have written superbly of Polish affairs, notably of the Solidarity period (1980–81), its preparation and its aftermath. Time and again I referred to Neal Ascherson's *The Polish August* (Penguin, 1982) and Timothy Garton Ash's *The Polish Revolution* (Random House, 1985) for their meticulous yet engaged reading of Solidarity and its (dis)contents. (It was Garton Ash who took down the words to the farmer's poem about wanting a "life of dignity.") The American journalist Daniel Singer, in *The Road to Gdansk* (Monthly Review Press, 1982), and the French journalist Jean-Yves Potel, in *The Summer before the Frost: Solidarnosc in Poland* (Pluto Press, 1982), both cover the events leading up to the formation of the Communist world's first sustained independent trade union, focussing on the class experience of the workers. Under the editorship of American scholar Abraham Brumberg, various Polish academics and journalists unearth the social and cultural roots of Solidarity in *Poland: Genesis of a Revolution* (Vintage, 1983), from protests against meat shortages to student unrest.

Before there was revolution there was the Party. The classic exposé of the workings of the mind of the intelligentsia in the "people's democracies" remains Czeslaw Milosz's elegant and pitiless *The Captive Mind* (Random House, 1990), first published in English in 1951. Not that the Party did not have its true believers, especially among the postwar generation that subscribed to the "Polish road to socialism" – Janina Bauman, for example, whose memoir *A Dream of Belonging* (Virago, 1988) describes her and her husband's fall into disfavour and then disbelief during the Party's anti-Semitic purges in 1968. The Polish journalist Teresa Toranska, working in the brief uncensored interlude of Solidarity's heyday, managed to interview an entire rogues' gallery of aging Party luminaries who, in her *Them: Stalin's Polish Puppets* (Harper Collins, 1988), admit to the most damnable – and sometimes heart-wrenching – ideological contradictions. For an inside look at how censorship worked in post-Stalin Poland, read *The Black Book of Polish Censorship*, ed. Jane Leftwich Curry (Vintage, 1984), a mind-boggling catalogue of official inanities and paranoia.

People's Poland immediately had its critics, some of whom were gathered in the American anthology *Bitter Harvest,* ed. Edmund Stillman (Praeger, 1959) – Adam Wazyk, for example, and his "Poem for Adults," and the young radical philosopher Leszek Kolakowski, whose "What Is Socialism?" was one of the early challenges by disenchanted socialists to the hardening Party line. Intellectuals and artists, even when "disloyal," have always been a kind of conscience in Polish society, monitoring the moral well-being of their fellow citizens. The dean of such barometers is Kazimierz Brandys who, in *A Warsaw Diary 1978–81* (Chatto & Windus, 1984), is caustic about everything from the "abnormality" of Polish writers to the moral significance of hunger strikes. More absurdist is the prolific novelist Tadeusz Konwicki; see, for example, *The Polish Complex* (Penguin, 1984) and *Moonrise, Moonset* (Farrar, Straus & Giroux, 1987). Marek Nowakowski's *The Canary* (Dial Press, 1984) is a deadpan observation of the grotesquenesses of life under martial law from 1981–83. Two western philosophers have written critically of totalitarianism on the Left: Jean-François Revel in *The Totalitarian Temptation* (Penguin, 1978) and Bernard-Henri Lévy in *Barbarism with a Human Face* (Harper Colophon, 1979).

The latest generation of artists/intellectuals to have made an impact on Polish politics were formed as students during the university uprisings of 1968; these events are given their context within earlier uprisings in Jakub Karpinski's *Countdown: The Polish Upheavals of 1956, 1968, 1970, 1976, 1980* (Karz-Cohl, 1984) and within the international New Left in George Katsiaficas's *The Imagination of the New Left* (South End Press, 1987). Adam Michnik, one of the most uncompromising of that student generation, expounds eloquently and wisely in *Letters from Prison* (University of California Press, 1985) on questions of democracy, opposition, collaboration and revisionism in their Polish context. For Polish literature under seige (censorship, linguistic pollutions, samizdat), read one who lived through it, the poet Stanislaw Baranczak, whose *Breathing under Water and Other East European Essays* (Harvard University Press, 1990) is the source of the Wislawa Szymborska quote.

Post-Solidarity social movements also left their mark on political evolution. A Helsinki Watch Report from 1987, *op. cit.*, details the activities of WiP (Freedom and Peace). *Forum Polek: Polish Women's Forum* is the published proceedings of a feminist conference held in London in 1986 and the source of the sociological data on the situation of women.

For details of the life and death of Father Jerzy Popieluszko, see *The Way of My Cross* (Regnery Books, 1986), a collection of his sermons, and *The Deliberate Death of a Polish Priest,* a playscript by Ronald Harwood (Applause Theatre Book Publishers, n.d.).

See C. M. Hann's *A Village without Solidarity* (Yale University Publishers, 1985) for a history of Polish-Ukrainian rural relations in southeast Poland and, for information on Akcja Wisla, John Basarab's essay "Post-War Writings in

Poland on Polish-Ukrainian Relations 1945–1975," in *Poland and Ukraine: Past and Present,* ed. Peter J. Potichnyj (Canadian Institute of Ukrainian Studies, 1980). T. Karabovich's *"Znak spohadu"* in *Nashe Slovo,* 23.11.1986, gives the Polish-Ukrainian journalist's account of the abandoned church. Adam Zagajewski's poem "To Go to Lvov" is from his *Tremor* (Farrar Straus & Giroux, 1987) and the Julian Przybos poem "Mother" is in *Postwar Polish Poetry,* ed. Czeslaw Milosz (Penguin, 1970).

The account of the last days of the Warsaw uprising (*"They worried most about their rifles..."*) is from J. K. Zawodny's *Nothing but Honour* (Hoover Institution Press, 1979). Mareck Garztecki's article was published in the January 9, 1982, edition of *New Musical Express.*

UKRAINE

Orest Subtelny's *Ukraine: A History* (University of Toronto Press, 1988), wide-ranging, measured and very readable, was the basic text in my reading of Ukrainian history from its beginnings and is the main source of details concerning the misery of turn-of-the-century Galician peasants, along with John-Paul Himka's compelling *Galician Villagers and the Ukrainian National Movement in the Nineteenth Century* (Canadian Institute of Ukrainian Studies, 1988).

Data on seventeenth-century Ukrainian literacy came from *Clandestine Essays* (Ukrainian Academic Press, 1976) by Ievhan Sverstiuk. *"The farmers collapsed, struggled to their feet..."* is from Vasyl Kostashchuk, *Volodar Dum Selianskych* (Vydavnytstvo "Karpaty," 1968).

The source of the revisionist interpretations of Cossack society (and of the information on Tatar slave trading) is Linda Gordon's *Cossack Rebellions: Social Turmoil in the Sixteenth Century Ukraine* (University of New York Press, 1983), a bracing revisit of the Cossack myth first encountered by western readers in Nikolai Gogol's *Taras Bulba* (many editions).

Robert Conquest's *The Harvest of Sorrow* (University of Alberta Press/Canadian Institute of Ukrainian Studies, 1986) is one of those formerly "right-wing" works now proved to be authoritative on the subject of the Ukrainian famine. The Mykola Khvylovy anecdote from the famine is from his *Stories from the Ukraine* (Philosophical Library, 1960). Wislawa Szymborska's poem "Starvation Camp near Jaslo" appears in *Postwar Polish Poetry, op.cit.*

There is a tremendous literature concerning dissidence in Soviet Ukraine, none more gripping and poignant than Leonid Pliushch's memoirs *History's Carnival* (Harcourt Brace Jovanovich, 1979). This is one of the sources of details concerning the life and death of Alla Horska. Another is *Ukrainian Herald* 4 (Cicero Press, n.d.), which, along with other issues of the *Herald,* regularly made available to the West reports on clandestine cultural and political activity in the 1960s and 1970s. Vyacheslav Chornovil's *The Chornovil Papers*

(McGraw-Hill, 1968) was another early report and is the source of the quote from Panas Zalyvakha's prison letter. The "granddaddy" of Ukrainian gulag writing is Valentyn Moroz's *Report from the Beria Reserve* (Peter Martin Associates, 1974), followed by Ivan Dziuba's sensational *Internationalism or Russification?* (Monad Press, 1974) and the novelist Mykhailo Osadchy's *Cataract* (Harcourt Brace Jovanovich, 1976). For a foreigner's account of the gulag experience, read the harrowing *A World Apart* by Gustav Herling (Oxford University Press, 1987). Political prisoner Danylo Shumuk eventually was released and deported to Canada; his *Life Sentence: Memoirs of a Ukrainian Political Prisoner* (Canadian Institute of Ukrainian Studies, 1984) is an almost unbelievable account of a virtual lifetime of incarceration. Canada's own John Kolasky, in *Two Years in Soviet Ukraine* (Peter Martin Associates, 1970), anticipated the repression.

A number of useful anthologies and studies have appeared from the Canadian Institute of Ukrainian Studies. In addition to those already mentioned, I found particularly useful *Ukraine after Shelest*, ed. Bohdan Krawchenko (1983) and *Politics and Society in Soviet Ukraine 1953–1980* by Borys Lewytzkyj (1984).

For the anecdote of Volodymyr's conversion to Christianity, see *Medieval Russia's Epics, Chronicles and Tales*, ed. Serge A. Zenkovsky (Dutton, 1963). Plano Carpini on the Mongol devastation is cited in *Lord and Peasant in Russia* by Jerome Blum (Princeton University Press, 1972). It was the Yugoslav writer Danilo Kis who wrote of the smell of hops in St. Sophia in his story "The Mechanical Lions," in *A Tomb for Boris Davidovich* (Penguin, 1980), and it was the Ukrainian filmmaker Oleksandr Dovzhenko who lamented the loss of Kievan monuments in his diaries *The Poet as Film-maker*, ed. Marco Carynnyk (MIT Press, 1973). Andrew Suknaski's poem "What Is Remembered" appears in his book *In the Name of Narid* (The Porcupine's Quill, 1981). Ivan Franko's "The Emigrants" has been widely anthologized; one place it appears is in his *Poems and Stories* (Ukrainska Knyha, 1956).

Orysia Tracz, writing in *Forum* (Spring 1988), was a valuable source for harvest rituals.

The following periodicals helped me in my research: *Labour Focus on Eastern Europe* (London), *Across Frontiers* (Berkeley, now defunct), *East European Reporter* (London, now Budapest), *Index on Censorship* (London), *L'Alternative* (Paris), *Ukrainian Weekly* (Jersey City) and *Cross Currents* (Ann Arbor).